The Vampire as Numinous Experience

The Vampire as Numinous Experience

Spiritual Journeys with the Undead in British and American Literature

BETH E. MCDONALD

McFarland & Company, Inc., Publishers
Jefferson, North Carolina, and London

LIBRARY OF CONGRESS CATALOGUING-IN-PUBLICATION DATA

McDonald, Beth E., 1950–
    The vampire as numinous experience : spiritual journeys with
the undead in British and American literature / Beth E. McDonald.
        p.   cm.
    Includes bibliographical references and index.

    ISBN-13: 978-0-7864-1947-0
    softcover : 50# alkaline paper ∞

    1. Horror tales, English — History and criticism. 2. Vampires
in literature.   3. Religion and literature — English-speaking
countries.   4. Horror tales, American — History and criticism.
5. Belief and doubt in literature. 6. Spiritual life in literature.
7. Good and evil in literature. 8. Immortalism in literature.
9. Future life in literature.   I. Title.
PR830.V3M36   2004
820.9'375 — dc22   2004010996

British Library cataloguing data are available

©2004 Beth E. McDonald. All rights reserved

*No part of this book may be reproduced or transmitted in any form
or by any means, electronic or mechanical, including photocopying
or recording, or by any information storage and retrieval system,
without permission in writing from the publisher.*

Cover image: Photo illustration by Mark Durr

Manufactured in the United States of America

McFarland & Company, Inc., Publishers
    Box 611, Jefferson, North Carolina 28640
        www.mcfarlandpub.com

Acknowledgments

This book began as a doctoral dissertation, so I wish to acknowledge my committee. Dr. Stephen Tabachnick worked tirelessly as the chair of my committee, giving me advice and encouragement. I would also like to thank Dr. Lawrence Frank, Dr. Michael Morrison, and Dr. James Madison Davis for being part of the committee and giving me such valuable feedback in the revision process. A special acknowledgment and thank you is due Dr. George Economou, who chaired my Master's committee and served on the Doctoral committee. These five people not only advised me on the project, but also, as colleagues and friends, still provide me with support in my writing endeavors. A special note of appreciation goes to my husband Michael for putting up with all the years of doctoral study, research, and writing.

Table of Contents

Acknowledgments — v
Preface — 1

One • Dreadful Revelations:
The Numinous and the Vampire — 11

Two • Surrendering the Self:
The Numinous and the Vampire in
Coleridge's "The Rime of the Ancient Mariner" — 39

Three • Recreating the World:
The Sacred and the Profane in
Bram Stoker's *Dracula* — 86

Four • Eros and the Thanatotic Hero:
Anne Rice's *Vampire Chronicles* — 129

Conclusion: Vampires for a New Age — 169
Chapter Notes — 183
Works Cited — 187
Index — 195

Preface

Writers such as Samuel Taylor Coleridge invited the vampire into the pages of British Romantic literature. His readings, not only of early eighteenth-century treatises such as *Traité sur les Apparitiones des Esprits, et sur les Vampire* (1746) by Benedictine abbot and religious scholar Dom Augustin Calmet, but also of the German Schauermärchen or horror tales which grew out of the continental interest in the existence of the vampire, were to influence the Gothic literature of nineteenth-century Britain. From such poetic parentage as Heinrich August Ossenfelder's "The Vampire" (1748), Gottfried August Bürger's "Lenore" (1773) and Johann Wolfgang von Goethe's "The Bride of Corinth" (1797) were born the first of the British Romantic vampires: Robert Southey's "Thalaba the Destroyer" (1797); Samuel Taylor Coleridge's "Christabel" (1797–1801) and "The Rime of the Ancient Mariner" (1797–1817); John Keats' "La Belle Dame Sans Merci" (1819) and "Lamia" (1819); Mary Wollstonecraft Shelley's *Frankenstein* (1818) and John Polidori's *The Vampyre* (1820). Out of the literary bloodlines of the Romantic vampire then was born their Victorian offspring, created by prose writers who, like Shelley and Polidori, had come under the spell of the glittery-eyed fiend and his lovely, pale sisters. One need only read the serialized *Varney, the Vampire* (1847), Charlotte Brontë's *Jane Eyre* (1847), or Emily Brontë's *Wuthering Heights* (1847) to realize that the vampire was thriving in early Victorian Britain. He, and she, would continue to evolve in the later decades of the nineteenth century in works like J. Sheridan Le Fanu's "Carmilla" (1872) and Bram Stoker's *Dracula* (1897). Emigrating to America along with countless other British and continental citizens, literary vampires have continued producing their bloodthirsty progeny from Edgar Allan Poe's "Berenice" (1835) and "Ligeia" (1838) to works such as *The Vampire Tapestry* (1980) by Suzy McKee Charnas, the various novels of the vampire Count Saint-Germain by Chelsea

Quinn Yarbro, the prolific novels of Poppy Z. Brite, Brian Lumley, Paul F. Wilson, and, of course, the *Vampire Chronicles* series of Anne Rice (1976–1998), whose new vampire series *New Tales of the Vampires* carries on the stories of the older vampires who appeared as supporting characters in *Vampire Chronicles*.

The purpose of this study is to investigate the experience of the numinous in a specific category of Gothic literature, which employs a vampire as the primary focus of its action, regardless of whether that figure is literal or metaphoric. I have, therefore, chosen to discuss the use of the vampire figure as a representation of the numinous over several literary periods in a kind of super-religious context that goes beyond the realm of traditional religious systems. The texts examined in the following chapters include both poetry and fiction, written at or near the ends of their respective centuries by both British and American authors. At the ends of centuries and millenniums, many humans suffer a sense of spiritual alienation exacerbated by fear of the unknown on such a momentous threshold of time; as a result, they often begin to question their spiritual beliefs. My study explores how at the ends of the last three centuries (and one millennium) these particular authors have used the numinous qualities of the vampire to convey a human sense of alienation from the divine and a desire to overcome that alienation.

For this discussion I have chosen to define the idea of the numinous as it was developed by Rudolf Otto in *The Idea of the Holy* and to expand upon that concept with several later examinations of the experience of the numinous based on Otto's primary work. While expressing the physical, non-transcendent, and isolated state of the individual human being, as a numinous figure, the vampire also represents the transcendent agent through which individuals and societies may confront questions about their innate goodness or evilness and the condition of their belief in the divine and in the possibility of an afterlife. In this study, therefore, I argue that a textual experience of the numinous in the form of the vampire propels the subject of the experience on a spiritual journey involving both psychological and religious qualities, and that through that journey the reader, and possibly the main character, begins to understand the value of his or her existence in the world and to negotiate a new relationship with the divine.

I have chosen to divide the body of this book into chapters dealing with the Romantic, Victorian, and late twentieth century periods. My purpose in this work is not to make judgments about the numinous in particular periods based on only one work or author. I have simply chosen the best representative works of their respective periods and analyzed how the numinous figure of the vampire was used in service of the theme of spiritual journey. Chapters Two and Three each examine one work by one writer from a particular period. Chapter Four, however, explores the numinous in relation to a particular character through a series of texts by one writer. For the Romantic period I have chosen to analyze Samuel Taylor Coleridge's "The Rime of the Ancient Mariner" (1798), basing my use of this poem as a vampire text on James B. Twitchell's arguments for that perspective in *The Living Dead*. No analysis of the vampire in literature would be complete without the now classic vampire Dracula; therefore, as a representative of vampire fiction in the Victorian period, I have examined Bram Stoker's *Dracula* (1897). For the late twentieth century, I have selected the first five books of Anne Rice's popular *Vampire Chronicles* (1976–1995) for analysis. Despite the fact that I am considering the vampire figure as a representative of the numinous in all the chapters, rather than using one text dealing with the numinous concept as a foundation and following that particular thread through the texts of all three centuries, I have chosen a different perspective on the numinous for each chapter. With this method, I hope to show how an experience of the vampire as a numinous figure can be analyzed on both its psychological and religious levels.

Chapter One. Dreadful Revelations: The Numinous and the Vampire

The introductory chapter of this work has been used to clarify several questions that must be dealt with in order to begin an analysis of the vampire as numinous figure in any period. These questions include: how to reconcile the linguistic construction of an experience of the numinous with the idea that the numinous, by definition, is indescribable; the philosophical question many might ask about whether the divine, in any form, truly exists and where belief, or lack of it, in the divine might enter into an encounter with the numinous; and whether a discussion of the experience of the numinous in literature should be approached from a purely psychological point of view, a purely religious one, or a combination of the two perspectives.

Chapter Two. Surrendering the Self: The Numinous and the Vampire in Coleridge's "The Rime of the Ancient Mariner"

In Samuel Taylor Coleridge's "The Rime of the Ancient Mariner" the poet returns to the traditional conventions of the romance genre and to romance's more popular ballad form to tell a tale of marvelous events. However, although he uses more general human types to populate his ballad, I believe that the story represents an individual human experience of the Mariner's spiritual journey. While one may wish to question the reliability of the narrator of this experience based on the reactions of other characters to him, on his sense of isolation from humankind, and on the dream-like quality of the events, one eventually has to accept the event as true to the Mariner's individual perceptions. His physical self gives the best evidence of the truth of his tale.

While other Romantic poets, and even other texts of Coleridge's, most notably "Christabel" (1798), offer a range of vampires to examine for Romantic tendencies toward individualism, in order to concentrate on the subject of the numinous in vampire literature, I have chosen, in chapter two, to focus my discussion of the Romantic vampire on the metaphorical use of that figure in the poem. In this chapter, I have relied on John Curtis Gowan's *Trance, Art and Creativity* as a foundational study of the process of numinous contact in which he discusses three levels of encounter between the individual conscious *ego* and the numinous. Here the *ego* is defined both philosophically and psychologically, as the conscious self experiencing the world through the senses and as the part of the psyche seeking to control the darker impulses of what Freud calls the *id*. Each level of contact between the self and the numinous entails a reshaping of the individual's orientation to the reality perceived through the senses and can be identified by some loss of ego and, therefore, of some degree of control over the forces of the *id*. At the most primitive level the process of numinous contact may involve aspects of possession, hypnosis, and madness, which are characterized by involuntary loss of the ego; while the more controlled level of artistic contact incorporates an environment of myth, ritual, and archetype, where loss of control may or may not be voluntary. The highest level of contact is a sort of shamanistic, magical surrender of the self where the revelatory experience can be communicated to others in order to transform their view of reality.

While, for a poet such as Coleridge's contemporary William Wordsworth, sublime nature provided a most revelatory path in a poem like "Tintern Abbey," for Coleridge and his Ancient Mariner the sublime seems only a threshold or door to the divine. A return to the numinous in the form of the more primitive Gothic past, superstition and the supernatural, and the sublime natural world gave Coleridge a way to interrogate the individual's relationship with the divine. In "The Rime of the Ancient Mariner," the most extreme sublime experience, contact with the numinous, gives supernatural, rather than natural, form to divine truth. An analysis of the Ancient Mariner as a vampire figure in Coleridge's text can demonstrate not only the relationship of the Romantic artist to his audience and his creative product, which James B. Twitchell proposes in *The Living Dead*, but also the numinous process through which the lone Romantic poet becomes the artist. Combining a psychological reading with a religious one, I believe that as the different levels of loss of ego are experienced, the creative process can be characterized as a spiritual journey, first of isolation and alienation at the primitive level, then of reintegration as the subject of the numinous encounter moves through the artistic and creative modes. Once the artist has reached the creative mode the emphasis shifts to the relationship of artist and audience as the creative product is communicated to the listener or reader. At this point in the process, the audience of the tale must also encounter a manifestation of the numinous, first in the primitive mode of isolation as the hypnotic aspects of the artist and tale take hold of the imagination, and, finally, in the reintegrative artistic and creative modes as the audience makes meaning from what Gowan designates to be the pre-conscious images that are evoked by both the creative product and the artist. As meaning is made through communication of the creative product's message, the individuals who comprise the audience imitate the artist by effecting a transformation of their own cosmic understanding.

My discussion not only shows how these levels of numinous contact are variously exhibited in Coleridge's poem, but also analyzes how the negative numinousness of the vampire figure works as a positive example for revelation, transformation, and healing for the individual who feels separated from the divine. Although the Mariner seems to have compromised his belief in God through his isolation from his home community and through his killing of the albatross, he has not lost his faith completely; and once he is confronted by the negative numinous in the form of Life-in-Death, he feels his longing to reestablish his relationship with the divine. The Mariner, as artist, subsequently reunites with the divine through the levels of artistic and creative contact with the numinous by creating an individual prescription for redemption which he introduces into society as the tale of his experiences. By telling his story, he attempts to atone for his sins and creates a relationship with the divine. Though the Mariner is still an outsider as far as his fellowman is concerned, through both his outward appearance and his tale he serves as an example for the larger community, enabling humanity, one person at a time, to recognize its isolation from the divine and to attempt a reunion with the cosmos through acceptance of the moral of the his tale.

Chapter Three. Recreating the World: The Sacred and the Profane in Bram Stoker's Dracula

Not only is *Dracula* now considered the classic vampire text, but the attitudes and ideas of the characters also represent the late Victorian mindset in regard to several important issues of their day, including the importance of business and their own desires for advancement in society, the significance of their culture in their own minds, and their concern over what the influx of foreign influences might do to their British culture and to the competition for place in society. Juxtaposed against these fears is their need for belief in a God who seemed all too absent in their busy, upwardly mobile lives, and their resultant feelings of spiritual poverty as they desired a reconnection with the divine, but had no real faith that it would or could happen.

With this novel, Stoker transforms the epistolary style of earlier, realistic novels, such as *Pamela* (1740–42) and *Clarissa* (1747–48) by Samuel Richardson, into the transcription of a Gothic nightmare whose multiple versions might raise doubt as to the reliability of any of the versions, despite Stoker's use of realism to describe setting and characters. However, when Jonathan Harker finally realizes what the women of castle Dracula and Dracula himself represent, he feels the weight of the truth of the events that have transpired. Later, when Mina Harker transcribes all of the characters' individual stories and combines them into one, acceptance of the situation as real must follow. Once she has put the events in perspective, the fears of the individuals become the fears of society; and, if society is to be protected, the individuals, now as a combined force, must use their powers to destroy the threat of Dracula and his women. In their search and destroy mission against the vampires, the individuals within the group call on their faith, imagining themselves to be crusaders, who must go on a more secular version of the spiritual journey to uphold what they value as sacred in British society.

For this discussion, I have taken S. L. Varnado's essay "The Daemonic in *Dracula*" from *Haunted Presence: The Numinous in Gothic Fiction* (1987) as a base point. Varnado's discussion is based to a great degree on Otto's *Idea of the Holy* and, more slightly, on religious historian Mircea Eliade's interpretation of Otto's work in his discussion of the sacred and profane features of early religions. Although Varnado interprets the story of *Dracula* as the universal, age-old opposition between the forces of chaos and order, he does little to illuminate how manifestations of the numinous as sacred and profane polarities are reflected as themes within the text. Instead, he concentrates on the emotions of Jonathan Harker as he succumbs to the qualities of the numinous that are manifested in Dracula's character. Therefore, my discussion employs Eliade's critical studies of world religions to illuminate the thematic, mythic patterns of sacred and profane space and time within the text. This examination leads eventually into a discussion of faith and belief and why it is important to late Victorian culture that the vampire be destroyed. As the humans in the text confront the numinous qualities of Dracula, they must also confront their own apathetic faith in God, leading them to reenact mythic rituals in order to reestablish their relationship with the divine.

While there is artistry in the characters' storytelling, as there is in "The Ancient Mariner," salvation for the group in *Dracula* does not come through the penitential telling of a tale, but through another more primitive act, the resacralizing of their world through the ritual staking of the vampire.

Preface

Although the Mariner and Dracula are both characterized as eternal wanderers and vampires, Dracula does not get to tell his story as the Mariner does; nor is he allowed to take part in the cosmic healing of society. As the negatively numinous vampire, Dracula is meant to be sacrificed so that society may continue on its already established course.

Although faith does become an issue for the protective powers in the story, that faith serves the purposes of the humans, rather than the humans being employed in the service of the faith as the Mariner is in Coleridge's Romantic poem. At the end of the story, the reader is still left with a sense of the Victorian's lack of faith, as the heroes of the action seem to simply be reestablishing the more secular sacredness of their current nationalistic, profit-making society, instead of reuniting with divine power and remaking their world in a more religious context as the Ancient Mariner does with his tale.

Chapter Four: Eros and the Thanatotic Hero: Anne Rice's Vampire Chronicles

For chapter four, I have chosen to concentrate on Anne Rice's *Vampire Chronicles*. In her stories of the vampire Lestat, Rice uses the autobiographical technique to provide an individual experience of the human condition through the eyes of the vampire. As individual memoirs and purportedly *true* histories of her vampire character's life, these tales lay claim, as do Coleridge's poem and Stoker's novel, to an individualistic and realistic approach to the telling of the tale; however, the ambiguousness and hesitation of the fantastic in her texts is less focused on feelings than the other two texts and more focused on the questions Lestat asks about who he is, what he is, and what his spiritual fate will be.

The difference between Rice's vampire Lestat and the vampires of Coleridge and Stoker is that Lestat is clearly the hero of the story; it is his search for divine truth with which the audience identifies. As the hero, Lestat is all too human, creating a world that mimics the one he has been banished from wherever possible. Unlike the Mariner and the main characters of *Dracula*, whose experiences of the vampire require them to fall back on a wavering belief in God, Lestat is a self-proclaimed atheist. Regardless of his disbelief, however, his experiences with the vampire

Preface

Magnus, and of the vampire life, serve to underscore for him that the divine does exist in some form and that he is now alienated from it with no possibility of reunion in the afterlife.

However, there are similarities between the vampires, as well. Through the five books of the *Vampire Chronicles* that deal with Lestat's story, Lestat searches for the meaning of his existence in the history of vampires, in the human life he has left behind, and, finally, in a meeting between himself, God and the Devil. Like the Mariner's story, Lestat's is one of moral dilemma. The question he often asks himself is how one continues to *be* good when one is so obviously evil because he is a vampire. Just as the Mariner seeks out only those who need to hear his tale and finds grace through the penitential telling of his story, Lestat does not kill indiscriminately, but looks for victims who have done evil, thinking that by doing so he might possibly negate his own evil in some way. In spite of his moral attitude, Lestat shares much with Dracula, also. While Dracula is perceived as evil by the heroes of Stoker's tale, his potential for goodness lies in his own heroic past. However, that past is overshadowed by his present desire to be the master of all and his need to survive by drinking blood. Lestat's heroic past, on the other hand, is what makes him moral, so that he must be a hero as a vampire. As a representative of divine power, Lestat is described in terms of angelic proportion and lives up to his godlike stature as he saves not only those he loves, but also the world, from death and destruction. In *Memnoch the Devil*, when Lestat finally meets both Satan and God, God produces a sense of guilt in Lestat, guilt that he would even consider becoming God's adversary. At the same time, he is tempted by Satan to join the forces of the rebels of heaven. Although he refuses to serve either God or Memnoch, on his return to earth he is aware that whatever action he takes in the future could very well be done unintentionally in the service of one or the other. While the Mariner and the characters in Dracula tell their tales in hopes that no proof is needed, Lestat refuses to provide the proof — a taste of the blood of Christ — that would convince his fellow vampires of the truth of his tale. Instead, he leaves them with the statement that his individual account is all there is — take it or leave it.

Preface

Conclusion. Vampires for a New Age

This study has explored how three writers in three different literary periods used the vampire to convey a human sense of alienation from the divine and a desire to overcome that alienation by arguing that a textual experience of the numinous in the form of the vampire propels the subject of the experience on a spiritual journey involving both psychological and religious qualities. In the conclusionary chapter, I offer an overview of some of the more marginal subjects that have been finding a voice in vampire literature in the years since Anne Rice's Lestat first brought her readers into the light. However, since this chapter is also meant to discuss the vampire of the twenty-first century, I have included a short discussion of Rice's character Lestat and his continuing spiritual journey as it is developed in three works Rice has published since the turn of the century: *Merrick* (2000), *Blackwood Farm* (2002), and *Blood Canticle* (2003). In these texts Rice further describes Lestat's personal spiritual journey through both his own words and those of others who know him, taking him further along the road to faith than ever before.

Who can truly say where these vampires will take us in the course of the twenty-first century? Will the new vampires be heroes, villains, victims, or saints? Whose voices will speak from their throats? It is my hope that many more voices that are considered marginal will find articulation in the vampire literature of the new millennium. We are all human after all!

• ONE •

Dreadful Revelations
The Numinous and the Vampire

Before attempting to examine the vampire as an experience of the numinous, several issues must be addressed. These issues include: the problem of how to reconcile the textual construction of an experience of the numinous through language with the idea that the numinous, by definition, is indescribable; the philosophical question of whether the divine in any form truly exists and where belief in the divine enters into an encounter with the numinous; and whether a discussion of the experience of the numinous in literature should be approached from a purely psychological point of view, a purely religious one, or a combination of the two perspectives. The problem of textual construction and the ineffableness of the numinous can be resolved, or at least clarified, in a discussion of the conventions of realism and the fantastic or Gothic text. Questions of the existence of the divine, of whether a preconceived belief in that existence is required in an experience of the numinous, and of the psychological versus the religious approach can be examined in a discussion of the definition of the numinous and the connection of an experience of the numinous to both the psychological and religious realms of knowledge.

Realism, the Fantastic, and the Numinous

In *The Rise of the Novel: Studies in Defoe, Richardson and Fielding*, Ian Watt attributes the development of the novel in the early eighteenth century to the advent of realism as a philosophic viewpoint, to the rise of the middle class as an important contingent of the reading public, and to the influence of the courts of law. Drawing on the work of philosophers, such as René Descartes' *Discourse on Methods* (1637) and John Locke's *Essay Concerning Human Understanding* (1690), Watt argues that "modern realism ... begins from the position that truth can be discovered by the individual through his senses" (12). With its use of realism, the novel "attempts to portray all the varieties of human experience" (11); and, therefore, the importance of realism lies not in what kind of experience is portrayed, but in how that experience is presented to the reader.

In Watt's estimation the most important problem that realism foregrounds is "the problem of correspondence between the literary work and the reality it imitates" (11). Watt locates the basis of this problem in the diametrically opposed philosophies of earlier literary periods and the more modern one in which the novel developed. He suggests that, just as many philosophers of the eighteenth century rejected universals and abstractions, many of the eighteenth-century novelists turned away from the formal conventions and traditional plots of earlier literary works based on universal subjects such as myth, history, and legends.

While acknowledging Ian Watt's work as the most successful of past studies on the novel, in *The Origins of the English Novel 1600–1740*, Michael McKeon addresses problems he feels are inherent in Watt's discussion, including Watt's argument for the rise of realism. McKeon argues that the historical situation of the emergence of the novel is more complicated than Watt envisioned it, that the changes that influenced the writers over time came not only from philosophical viewpoints, socio-economic advancements, and the influence of courts of law, but also from the effect of the religious and scientific movements of the various periods and from the rise of the print media itself. McKeon's main criticism of Watt's study is that Watt did not extend his research far enough into the history of literature to give an accurate view of how realism became part of the literary tradition. Therefore, while Watt believes the eighteenth-century novelists were rejecting tradition, McKeon sees the new novelistic convention of realism grounded in the traditions of the past. From McKeon's perspective, the literary romance grew out of earlier oral traditions as the conventions of myth were employed in the service of believability. Drawing on the archetypalist theories of Mircea Eliade, Claude Lévi-Strauss, and Northrop Frye, McKeon argues that the novel emerged from the genre of romance, which itself was grounded in the mythic stories of many primitive tribal societies.

However, McKeon maintains that another problem arises in the use of archetypalist theory to trace literary history. As Watt's approach relied on differences between genres, archetypal theory tends to "overemphasize continuity and identity" (McKeon 10). In the antithesis of these views, however, McKeon finds hope for a comprehensive theory of genre. The historical evidence McKeon gathers to support his premise indicates that the conventions of myth were never exhausted, but simply destabilized and changed into the conventions of romance. Claiming that early writers of romance employed some characteristics of *formal realism*, McKeon argues that the differentiation between factual and fictional literature was already becoming established long before the novel's emergence as a genre in the early decades of the eighteenth century, and that the conventions of romance were never entirely replaced by those of realism. In a study that attempts to trace the movement of these overlapping genres through history, McKeon takes a dialectic approach, examining how the literature of each period handled questions of truth and virtue in an atmosphere of alternating pressures from "naïve empiricism ... [and] extreme skepticism" (21) motivated by conservative and progressive ideas. He maintains that through the changes wrought under these pressures, the conventions of realism and the novel itself were born; by the end of the eighteenth century, he argues, the idealism of romance had weathered a long re-evaluative process which gave rise to the romantic movement and "the secularized, human spirituality of the aesthetic" (419).

While McKeon's study of realism's genealogy is interesting and useful at various points in this discussion, Watt provides knowledge that is more practical to begin a discussion of realism and the individual human experience. Watt maintains that in relating human experience, the eighteenth-century novelists adapted traditional prose styles in order to reflect their claims of "complete authenticity" (27) and faithfulness to the human experience. In order to recreate the unique experience of the individual as faithfully as possible, characters had to be presented as particular people with proper names that demonstrated their individuality rather than names that reflected a general type of human being. Many early novelists also found that the Aristotelian unities of time and space had to be particularized along with the characters. Time and space became important facets of presenting a particular setting and character realistically. Time also became important in realism because the concept of time allows the self-aware person to see a cause and effect relationship between past experience and present action.

If the novel with its conventions of realism promises an authentic account of human experience, the novelist must seek to satisfy the readers with details that reflect the individuality of the characters and the specifics of time and space in which the characters act and speak. The problem with the individual experience in literature, as in life, lies in the same particularity that makes the experience realistic or believable. McKeon's principle of reversals shows itself at this point, because the realistic novel might be considered a product of *naïve empiricism*, seeking to provide an authentic version of the world; however, in McKeon's analysis, *extreme skepticism* is always waiting in the wings. An attitude of skepticism toward a text tells the reader that this particular version of events is not the only version, and the questions of truth and virtue must be applied to elements of the text in order to ascertain whether this particular version can be trusted. Since language is the medium of text production, the details of an individual human experience are presented in the realistic novel with "a more largely referential use of language than is common in other literary forms" (Watt 32). Realism, therefore, makes fewer demands upon the imagination of the reader; however, a genre such as the fantastic makes larger demands on the audience because use of the conventions of the fantastic causes the reader to question the truth of the individual experience. Questioning the truth or authenticity of an account of human experience underscores the probability of multiple interpretations, which in itself implies the possibility of there being no definitive interpretation. This lack of interpretability produces a feeling of chaos in the imagination of the reader, a chaos that challenges the individual's comprehension of order within his own life.

It is this chaos, this lack of interpretability, which concerns theorist Tzvetan Todorov. In *The Fantastic: A Structural Approach to a Literary Genre*, he writes, "in a world which is indeed our world, the one we know, a world without devils, sylphides, or vampires, there occurs an event which cannot be explained by the laws of this familiar world" (25). Seeking a linguistic basis for the structural features he sees in fantastic texts, Todorov places the interpretation of meaning secondary to the effect produced by language. Despite his assertion that one cannot "define the fantastic in terms of opposition to the faithful reproduction of reality" (36), an overview of the conventions of fantasy as he developed them placed against Watt's conventions of realism helps to lay the foundation on which to build a discussion of the numinous.

In his study, Todorov places the fantastic at the center of a spectrum of reaction to the chaotic events. However, it is the reader, and sometimes the main character, who decides whether "laws of reality remain intact and permit an explanation of the phenomena described ... [or] if, on the contrary, ... new laws of nature must be entertained to account for the phenomena" (*Fantastic* 41). Once the reader or character has chosen to believe in either natural or supernatural causes for the events encountered, he or she has entered the genres of either the uncanny or the marvelous, respectively. Works that maintain the hesitation of the character for a long period but in which ultimately the decision is made between natural and supernatural causes are relegated to the sub-genres of fantastic-uncanny or fantastic-marvelous that lie between the central pure fantastic realm and the two extremes of pure uncanny and pure marvelous. According to Todorov, the truly fantastic can be found only in the uncertainty and hesitation of the subject who suffers from the lack of interpretability that characterizes the text. From a structuralist viewpoint, the reader ultimately decides what texts are fantastic, as in the process of reading he or she identifies with a character in the story and attempts "to reconstruct the story the text is telling" (*Genres* 125) through that character.

Todorov further delineates conditions that must be met if a text is to be considered fantastic. Not only *must* the reader accept the textual world as populated by real people, identify with one or more characters in that world, and experience the hesitation between natural and supernatural explanations, but the hesitation felt by the reader also *may* be experienced by one or more of the characters in the text. In this way the hesitation felt by the reader becomes a theme of perception within the text. The reader's attitude toward the text must also be such that the reader rejects both allegorical and poetic ways of reading the text in favor of reading the events as real and unexplainable. To read allegorically is to read events as being significant of more figurative meanings, of standing for something else. To read poetically would be to read the events as literally true but with the added awareness that they are not. To accept some event as fantastic, however, requires that we not know whether the event is real or not. Seeking the linguistic foundations for the structural features he sees in fantastic texts, Todorov attempts to explain the system of language that makes the literary effects of fantasy possible by relying on the verbal, syntactical, and semantic features of language.

The verbal factors of Todorov's structuralist theory are constituted in what Todorov refers to as "ambiguous vision" (*Fantastic* 33), manifested verbally by the mode, time, perspective, and voice of the fictional discourse. Mode of discourse pertains to "the degree of exactitude" (Todorov *Poetics* 29) with which the events of the plot are evoked in the text. The ambiguous vision of the fantastic text is produced through a manifestation of mode that transgresses realistic conventions with the use of figurative discourses such as exaggeration and metamorphosis. Time involves the relationship between two temporal lines that have been juxtaposed within the text: that of the "universe represented" within the text and that of the "discourse representing it" (29). In a fantastic text, time is manipulated with foreshadowing techniques and pacing to condition the reader to the coming fantastic event and build tension to which the reader reacts. Perspective or vision involves the point of view from which the story is told, as either objective or subjective. Objectively, the reader is informed about what is perceived; subjectively, the reader discovers information about the perceiver of the action or object. In regards to the reader's degree of knowledge about the fictive world, two things are important: first, the extent of the vision or the angle from which events are observed, as either internal or external, and second, the depth or degree of vision. Narrative voice concerns the agent of the construction of the fictive universe. The narrator establishes the principles on which judgments of value and reality are made in the text and conceals or reveals the character's thoughts and actions in order to move the story along the path it must follow to its climax. Involved along with the narrator is the "narratee," who, as Todorov says, "is not the real reader, any more than the narrator is the author" (40). The narratee, he or she to whom the fictive discourse is addressed, does, however, serve as a liaison between narrator and actual reader, characterizing the narrator, bringing out themes, advancing the plot, and showing the actual reader how to read the text.

In his essay "Reading as Construction," Todorov maintains that "only referential sentences allow construction to take place" (68); however, in reading fantasy, though the sentences themselves must be referential in order for the reader to construct the fictive universe, the ambiguity of vision suffered by the narrator undercuts the constructive process, forcing a *de*-construction to take place at the same moment of construction. In this *de*-constructive process, gaps of knowledge and belief appear in the story through the modalization of doubt and the ambiguity of vision. In Todorov's theory, the second feature of language that is important to production of the fantastic is the syntactical character of the structure. Syntactical structure involves the reactions of characters to the events seen as formal units of language utterance. These utterances can be logical, temporal, or spatial. Realistic fictional works are structured in accordance with temporal and spatial order and with the logical constraint of cause and effect. However, in the fantastic text, syntactical structures involve the reactions of the characters to the events. These reactions can be seen as formal units that Todorov articulates as: "I + verb of attitude + modalization of that verb in the direction of uncertainty" (*Genres* 24). Ambiguity results syntactically with the use of a verb and the modalization of that verb toward uncertain vision. The pronoun *I*, representing the reader of the text as guided by the narrator within the text, and subject to the same ambiguity of vision which the narrator suffers, responds to the fantastic events recounted within the text with some form of attitudinal reaction characterized by words such as *believe* or *think*. However, the hesitation that Todorov characterizes as the most important element in the reader's reaction to the fantastic comes into play here. The reader experiences the narrator's ambiguous vision as the narrator modalizes the verb of attitude through use of the imperfect tense to establish "distance between character and the narrator" (*Fantastic* 38) and with adverbs that suggest ambiguity, hesitation, and doubt. In this way, the fantastic text is both logically and temporally shifted toward a feeling of uncertainty over the events, rather than toward sureness of a natural or a supernatural causality.

Although spatial order is often considered more important in poetry than in prose, it also has its application in the construction of a fantastic text. Todorov defines spatial order as "the existence of a certain more or less regular disposition of the units of the text" (*Poetics* 46). In terms of syntactic elements of a text, spatial order involves organization of the text in symmetrical patterns involving repetition, gradation, parallelism, and thesis/antithesis. Repetition and gradation, in which each repeated manifestation of a fantastic event becomes gradually more obvious, more *real* to the character and reader, and more threatening to the character's and reader's already tenuous hold on the reality of the overall chain of events work together to produce a spatial structure in which the repeated events form the impetus for the plot and the thread which ties the actions of the characters together. On the other hand, parallelism and thesis/antithesis form spatial structures with the use of doubling and polarities that manifest themselves in events and characters which split the discourse of both plot and characters into separate threads to be rewoven in the reader's mind. These doublings and polarities then become themes of the self and the other so important in the development of fantastic texts.

In the development of themes, the semantic aspect of structuralism becomes important. The semantic properties of Todorov's structuralist theory involve relationships "of meaning and of symbolization" and of "configuration, of construction" (*Poetics* 14). In terms of meaning and symbolization, "a certain signifier *signifies* a certain signified, a certain phenomenon *evokes* another, a certain episode *symbolizes* an idea, another *illustrates* a psychology" (14). The power of meaning and symbolization is the power to evoke the existence of one thing through the manipulation of another. With configuration or construction, cause and effect logic links the phenomena. The *antitheses* and *gradations* of the manifestation of phenomena, instead of the symbolization, form the relationships between characters, and word combinations form the relationships of those things or people juxtaposed. Meaning and symbolization are paradigmatic, relying on repetition and parallelism to create patterns, while configuration and construction are syntagmatic, relying on the reactions of the characters to provide causality. In fantastic literature, the syntactical reactions of the characters to repeated events represent themes of perception and of its notation by the character. The problems and awareness of ambiguous perception are manifested in the fantastic text as polarizing themes of the self, involving divisions of personality or doubling, as the play of dream and reality, and as the play of mind and matter. These themes can be represented as what Todorov calls "themes of discourse" (*Fantastic* 39), involving qualities of otherness in which the relationship of man with his unconscious, with his own feelings of desire for both sexual gratification and violence, become important.

By virtue of its structural focus, Todorov's theory of the fantastic puts the burden of construction of the text upon the reader's shoulders. In order to experience the hesitancy which Todorov feels to be the main requirement of the fantastic text, the reader must constitute the ambiguous vision of the narrator through his or her reading of the verbal, syntactic, and semantic structures in the text. If we consider the numinous to be an effect of the language of a text, just as the fantastic is, we now must question where an experience of the numinous should be situated in terms of the conventions of both realism and the fantastic.

For Rudolf Otto, whose work *The Idea of the Holy: An Inquiry into the non-rational factor in the idea of the divine and its relation to the rational* defines the experience of the numinous, the Gothic is the most numinous of literary genres, due to its use of sublime and daemonic conventions, such as mountainous crags, glaciers, ice flows, and ruined castles; and since Otto's definitive study, other works such as Devendra P. Varma's *The Gothic Flame* have appropriated Otto's phrase *the numinous* to describe the Gothic as the "quest for the numinous" (206), a quest Varma characterizes as having been brought on by religious decline and by humanity's need to find a new outlet for its guilt and fear. Varma likened this quest to "an almost archetypal impulse" (211) that drives the individual to attempt to experience the infinite within a finite existence. Almost four decades later Vijay Mishra returned to Varma's earlier work on the numinous to redraw the symbols of the quest and flame, discussing the idea of the numinous under the title *The Gothic Sublime* by drawing on philosopher Edmund Burke's eighteenth-century aesthetic theory put forward in *A Philosophical Enquiry into the Origins of our Ideas of the Sublime and Beautiful* (1756). Following a psychological approach, Burke regards the sublime as a phenomenon of power because issues of power most often arise in an exchange where "terror, the common stock of every thing that is sublime" (64) is felt at the possibility of pain or the danger of death. An object or person of superior strength is considered dangerous by those who are weaker because they fear that power or strength will be used against them or those they love. In addition to being of superior strength, to evoke the fear of the possibility of pain or death, the object of terror must be perceived as obscure in some way; for, if a person can ascertain the full extent of a danger, a great deal of the fear vanishes. Burke also catalogs concepts and aspects of nature which can produce sublime feeling, including aspects of privation such as darkness, solitude and emptiness which evoke feelings of mankind's essential loneliness, and features of dimension such as vastness, infinity and magnificence which draw attention to the littleness of the human being in the grand scheme of the world. Burke believed that through the contemplation of sublime nature humans could move to contemplation of God and their relationship with Him. Using the concept of the sublime to investigate the Gothic, Mishra finds that at its heart the Gothic is unable to present meaning because the "sublime threatens our very capacities of cognitive judgment" (16).

Mishra's characterization of the Gothic sublime as a threat to the human capacity for apprehension must take us back to Todorov's theory of the fantastic genre. If we are to define the numinous as a textual construct within the Gothic genre, we must take a page from Todorov and situate the numinous in terms of realism and the fantastic. In order to place the conventions of the numinous in literature somewhere between those of realism and the fantastic, and to answer the questions of the ineffableness of an experience of the numinous and the existence of the divine, we will turn to Rudolf Otto's *Idea of the Holy* for a definition of the numinous as a religious experience.

Drawing on ideas from Immanuel Kant's *Critique of Pure Reason* (1781) and *Critique of Judgement* (1790), Otto incorporated into his own theory Kant's idea of *a priori* knowledge obtained through experience, interpreting Kant as dividing judgements based on experience and knowledge from those based on logic and rational concepts. According to Otto, a deity is characterized by concepts, such as "spirit, reason, purpose, good will, supreme power, unity, [and] selfhood" (*Idea* 1). A rational religion is based on the definition and analysis of, and consequent belief in, the manifestation of these concepts rather than on emotional responses to experiences. However, human knowledge of these concepts can only rest on faith because "knowledge of God and eternity, and the real value, transcending space and time, of our own inner being" (Otto *Naturalism and Religion* 11) cannot be established only through reason and scientific study.

For Otto, the rational, conceptual aspects of the sacred, though an essential moral and ethical part of the religious experience, do not define it entirely. Religion also has a non-rational nature, which, neither in opposition to, nor superior to, reason, is still beyond the conceptual foundation of knowledge which reason posits. In *The Idea of the Holy*, Otto's purpose is to balance the non-rational, mysterious quality of the sacred against the human tendency to reduce the experience to something within

One • Dreadful Revelations

our own limits of understanding. To help define this non-rational experience, Otto coined the word *numinous* from the Latin *numen* to signify not only the divine, but also to designate that "feeling which remains where the concept fails" (Otto *Idea* Foreword by the Author to First Edition n.p.). Otto conceives this feeling not as emotion per se, but as a subjective awareness that cannot be arrived at conceptually, and through which the observer of the sacred comes to comprehend and acknowledge the numinous object or situation. An experience of the numinous as an instance of awareness of the sacred is "perfectly *sui generis* and irreducible to any other" (*Idea* 7), and, as such, is ineffable and beyond the power of language to describe. Otto, however, seeks to express the inexpressible experience by articulating its attributes as *"mysterium tremendum et fascinans"* (Varnado *Haunted* 1), a frightening mystery, which is, at the same time, fascinating and enticing.

The attribute that Otto calls *mysterium* is defined as being beyond the scope of human understanding because in the experience of the numinous the individual encounters "something inherently 'wholly other'" (*Idea* 28) and is struck with a sense of awe and confusion. It is this reaction to the otherness of the numinous object that delineates the first necessary attribute of the numinous. To be a mystery, the numinous must be perceived as an objective entity, something outside of the observer, obscure in its own way and, therefore, puzzling. The mysterious nature of the numinous allows the hesitation of which Todorov speaks in terms of the fantastic also to be part of the conventions of the numinous. In the mystery and the puzzlement it produces, there exists a modality of doubt that leads to reader hesitation as to what the experience means and as to whether the experience is real or not. However, the subject of an experience of the numinous must eventually perceive the experience as real in the sense that it represents the other as opposed to the self of the subject.

The feeling brought on by the mysteriousness of the numinous object is then strengthened by the addition of the adjective *tremendum* in Otto's definition. Now the mystery evokes more than wonder; it evokes fear. While Todorov feels that fear does not necessarily need to be present in the fantastic text, for Otto, this feeling of fear or dread "implies ... a category of valuation" (*Idea* 15) outside ordinary human experience, in other words, a new way of seeing, experiencing, and knowing the world. In Otto's definition, *tremendum* or dread is characterized by the elements of awefulness, overpoweringness, and energy, which work together to produce the dread inherent in an experience of the numinous. The awe and natural fear evoked by the sight of a raging ocean, a mountain lightning storm, or the unbroken expanse of a starlit night sky may sweep one with a feeling of what Immanuel Kant referred to in *Observations on the Feeling of the Beautiful and Sublime* as the *noble* sublime (48), a recognition of the self in relation to a divine Being who not only made man, but also created the immensity of the natural world which surrounds him; or, as *tremendum*, the mystery may "burst in sudden eruption up from the depths of the soul with spasms and convulsions, or lead to the strangest excitements, to intoxicated frenzy, to transport, and to ecstasy" (Otto *Idea* 12).

However, it is not the degree or intensity of the fear that is most important, according to Otto; it is that the person not only trembles before something apparently absolute and powerful, but also that the person is left with a sense of the self's insignificance in relation to that absolute power. This sense of utter powerlessness comes into play with the addition of the second element of *tremendum*, which Otto describes as "absolute overpoweringness" (*Idea* 19). The submergence of one's own significance in relation to the absolute power of the numinous object engenders a feeling which Otto calls "'creature-consciousness'" (10), comparing it to being, like the Biblical Abraham, "but dust and ashes" (Otto *Idea* 9, Gen. 18:27) before that which is "supreme above all creatures" (*Idea* 10). The character of this overpoweringness is verbally inexpressible, suggestible only through the person's reaction to it, which must be personally experienced in order to be comprehended as a sense of powerlessness before what is perceived as an absolute power.

The subject's sense of the power of the divine also involves the third element of *tremendum*, "'energy'" (Otto *Idea* 23), which Otto, expanding on the work of Johann Gottlieb Fichte, defines as the "will, force, emotional temper" (23) of the numinous. The numen is understood to be dangerous, having the ability and the perceived intent to inflict pain or death. The force of the numinous is durable and unstoppable, living and urgent, seeking, in the perception of the subject, consummation with and consequent annihilation of the subject of the experience. For Otto, an individual's dread of this presence produces a sense of his or her own creatureliness and mortality. This sense of one's own mortality in the face of the absolute power and immortality of a divine power evokes fears of the destruction of the self and these fears, in turn, engender their own understanding of the "transcendent as the sole and entire reality" (21) and an estimation of the self as "something not perfectly or essentially real" (21).

For Otto, the element of *tremendum* also may indicate a negative experience of the numinous in which the "daemonic element is emphasized" (Varnado *Haunted* 15) and the sacred and profane "value elements" (35) are inverted. In the negatively numinous, the sacred aspects become profane and the awe and dread of *tremendum* increase to the point that fear reduces the individual to "horror and shuddering" (Otto *Idea* 13). In order to explain his theory of the negative numinous, Otto draws on the work of Jakob Böhme, a German mystic of the early seventeenth century. Otto interprets Böhme as saying that comprehension of the earthly world and its relation to the divine begins in man's experience of "the 'primal bottom', the supra-rational identification of good and evil in an Indifferent" (106). The numinous as an indifferent entity demonstrates that the character of the divine is two-fold, consisting of "goodness and love on the one hand and fury and wrath on the other" (106). In a footnote, Otto defines the "negatively numinous" as produced more by "*mysterium horrendum*" than by "*mysterium tremendum*" by virtue of the "mere potentiality of evil" (106–7) comprehended in an experience the numinous as the subject's perception that the event or figure has the ability to do harm. Though the negatively numinous figure or event is considered as opposed to the more positive power of the numinous as holy because of its potential for evil action against the subject, Otto still defines it as arising from the same fount of religious development as did mankind's perception of God. It is, therefore, through both the positive and negative attributes of the numinous that the individual may perceive the sacred once again as present in the world. The negative numinous includes the perception of such manifestations as demons and ghosts; however, Otto's discussion of the negative numinousness of these creatures does not link them necessarily to the profane in the human sense of being powerless, profane objects confronted by the power of sacredness. According to Otto, the profane is the quality of powerlessness and creatureliness the *earthly being* feels when confronted with the power of the sacred, whether that power is objectified as a heavenly being or as a negatively numinous lower form of the divine such as a ghost or demon — or, I would assert, a vampire — which, by virtue of their numinousness, have some touch of the divine to them and, therefore, are objects of so-called value or power as opposed to the lack of power felt by the subject.

As a further quality of the numinous, the mysterious factors of the numinous are influenced by the element of fascination which can be defined as a quality of attraction through which the experience "entices the imagination, awakening strong interest and curiosity" (Otto *Idea* 28). Dread and fascination combine in a "harmony of contrasts" (31); so, while the numinous is dreaded for its power to destroy the self, the subject of the experience is also drawn toward the numinous through a kind of enchantment that "that captivates and transports ... with a strange ravishment" (31), a kind of vertigo of the soul in which the subject fears the abyss below but cannot help but be drawn to take a step toward it.

According to Otto, the human awareness of the divine began as a feeling of "'daemonic dread'" (*Idea* 32) evoked by the awe-full majesty of the mystery that the divine represented, but a part of the fascination of an experience of the numinous is that same mystery. Eventually, as Otto interprets religious history, human beings attempted control the mystery of the divine world, and even to identify themselves with it. In effect, individuals sought to lose themselves in the experience of the numinous in order to understand the mystery more clearly. To move closer to the divine, humans adopted certain spiritual response systems, including "'magical' identification of the self with the numen ... [and] 'shamanistic' ways of ... self-fulfilment in exaltation and ecstasy" (33).

From Otto's viewpoint, this transactional relationship with the numinous, though it exists beyond moral concepts in and of itself, creates a category of value from the feeling of the unworthiness of the self, society, and of "existence in general" (*Idea* 50) that the subject perceives in the experience of the numinous. The subject's perception of powerlessness and insignificance is not moral as such, but is a "feeling of absolute 'profaneness'" (51) which, if accepted, must, in turn, suggest a correspondent positive value for the more powerful representation of the numinous. Otto suggests that, through acknowledgement of feelings of profaneness, and through the resulting submissiveness in the face of the power of the divine, humans began to perceive themselves as sinful and to look for ways to atone for that supposed sin. The subject feels the need of protection against the possible wrath of the divine, a kind of "shelter from the *tremendum*" (54). This act of protection becomes a consecration in which the subject approaching the divine rises above his or her earthly, profane existence to be manifested as numinous and, therefore, prepared "for intercourse with the numen" (54). Atonement for sins is an act of covering, necessary due to the lack of value the sinner feels in relation to the value of the numen. Longing to transcend his or her sense of unworthiness, the individual manifests a need for what might be called proactive atonement; and the absence of worth felt in relation to the numinous becomes a moral value in terms of the individual's relationship with the divine.

In Todorov's schematic of the fantastic, uncanny, and marvelous, the fantastic can only exist in a moment of hesitation characterized in similar terms to the ambivalent feelings of fascination and fear that Otto attributes to an experience of the numinous. If one accepts Otto's definition of the numinous, one might be tempted to interpret the numinous as fitting into Todorov's pure fantastic mode because the experience begins with a hesitant feeling due to the mysterious quality of that event. However, to continue in a condition of hesitation over the reality of the events would only produce hesitation in relation to the power polarities in the novel and, therefore, in relation to the formation of moral values and to the character's possible relationship with the divine in the end. In my analysis, an experience of the numinous eventually must be perceived as real by the character and the reader in order that the anxiety and fear felt through the dynamics of power and powerlessness be at their greatest strength to lead the subject to a change of moral attitude. Therefore, the conviction that an experience of the numinous is real is necessary to acceptance of the action of the plot and to the evaluation of the moral stand the text puts forward in the end. Since an encounter with the numinous, particularly in the form of the vampire, cannot be explained by the laws that govern empirical reality, at some point in the plot, the reader and the main character in the text must accept that new laws control the manifestation, and that they simply do not understand the laws that govern the event. This shifts the conventions of the numinous into the realm of the marvelous; and the text employing numinous conventions, although informed by the experience of hesitation that characterizes the fantastic, must give way in some degree to realism's assertion of the authenticity of the account and to a more referential language of belief in the reality of the experience.

Otto's definition of the experience of the numinous also brings up the questions of how to reconcile the construction of a text through language with the idea that the numinous is indefinable and, therefore, inexpressible and of whether the divine exists and if belief in the divine is necessary to an experience of the numinous. Accepting Otto's definition of the numinous as indescribable and beyond language, yet recognizing that in a text the numinous must be described in language, we must conclude that just as in Todorov's theory of the fantastic, in literature an experience of the numinous would include references to feelings and thematic polarities. The feelings in the text employing the numinous conventions would include the mysterious, frightening, and fascinating elements of the numinous event or object and the thematic polarities, such as power and powerlessness, life and death, and the sacred and profane, that call into question the character's belief in the existence of the divine. When the mysterious qualities of an experience of the numinous cause such dread that the character is filled with horror at the absolute power represented and at the potential for harm perceived in that power, and when the fascination the subject feels toward the numinous event is not simple longing or curiosity, but a violent seductive urge to lose oneself in the experience, and, thereby, to risk the immortal soul, the subject feels a sense of annihilation that has spiritual implications.

In Todorov's theory of the fantastic, hesitation is an end in itself; in relation to the numinous text, it is a means to an end — the examination of the character's and reader's ground of existence. In the "harmony of contrasts" (Otto *Idea* 34) that Otto defines as terror and fascination, we find what Todorov calls hesitation over the reality of the events. In this hesitation, as it is reflected in the numinous conventions, the reader may discover themes that reflect the polarities of sacred and profane, of life and death, and of power and powerlessness. The purpose of the numinous event, however, is not continued hesitation, but a challenge of the rational beliefs of the individual who sees this event as real but as controlled by laws beyond the scope of the empirical world; and this challenge sends the individual on a journey into the irrational side of experience to clarify the grounds of his or her spiritual existence.

The conviction that this experience is real brings up other problems in a discussion of the numinous. The relationship of the character to what he or she perceives to be a divine presence gives a clue as to where belief in the divine enters into a discussion of an encounter with the numinous.

One • Dreadful Revelations

The purpose of this discussion is not to prove the existence of the divine, but to argue that initial belief does not necessarily matter for one to experience the numinous. The problem of the divine's existence and its solution can be found in the hesitation the character feels about the reality of events. The hesitation produced by the sense of mystery over the reality of the events suggests the individual's hesitation between total belief in the existence of the divine and the possibility that the divine does not exist at all. However, the important question is not whether the character or reader believes whole-heartedly in the existence of a divine being, but how belief or disbelief influences that character's or reader's experience of the numinous.

In *The Future of an Illusion* (1927), Sigmund Freud posits the origins of religion as the sense of helplessness that primitive individuals felt in relation to the power of natural forces such as disease and death. He argues that to avoid the feeling of helplessness evoked by the forces of nature individuals banded together to create civilizations or cultures that would defend them against their feelings of helplessness. In order to reduce the anxiety they felt over their powerlessness, primitive individuals supposedly assigned human attributes to the forces of nature so they might approach them in the same manner of appeasement and influence as they did the more powerful humans in their society. Freud argues that the origins of this action are to be found in the sense of helplessness felt by the child in relation to the parents. For Freud, this is an ambivalent relationship characterized both by fear and by a sense of safety. The parents, especially the father, are feared because of their obvious power, yet they are also perceived as protective because of that greater power. As primitive individuals and societies recognized the power of the natural forces around them they turned the personified forces of nature into gods by giving them "the character of the father" (21) through attributes such as "wisdom, ... goodness, ... [and] justice" (24). In terms of psychology, these attributes of the divine were eventually "condensed" (24) into the form of one God which Freud feels uncovers the relationship with the father behind every divine figure. Despite the fact that these attributes of the divine are often put forth as divine revelations by different civilizations in different epochs, the revelations themselves cannot be authenticated because they are based on individual experiences. Over time, Freud maintains, people discovered that scientific laws controlled natural forces; however, as the forces of nature were divested of their human attributes, people still felt a sense of helplessness, now joined with a sense of longing for the lost father and the lost gods. These individuals expected the divine powers to appease their fears of the natural world and of the inevitability of human destiny and to hopefully reward them for the hardships suffered in life. When the divine failed in its tasks to rid individuals of terror and to reconcile them to their mortal fate, morality became the gods' "true domain" (22).[i]

Regardless of Freud's argument that religion is born from and sustained by the feelings of helplessness felt by the child and by primitive individuals, he feels that the illusion of religion, the fiction of the system, is necessary to control the despair individuals might feel without it and to provide the moral structure that would not be present without it. Just as Kant, who was unsure of God's existence, felt that individuals should live their lives as though God existed, Freud seems to be indicating that regardless of whether the divine truly exists or not, one should live life as though it does in order to have a moral code by which to live.

The existence of the divine is truly a mystery to humanity; however the question of whether one should believe in the existence of the divine is really a moot point in terms of literary analysis. As Otto defines an experience of the numinous, it requires that the individual encountering the numinous perceive the experience as an objective reality; however, at the outset of the experience, it is not necessary that the person believe in God or any other manifestation of the divine for the person to perceive this manifestation as real. It is through the experience of the numinous and the moral outlook engendered by that experience that the subject comes to view the event as representative of divine power. In Coleridge's "The Rime of the Ancient Mariner," the Mariner's belief has suffered from his isolation from traditional religion while he is at sea and from the crime he has committed against nature. Although his spiritual journey continues indefinitely since he must travel from place to place fulfilling his penance by telling his tale, he does end up transformed, with a new moral outlook, an outlook for which he wants the reader and the Wedding Guest to take his story as proof. In Stoker's *Dracula*, the religious beliefs of the British society, represented by the community of characters who search for and destroy Dracula, have been forgotten or, at least, compromised by the late nineteenth-century concentration on profit and professional advancement. Having begun their journey with no proof their experience of the vampire was real, at the end they need no proof of the authenticity of their experience. They have lived the nightmare journey. In Rice's *Vampire Chronicles*, Lestat has never believed in God, only in those who represent God. At the end of his tales, he ends up transformed; but his story is the only proof he will give others of the truth of his experience, because in the end he still is not sure of his beliefs. However, he has moved forward a little: no longer an atheist, he now might be labeled an agnostic.

The last question to be addressed is whether an experience of the numinous should be considered a purely psychological issue, a purely religious one, or a combination of the two. Since an experience of the numinous is by definition indescribable and, therefore, can only be suggested through the subject's reaction to the experience, the numinous, though essentially considered an ecstatic and revelatory experience of a divine presence in the world, may also be considered a psychological experience. In "The 'Uncanny'" (1919), Sigmund Freud addresses the emotional effect he calls the *uncanny* in psychoanalytic terms. Although he admits his research into previous studies on the subject was not as thorough as he might have hoped, he attempts to clarify the features of the uncanny through an examination of the ambiguous definitions of *heimlich* that form the foundation of *unheimlich* or the uncanny. He follows this lexical discussion with an extended investigation of instances of the uncanny, particularly in literature. Asserting that the uncanny effect is produced by whatever "arouses dread and horror" (219), Freud feels that what is feared in an uncanny situation is the perceived intent and ability of the uncanny to harm the individual. This idea leads him back to a more primitive understanding of cosmic origins in which people populated their world with "the spirits of human beings" (240). However, he also underscores the inability to describe the uncanny and the feeling of hesitation by calling attention to the various and complicated definitions from which the term arose and finding that the meaning of the original German *heimlich* is ambiguous at best.

As hesitation must be present in Todorov's theory of the fantastic, so Freud feels that for an event to be considered uncanny, the reader must be uncertain as to whether events are real or not; however, the focus must not be on the uncertainty but on the feelings evoked by it. He argues there must be a sense of helplessness, much like the feeling of helplessness one feels in some dreams. Freud feels that the frightening situations that one defines as uncanny can be traced back to what is familiar. However, for Freud, as for Todorov, uncertainty must be present; therefore, the familiar cannot be recognized as familiar.

These familiar, yet unfamiliar, events are remnants of what Freud refers to as the "animistic stage in primitive men" ("'Uncanny'" 240) that has been outlined earlier in this introduction's discussion of *The Future of an Illusion* (1927) and was developed also in *Totem and Taboo* (1913). An experience of the uncanny occurs in two ways: when repressed "infantile complexes" ("Uncanny" 249) are triggered by some incident or "when primitive beliefs which have been surmounted seem once more to be confirmed" (249). However, Freud does not view these uncanny manifestations as occurring independently of one another; rather, he sees them as interconnected because he feels that primitive belief systems originated from those "infantile complexes" (249). Understanding the foundation of these types of uncanny episodes also does not necessarily preclude belief that their content is based in reality. Freud argues that familiar events are repressed by the psyche and turned into feelings of anxiety that are then manifested as the uncanny when the event recurs in some form; and, for Freud, the event over which people experience the greatest degree of uncanny feeling is death. He argues that religion posits life after death to ease those fears.

In literature, Freud feels, the uncanny depends for effect on the fact that the content of the text is not submitted to a test of reality. Readers accept the world the writer has created along with the assumptions of the characters in that world. If the writer depicts reality, however, he must also allow for the circumstances of life that provoke uncanny sensations. Freud argues that people are essentially passive and indifferent to the real experiences of their lives and "are subject to influence of [their] physical environment" ("Uncanny" 250); but the storyteller has a "peculiarly directive power" (251) over the readers and can create moods and emotions that lead them toward the uncanny.

In light of the uncanny's ability to cause fear and hesitation in the character and in the reader, one might be tempted to assume that Freud's theory is the same as Todorov's. However, while Freud defines uncanny events as arising from repressed childhood memories or surmounted beliefs from the primal childhood of the human race, Todorov characterizes the uncanny as events that, however extraordinary and unexpected they might be, can be explained through reasonable means. Todorov does admit, though, that if one accepts that "primal experience is constituted by transgression" (*Fantastic* 48) one can accommodate Freud's definition, regardless of the fact that it has not been proven. In accepting the possibility of Freud's definition being true, Todorov also accepts that the fantastic text can be subjected to a psychological reading. Todorov argues that in Freud's analysis of uncanny phenomena psychoanalysis fulfills two tasks. As "a science of structures," it "describes [the] mechanism ... of psychic activity" (149); and as "a technique of interpretation," it "reveals the ultimate meaning of the configuration ... described" (149). This is precisely what Todorov's theory of the fantastic attempts to do, to answer the questions of how the effect is caused and what it means. If we now draw a connection between Todorov's theory of the fantastic and Otto's theory of the numinous, we can see that Otto's theory can be analyzed psychologically, as well as religiously, since Otto's theory of the religious experience also deals with the effects of the experience and the resultant meaning of that experience. The meaning, however, is carried a step past the psychological into the realm of the spiritual because the thematic polarities, which for Todorov and Freud question the relationship of the reader and character to the world, in Otto's theory specifically interrogate the relationship of the reader and character to the divine.

Another psychoanalytic theory of literature and religion important to this discussion can be found in Julia Kristeva's theory of *abjection*. In *Powers of Horror: An Essay on Abjection*, Kristeva advances a theory of *abjection* that is akin to the theories of Todorov, Otto, and Freud. As a psychic act, abjection rejects whatever is deemed a threat to the identities of the individual self and the group to which the individual belongs. Kristeva argues that the *abject* has no "definable *object*" (1), at least not one that can be imagined or named by the conscious self. The only "quality of the object" (1) that the abject has is that it is "opposed to I" (1). In the act of abjection, Kristeva finds ambiguity not only in the opposition of self and abject, but also in the feelings of repulsion or fear and fascination that characterize the opposition. For Kristeva, meaning is excluded in the opposition of object and I when "a certain 'ego' [the abject] that merged with its master, a superego, has flatly driven it away" (2). However, Kristeva argues the object does not give in to oppression by the superego but continues to challenge it. Kristeva defines this opposition as "a brutish suffering that 'I' puts up with, sublime and devastated" (2) because the self imagines "that such is the desire of the other"(2).

The feeling of uncanniness that emerges from this sense of the other is greater than Freud's feeling of the uncanny; for Kristeva in this relationship "nothing is familiar" (*Powers* 5) and the self feels "radically separate, loathsome" (2) and unrecognizable. Oppressed by "a weight of meaninglessness" (2), the self feels itself to be "on the edge of non-existence and hallucination, of a reality that, if I acknowledge it, annihilates me" (2). At this point of creatureliness, to borrow Otto's term, "abject and abjection" (2) seem to be protective shields against annihilation. Kristeva calls this feeling of abjection "a narcissistic crisis on the outskirts of the feminine" (209) and connects it to the child's fear over the initial loss of the mother as an object of love and protection.

Kristeva defines abjection as "the other facet of religious, moral, and ideological codes on which rest the sleep of individuals and the breathing spells of societies" (*Powers* 209). These codes or systems of civilization are "abjection's purification and repression" (209); however, according to Kristeva's theory the return of the repressed facets of these codes is apocalyptic and represents our "religious crises" (209). For this aspect of her theory, Kristeva has borrowed from Freud's argument that civilization's systems, including religion, provide protection for the individual against the powers of nature and other human beings, and that, in turn, civilization also exerts privations on individuals which repress their actions. The only difference Kristeva sees between the abject on a personal level and on a religious one is that on a religious level we are no longer willing to have an intimate encounter with the abject because "we have lost faith in One Master Signifier" (209). In our concentration on the everyday acts that keep our personal fears at bay, we have ignored the ultimate relationship of abjection — our relationship with the divine.

In literature Kristeva finds the "full power" of the abject represented in "the religious imagination" (*Powers* 207), calling "all literature ... probably a version of the apocalypse that seems ... rooted ... on the fragile border ... where identities (subject/object, etc.) do not exist or only barely so — double, fuzzy, heterogeneous, animal, metamorphosed, altered, abject" (207). For her, the meaning and power of horror is based on her theory of abjection, representing human crises at a most intimate level; and "because it ... decks itself out in the sacred power of horror, literature may also

One • Dreadful Revelations

involve not an ultimate resistance to but an unveiling of the abject: an elaboration, a discharge, and a hollowing out of abjection through the Crisis of the Word" (208). This theory has a great deal in common with Aristotle's theory of catharsis through pity and terror, both feelings which cannot be articulated perfectly; and, indeed, Kristeva feels the writer composes in just such a condition, "being possessed by abjection, in an indefinite catharsis" (208).

The last psychoanalytic theory I would like to draw on in the discussion of whether the numinous should be considered purely psychological, purely religious, or both is Carl Jung's archetypal theory. In a published lecture "On the Relation of Analytical Psychology to Poetry" (1966), Jung argues that although the process of creativity can be examined psychologically, its essence cannot be. Similarly, he feels that religion can only be subjected to psychological scrutiny in terms of its phenomenological aspects and not its essence. Jung labels as *extraverted* the type literature in which the writer's deliberate design is secondary to the demands made by the work itself. As such, the author's creative process takes place on a subconscious level until the ideas are strong enough to manifest themselves at a conscious level. However, consciousness does not necessarily mean assimilation, only perception. As perception, the work of the psyche cannot be deliberately organized, repressed or duplicated on the conscious level. Jung feels that these subliminal ideas come not from the personal unconscious but from the *collective unconscious*, a realm of "unconscious mythology whose primordial images are the common heritage of mankind" (80). Although Jung uses mythological terminology to describe his theory, it is remarkably close to Freud's argument that repressed events are connected to primal experiences. For Jung, these psychic images are "the instincts and archetypes" (80) that have survived in our psyche from the time of human primordial existence. As *a priori* ideas, the experience of these representations can only be confirmed through the results of their manifestation and, in literature, can only be reconstructed in the mind of the reader through contemplation and analysis of the completed text. The primordial archetype can be "a daemon, a human being, or a process—that constantly recurs in the course of history or appears wherever creative fantasy is freely expressed ... [and] essentially, therefore, it is a mythological figure" (81). The appearance of this archetypal event or character results in an extreme sense of catharsis. At this moment, one is no longer an individual self, but has a sense of the racial memory of humankind. The author who gives form to these primordial representations universalizes the personal to produce in the reader a sense of the human emotions that connect us to the divine in the world. For Jung, creativity is a process of awakening the needed archetypal patterns, of organizing and refining them as part of a complete work.

In regard to the question of whether literature that foregrounds an experience of the numinous should be interpreted on psychological or religious terms, in another essay, "Psychology and Literature" (1966), Jung argues that both psychological and aesthetic principles are important in the analysis of works of art and the artists themselves; however, he does differentiate between *psychological* and *visionary* modes of creativity. When writing a psychological novel, Jung maintains, the author uses the real world experience. In the visionary mode of literature, however, the author transmits more unfamiliar experiences, born "from the hinterland of man's mind, ... from the abyss of prehuman ages" (90). Just as Otto has described the effect of the numinous, so for Jung, the primordial experience produces meaning through powerful emotional effects. He describes the primordial experience "chilling the blood with its strangeness" (90). Born from humanity's primeval existence, the representations of this experience are "glamorous, daemonic, and grotesque" (90). The suddenness and strangeness of an experience such as Jung describes shatters our human sense of reality.

When dealing with the visionary mode, the reader is "astonished, confused, bewildered, put on ... guard or even repelled" ("Psychology" 91) by the author's reminder of mysterious depths of the human psyche. The reader requires an explanation, a meaning, from these visionary experiences in literature; and it is not in the visionary material but in the experience that the material articulates that meaning is found. Jung admits that because of Freudian psychology's influence readers are inclined to believe that all psychical manifestations are founded upon personal conscious experiences that have been repressed. However, Jung's argument for a psychological interpretation of literature begins not with the personal but with the "primordial experience" (93). Regardless of how difficult it is to believe in the reality of a visionary experience, Jung argues that the vision is genuinely symbolic — authentic regardless of its mystery. Although, we experience the known world with our senses, it is our intuitions that signal that we are in the presence of events that have always been "mysterious, uncanny, and deceptive" (94). So indescribable is this experience that the writer or poet must turn to the archetypal patterns in order to articulate it. Jung defines an archetype as "morally neutral" (104), perceived as good or evil only on a conscious level and argues that archetypes in literature are compensatory in relation to the conscious attitude of the times. Representing the undeclared desires of the period or culture, these manifestations become a kind of wish fulfillment that foreshadows conscious shifts in perspective.

Jung treats the visionary experience as compensatory in that it thrusts readers into the abyss of primordial experience forcing them to participate in the re-balancing of the social psyche, as represented by both reader's and character's psyches, by confronting the demons of the abyss. As the reader identifies with the character in the visionary text, he or she must decide whether to believe in the reality of the event. Accepting that inclusion of an experience of the numinous would qualify a text to be visionary, in deciding that the events are real, the reader turns a psychological journey into a religious one by recognizing the feelings of powerlessness in relation to an absolute power that can be characterized as divine in some way. By realizing the spiritual implications of the danger the character faces in relation to the power of the numinous event or figure, the reader seeks moral meaning in that relationship. Since Freud, Kristeva, and Jung all see a psychological quality to religion, as well as to literature, it seems appropriate in this discussion to approach the spiritual journeys of the characters, and of the imagined reader, as both psychological and religious transformations caused by an experience of the numinous in the form of the vampire.

The Numinous and the Vampire

In dealing with the numinousness, particularly of a negative nature, of the vampire figure, the question now becomes why should the numinous be manifested in a negative experience like an encounter with a vampire. The answer lies in the idea that the Gothic genre posits the existence of the divine as problematic. If the numinous were manifested as a positive figure or event in the Gothic, the existence of the divine would be reinforced and not challenged. As a negative figure, the vampire better serves to question the character's search for transcendence and divine truth by arousing feelings of fear and fascination at the sense of divine mystery that the vampire represents. Transcendence is a liminal experience, an encounter at the threshold, where the individual reader must choose whether or not to give in to the potential of the mystery of the numinous. It is in these marginal features of the text where issues of divine truth and of faith and immortality come to the forefront, and where use of the vampire as a figure in literature can produce questions about the human condition. Individual readers experience the contrasting emotions of fear and fascination inherent in an encounter with the numinous and must seek their own answers to the moral and ethical questions of their existence.

As a literary figure, the vampire manifests Otto's definition of the numinous and causes hesitation and fear in the subject of the encounter in several ways. He or she is perceived by the main character as an objective presence and considered "wholly other" (Otto *Idea* 28); but, at the same time, the vampire is a mysterious figure. As something alien to the perception of the character encountering the presence of the vampire, the figure evokes the dread of *tremendum* and the sense of overpoweringness and energy as a feeling that he intends to do harm on a spiritual level. The characters affected by the vampires appearance recognize their own lack of power in relation to the vampire's power and feel a sense of helplessness. The quality of fascination as an element of the numinous also is reflected in the vampire as the power to hypnotize and to seduce its victims. The main character perceives the danger of complete annihilation but still is drawn to the vampire.

Not only does the vampire itself manifest all the attributes of Otto's numinous, but also, as a character in the text, the vampire represents a character caught on the margins of existence, one who has passed beyond being human but has not crossed the threshold into death. To be a vampire is to be in a state of suspended transcendence, caught at the edge of both the physical and the spiritual worlds, an insider and outsider at once. Unlike the numinous qualities of other Gothic characters, such as ghosts or spirits, or even thoroughly evil human villains, the vampire's numinous nature and the danger he or she poses to the human characters in the text hinges on the fact that the result of the encounter with the numinous may not be simply pain or death, but something far worse, far more frightening.

The negative quality of numinousness represented by the vampire causes even greater dread on the part of the observer because not only the life, but also the soul of the subject is in jeopardy. The victim faces the possibility of surviving an encounter with the numinous in the form of a vampire in a condition of hesitation, being caught forever on the threshold of spiritual release and human existence, of the sacred and the profane. Unlike a mortal antagonist such as Walpole's Manfred or Radcliffe's Montoni, however evil they might be, unlike even Shelley's Frankenstein or Maturin's Melmoth, who, despite their capacities of prodigious strength and seeming immortality, still do not have the power of the vampire to affect the relationship of the individual to the divine permanently, the power in the negatively numinous vampire is that of a divine creature with evil potential.

The numinous value, or sacred functioning, of the vampire myth lies in the influence that an encounter with the numinous has on the individual. In vampire literature, an encounter with a vampire works on both structural and thematic levels to produce, first, an effect or condition of perception which allows the reader, and perhaps the character, to experience a sense of powerlessness in the face of someone or some thing supernaturally powerful; and, second, through the feelings of fear and the accompanying themes of power and powerlessness, to reach an epiphany, a kind of catharsis of soul that brings the character to a new understanding of being-in-the-world. Those who come in contact with the vampire must question what it is to be human and mortal in this world; but the most important problem for all of the characters in the texts discussed in the body of this work is how does one relate to the divine in a world in which the divine may or may not be present, and in which faith may or may not be strong enough to vanquish the fear that the divine does not exist at all.

As a negatively numinous figure, the vampire serves as an example to the reader of what both the individual and the society can become when separated from the divine forces of the universe, but the vampire is more than simply an example of transgression and alienation. The use of the vampire figure in literature can increase an individual's awareness that the divine may not exist, but, at the same time, the vampire also provides the way in which the individual can affirm that existence, whether that affirmation comes through an understanding and acceptance of the mortal condition and a subsequent propitiation of the divine in light of that acceptance, or through the ritual destruction of the vampire in order to restore what the main character or characters perceive as sacred order to their mortal world.

• Two •

Surrendering the Self
*The Numinous and the Vampire in Coleridge's
"The Rime of the Ancient Mariner"*

> I considered the being whom I had cast among mankind, and endowed with the will and power to effect purposes of horror, ... nearly in light of my own vampire.... [Mary Wollstonecraft Shelley, *Frankenstein* 77][1]

During a lecture on the "General Character of the Gothic Mind in the Middle Ages" (1818), Samuel Taylor Coleridge explained how the sublime and numinous in Gothic art affect the human subject. According to notes of the lecture taken by Joseph Henry Green, Coleridge felt that gothic art "entirely depended on a symbolical expression of the infinite, — which is not vastness, nor immensity, nor perfection, but whatever cannot be circumscribed within the limits of actual sensuous being" (Coleridge *Literary Remains* 68) and which "impresses the beholder with a sense of self-annihilation" such that "he becomes, as it were, a part of the work contemplated" (69). Coleridge's commentary on the effect of Gothic art is remarkably close to Rudolf Otto's description of the feeling of the numinous in *The Idea of the Holy*, in which he characterizes the numinous as inexpressible because it "completely eludes apprehension in terms of concepts" (5). The subject of the encounter is filled with a sense of "nothingness" (10) to the point that he or she seeks to identify more closely with the numen. The numinous in the form of the more primitive Gothic past, superstition and the supernatural, and the sublime natural world provided Coleridge with a way to interrogate the individual's relationship with the divine. In "The Rime of the Ancient Mariner" contact with the numinous on several levels propels the Mariner on a spiritual journey.

In this poem, Coleridge returns to the traditional conventions of the romance genre and to romance's more popular ballad form to tell a tale of marvelous events. However, although he uses more general human types to populate his ballad, the story still represents an individual human experience. While one may question the reliability of the narrator of this experience based on the other characters' reactions to him, on his isolation from humankind, and on the dream-like feeling to many of the encounters, one eventually has to accept the event as true to the Mariner's individual perceptions. His physical self and his power to hypnotize are the best evidences of the truth of his tale.

Modes of Numinous Contact

In *Trance, Art, and Creativity* (1975), John Curtis Gowan, educational psychologist, researcher and writer in the fields of creativity and development, discusses the three illusions of space, time and human relationships that make up an individual's perception of the empirical world and how the laws that govern the relationship of a human being to the world change when one is thrust into an altered state of consciousness by contact with the numinous. Space is comprised of the objects that make up the world around us; time, of the events that happen to or around us; and personality, of the human relationships we experience. The ego, which Gowan considers the conscious self, initially, is in denial as to the possible existence of any other state of consciousness. It is contact with the numinous element which causes an individual to realize that another mode of consciousness exists; and the driving force behind a person's life becomes the desire to make a connection between the individual ego and the numinous. Here the *ego* is defined both philosophically and psychologically, as the conscious self experiencing the world through the senses and as the part of the psyche seeking to control the darker impulses of what Freud calls the *id*.

Gowan identifies three levels of contact between the ego and the numinous, which he terms trance, art, and creativity, respectively.[2] Each of these involves some degree of loss of ego and includes a number of procedures productive of an altered state of consciousness in which there is some kind of relationship formed between the individual subject and the

Two • Surrendering the Self

numinous and a degree of "dissociation or hair-raising uncanny affect involving awe or dread" (Gowan 3). Trance mode is a primitive method of numinous contact, characterized by an involuntary loss of ego control; and it is in this mode that Gowan finds Rudolf Otto's concept of the *mysterium tremendum* and the wholly otherness of the numinous object with its "uncanny qualities of awe, dread, horror, and loathing" (24) are most intensely experienced. Regardless of how primitive the experience might be in this mode, though, it often serves the purpose of healing and revelation for the individual. Under the greater ego control of the artistic and creative stages of numinous contact, however, encounter with the numinous is more tempered, as the uncanny qualities of the experience are veiled and the positive qualities of the experience emerge as creative products. These levels of contact are reflected in the poem as the Ancient Mariner's spiritual journey.

For Gowan, the process by which creativity evolves, both for an individual and for a species, is an odyssey through the three levels, from the primitive stage of dissociation that includes such influences as psychoactive drugs, trance and hypnotism, through the artistic phase of archetypes, dreams, ritual, myth and art, to the more meditative, creative level in which "intuition, transcendence, ecstasy, metamorphosis, and salvation" (Gowan 245) are ways of understanding and in which the knowledge of the numinous gained through these procedures can be communicated with others. When a person encounters a manifestation of the numinous, he or she moves from empirical reality to an altered reality and discovers in the journey a state of consciousness where "the larger laws which pertain to the metaphysical world ... are seen to operate" (12) and in which the universal connection of all things is understood. The subject in the primitive mode perceives the numinous with such dread and horror that conscious thought is impossible, while the subject of an artistic contact with the numinous element finds the numinous obscured and, therefore, "accessible aesthetically rather than cognitively" (250). However, in the creative or communicative mode, which allows the artist to approach the numinous through individual creativity, the numinous appears as a less frightening feature of what Gowan refers to as the "collective preconscious" (250), preferring that term to Jung's *collective unconscious* because his research shows that "this aspect of the psyche can sometimes be available to the conscious mind" (250). In a poem like "The Ancient Mariner," an encounter with the numinous gives supernatural, rather than natural, form to divine truth; and the Ancient Mariner becomes not only artist, but also a representative of the numinous, a vampire, as well, in his act of identification and creation.

Coleridge and the Modes of Numinous Contact

Although existing in a pre–Freudian culture, many Romantics, like Coleridge, would have been familiar with the altered states of consciousness brought on by contact with the numinous through use of drugs. Both Coleridge and his contemporary Thomas De Quincey found the series of fantastic drawings of prisons entitled "Carceri d' Invenzione" by Italian engraver and architect Giovanni Batista Piranesi (1720–1778) to be accurate representations of the sensations of expanded space and time felt under the influence of opium. In *Confessions of an English Opium-Eater*, De Quincey, a contemporary of Coleridge's and fellow opium user, describes how the sense of space and time "were both powerfully affected" (234) in his opium dreams. In the description of his dreams, De Quincey tells how buildings and landscapes took on Piranesian impressions of the vastness and magnitude of space such as "the bodily eye is not fitted to receive" (234). Time also appeared to expand so that he "seemed to have lived for seventy or a hundred years in one night" (234) and even at times beyond the limits of human duration.

In *The Milk of Paradise: The Effect of Opium Visions on the Works of De Quincey, Crabbe, Francis Thompson, and Coleridge*, M. H. Abrams establishes Coleridge's opium use before and during the production of "The Ancient Mariner." Drawing on letters, journal entries, reminiscences of acquaintances, and the existence of parallels between the attributes in Coleridge's poems and those of other poets who were definitely influenced by opium, Abrams traces Coleridge's use of the drug as far back as 1791. According to his research, it appears that the poet used opium consistently until 1796 and that there were "definite proofs of addiction" (28) in March, November, and December of that year. Abrams feels that the "sudden metamorphosis of technique ... and Coleridge's use of the supernatural theme" (36) point to the influence of the drug on Coleridge at this time in his career. He also mentions the distinct possibility that Coleridge was given opium in the form of laudanum as a child because he was by all reports a sickly child, as well as a sickly adult.

If one looks at Coleridge's "Pains of Sleep" (1803), one sees that he is suffering through a primitive phase of the numinous in his opium dreams, as he records a "fiendish dream" of "deeds to be hid which were not hid," and how with "powerless will/Still baffled, and yet burning still" he felt "desire with loathing strangely mixed" (Coleridge *Complete Works*, Vol. 1:389–90). As a numinous experience, triggered by the use of opium, Coleridge's frightening dream calls to mind Otto's discussion of the numinous, in which feelings of powerlessness and dread in the face of the *mysterium tremendum* are combined with an element of fascination, so that the numinous, though it frightens, draws man closer to the rapture at its center. In Abrams' analysis, the opium dreams led Coleridge to his line of study, and the detailed imagery gleaned from this research was "fused in the heat of his imagination" (39) to be consciously utilized later in the poem of his mariner. In this regard, Abrams sees the artist as alchemist, his mind the transforming agent through which the raw materials of his opium reveries and his research were "metamorphosed in the crucible of dreams" (40) to form an archetypal tale not only of individual crime and punishment, but also of universal sin and salvation.

Moreover, both the mystic and the drug user experience a singular sensation of weightlessness during their numinous experiences, a sense of floating on air, in which the subject is focused on the feelings of the upper areas of the body, most particularly, those of the head; and in "Ode to the Departing Year," written in late December, 1796, which Abrams' sites as proof that the poet was using opium before the composition of "The Ancient Mariner," Coleridge writes:

> My ears throb hot; my eye-balls start,
> My brain with horrid tumult swims;
> Wild is the tempest of my heart;
> And my thick and struggling breath
> Imitates the toil of death!
> [Coleridge *Complete Works*, Vol. 1:160]

In this passage, one can see evidence of Coleridge's preoccupation with the lightness of the body and with the sensations of the upper body. Coleridge's dedication to the poem, written to Thomas Poole, and quoting

The Vampire as Numinous Experience

Dr. Johnson's Preface to *Dictionary of the English Language* (1806), speaks of his illness just before the composition of the poem and excuses the poem as having been written "amidst inconvenience and distraction, in sickness and in sorrow" (Coleridge *Complete Works*, Vol. 2:1113). Although this poem also was written under the duress of illness, Coleridge was most likely using opium at the time, since it was his habit to use the drug for relief in times of illness; and, since the delirium of severe illness evokes similar numinous affects on the brain as drug use, at the time this poem was written Coleridge may have been suffering a numinous encounter in double doses, from the effects of pain and illness and from the drug used to alleviate the pain.

Like his Ancient Mariner, Coleridge had a sublime, if not numinous, power over his audiences. In "The Power of the Eye in Coleridge" Professor Lane Cooper discusses the "power of hypnotic fascination" (78) in the Ancient Mariner's eye in relation to Coleridge himself. Cooper also calls into evidence "The Color of Coleridge's Eyes," an essay by John Louis Haney, in which Haney draws together the comments of acquaintances of Coleridge, describing his eyes variously as "keenly penetrating" (Haney 424), "luminous" (426), and "actually glittering" (425). Moreover, in a letter to her friend Mary Hutchinson in June, 1797, Dorothy Wordsworth, Coleridge's contemporary and sister of William Wordsworth, remarked on the ocular power of Coleridge's eyes, writing that his gaze showed "every emotion of his animated mind" (De Selincourt 169). Borrowing an expression from Shakespeare's *A Midsummer Night's Dream* (V, i), she also noted that he had "more of 'the poet's eye in a fine frenzy rolling'" (169) than she had ever seen in anyone else's. In addition, John Sterling, a student of Coleridge's, recorded how, in his first interview with the poet, Coleridge's eye had a "glare in it, a light half earthly, half morbid" (Armour and Howes 345); this was "the glittering eye of the *Ancient Mariner*" (345).

If there was potency in Coleridge's gaze, his voice must have held some fascinating power, also. Dorothy remarked in the same letter that if "you hear him speak for five minutes" (De Selincourt 169), you forget his "plain" (169) appearance. Moreover, Coleridge seems to have been a sublime talker. Thomas Carlyle characterized the audience of Coleridge (himself included) as having been "swamped near to drowning in this tide of ingenious vocables, spreading out boundless as if to submerge the world" (Carlyle 54–55); but he admitted his willingness to listen on despite the near drowning. Upon hearing Coleridge preach in January, 1798, William Hazlitt also described the poet in sublime terms, describing how Coleridge's voice wafted over the audience "like a steam of rich distilled perfumes," and how on "the two last words, which he pronounced loud, deep, and distinct, it seemed ... as if the sounds had echoed from the bottom of the human heart, and as if that prayer might have floated in solemn silence through the universe" (Armour and Howes 243). This is the voice that captured the hearts of the faithful as a preacher; and this is the voice that wove the spell of the Ancient Mariner on his listening audiences.

In regards to the numinous qualities of the poem itself, Charles Lamb, in a letter to Wordsworth in January, 1801, on the publication of the new edition of *Lyrical Ballads*, noted in defense of Coleridge's poem that he "was totally possessed with it for many days" (Marrs 266) after first reading it. It is interesting to note that Lamb attributes the power of "The Ancient Mariner" to its evocation of "the state of a man in a bad dream, one terrible peculiarity of which is, that all consciousness of personality is gone" (266). It is not surprising then that Coleridge, with his power of eye and voice and his fiendish opium dreams, came to identify closely with the figure of the Mariner, particularly after his voyage to Malta in 1804. Coburn connects several journal entries in the second volume of *Coleridge's Notebooks* to his increasing identification with the Mariner figure. (See notes 1913 and 1996.) However, identification had begun almost immediately after the production of "The Ancient Mariner." In September, 1798, only a few weeks after publication of the poem, Coleridge left for Hamburg, Germany, on his first sea voyage. In letters written home during the journey, he refers to how the sight of his "native land retiring" (*Biographia Literaria* 309) from his view beyond the horizon called forth an "ardent prayer" (309) and mentions in association with the disappearance of land "the kirks, churches, chapels, and meeting-houses" (309) of his country. This reference is very like the words of the Mariner as he describes the ship leaving port. Again, in the same letter, Coleridge records seeing a duck swimming and "how interesting a thing it looked in that round objectless desert of waters" (319); here Coleridge is disappointed that the ocean's vastness does not seem to live up to the expectations he had built in his mind (and in the poem?), exclaiming how the "feeling of immensity" (319) he had expected turned out to be instead a "narrowness and *nearness*, as it were, of the circle of the horizon" (319). Just as he had described his mariner's world so narrowly circumscribed by the sea, the sky and the water snakes, Coleridge acknowledges his own sense of narrowed vision.

Metaphoric Vampires and the Numinous

To speak in terms of the numinousness of the vampire figure in "The Ancient Mariner" one must first justify the reading of the text as vampire literature; and to do this, one must realize, as James B. Twitchell, professor of English at the University of Florida, writes in *The Living Dead: A Study of the Vampire in Romantic Literature*, that "the Romantics ... rarely if ever wrote about vampires *as* vampires; instead the vampire was the means to achieve various ends" (38). In reference to reading "The Ancient Mariner" as a vampire text, Twitchell argues that "when Coleridge first sat down in 1797, he had planned to write a vampire poem" (146); however, in light of a note on "The Ancient Mariner" added to the 1800 edition of *Lyrical Ballads* by William Wordsworth, Twitchell also believes that pressure from his friend Wordsworth caused Coleridge to temper many of the more obvious resemblances to vampirism in later versions. Twitchell calls this note, which details the defects of Coleridge's poem, "rather patronizing" (158) and draws attention to the fact that he is not the first critic to feel this way. Critics such as Lowes, Empson, and Pirie have all found the note indicative of Wordsworth's probable disapproval of the poem.

Basing his reading of the text on the article "Coleridge's Revision of 'The Ancient Mariner'" by B. R. McElderry, Jr. and on John Livingston Lowes' *Road to Xanadu*, Twitchell draws heavily on Lowes' endnote references to underscore the probability that Coleridge had read information on vampire folklore. Lowes has established that Coleridge had read volume two of *Memoirs of the Literary and Philosophical Society of Manchester* and assumes that Coleridge would also have read the third volume, containing an article by John Ferriar on "On Popular Illusions and Particularly of Medical Demonology" in which he summarizes the work of several earlier authors on the nature of the occult, including vampirism. Although Coleridge's reading of volume three is only speculation, Twitchell reiterates Lowes' opinion that Coleridge hardly could have passed up this text in his reading on the supernatural. Both Lowes and Twitchell also note that Coleridge's habit of verifying his sources probably would have led him to follow up on this article by reading the Voltaire and Calmet sources summarized by Ferriar in the original. Using this evidence, circumstantial as it might be, Twitchell makes a strong case for reading "The Ancient Mariner" as a vampire text by referring to the "almost ... totemic" (*Living Dead* 147) representation of blood in the text, the Ancient Mariner's sucking of his own blood in order to speak, and the mesmeric effect of his eyes on his listeners.

Analyzing vampires in a Romantic context, Twitchell defines them to be more than "foamy-mouthed fiends with blood dripping from extended incisors" (*Living Dead* 3). Rather, he sees them as "participants in some ghastly process of energy transfer in which one partner gains vitality at the expense of another" (3). As Twitchell interprets the Romantic Movement two important characteristics were the relationship between the artist and "his inner self" (142) and his understanding of the exchange of energies "between artist, artifact, and audience" (142). In the Romantic period, the transfer of energy explicit in the vampiric act, a transfer which can be understood to include both the enervation felt by the victim and the obvious transfer of blood, often became an "elaborate metaphor" (142) for the more implicit energy exchange among artist, audience, and creative product. In this relationship the artist puts energy into the production of the creative work, and that energy is transferred to the audience as it listens to, reads, or otherwise experiences the artistic product. The audience then releases energy in reaction to the work and that energy is picked back up by the artist. In this respect, Twitchell defines the Ancient Mariner as a vampire figure representing a "surrogate artist ... who creates a work of art ... to be heard by an audience" (144), because, in Twitchell's opinion, through the telling of the tale energy is exchanged between the Wedding Guest and the Ancient Mariner. Contact with the numinous involves just such a relationship, in which the subject of the experience suffers a weakening of the conscious self and loss of vital energy in the face of the stronger numinous object.

Using Gowan's theory of numinous contact, analysis of the Ancient Mariner as a numinous vampire figure can demonstrate not only the relationship of Romantic artist, audience, and poem that Twitchell proposes, but also the numinous process through which the lone Romantic poet becomes the artist/prophet that Percy Bysshe Shelley describes in *A Defense of Poetry* (1821) as being part of eternity or the infinite through his poetry. As the different levels of loss of self are experienced, the creative process can be characterized as a journey, first of isolation and alienation at what Gowan characterizes as the primitive level of contact with the numinous, then of reintegration as the subject of the numinous encounter moves toward insight through the artistic mode, and on to communication of his newfound truth in the creative phase. My discussion not only shows how these levels of numinous contact are variously exhibited in "The Ancient Mariner," but also analyzes how the negative numinousness of the vampire works as a positive vehicle for revelation, transformation, and healing. As the use of the figurative vampire allows the poet to establish a connection between the vampire and the isolated self searching for a divine presence, the vampire in the poem not only shows humanity's alienation from the divine, but also becomes a vehicle to reunite the individual and the divine through the process of artistic creation and communication.

The central discussion of this chapter involves an interpretation of the poem in terms of the Ancient Mariner's numinous journey from alienation and disconnection to reintegration; however, the tale and the poem itself also evoke the various levels of numinousness for the audience and an examination of the audience's numinous or spiritual journey deals with the hypnotic influence of the Mariner's tale and the poem on the internal and external audiences, respectively. Final remarks treat the meaning of the numinousness of the vampire in the relationship between the artist, the poem, and the audience and how this relationship serves to reshape the relationship between human beings and the divine.

The Numinous Experience of the Ancient Mariner

As a representative of the Romantic artist, the Ancient Mariner journeys from the primitive, negative numinousness toward positive creativity and communication. Isolated from the divine in the primitive stage through his dread at the mystery and power of the numinous vampire figure, referred to in this discussion as Life-in-Death as she is in later editions of the poem, and through his resulting loss of ego because of that dreadful power, the Mariner recognizes his need for a relationship with divine power and seeks a reunion in the artistic phase as he gains insight into his alienated state by experiencing the condition of Life-in-Death himself. Eventually, he attains a degree of reintegration with the divine, and to some extent with society, as in the creative stage he is forced into the role of communicator carrying the cosmic message of divine unity to those who must hear his tale. The Mariner is associated with the divine by becoming not only the artist/prophet, but also the numen/vampire. Through his penance and through his existence as vampire/artist he serves as the vehicle for the Hermit, the Wedding Guest, and the broader reading and listening audience to relate to the world in a more spiritual sense. In the following discussion, I argue that the sublime experiences of the Mariner lead directly to an encounter with the numinousness of the vampire Life-in-Death. This experience of the numinous is important because, through it, he associates with divine power by becoming the artist and creating a tale that asserts a reunion with that power. This tale then may help others to reestablish their own relationship with the divine.

"My Heart Beat Loud": The Primitive Numinous and the Ancient Mariner

In *The Demon and the Poet: An Interpretation of "The Rime of the Ancient Mariner" According to Coleridge's Demonological Sources* (1983), Katherine Bruner Tave carries Lowes' *Road to Xanadu* study a step further. Feeling that many times he missed the implications of Coleridge's reading on the subject of the supernatural, she believes an interpretation according to these demonological sources, both spiritual and supernatural, can explain some of the more ambiguous and puzzling events in the poem. In her interpretation, therefore, the spiritual realm represents the good and the supernatural realm, the evil; and both the Ancient Mariner and the Wedding Guest suffer crises of faith through the struggle between these forces of good and evil. As she interprets the text, the Mariner journeys away from "established spiritual guidance" (50) and, later, possessed by evil demons for his role in the albatross's death, he causes despair and a loss of faith for the Wedding Guest. In her discussion, Tave calls attention to Robert Penn Warren's interpretation, in his essay "A Poem of Pure Imagination: An Experiment in Reading," as indicative of the allegorical qualities of the poem and its sacramental vision — the church being a representation of the spiritual community of man; the hill, an emblem, like Calvary, of the Christian's salvation in Christ; and the lighthouse, a figure of salvation and safety for Christians at the end of life. However, in "The Nightmare World of 'The Ancient Mariner'," Edward E. Bostetter argues that the end of the poem does not reveal Penn Warren's interpretation of a sacramental vision of the world, but instead provides the reader with the figure of an "eternally alienated Mariner alienating in his turn the Wedding Guest" (70). I would have to disagree in part with each of these interpretations. The Mariner's journey does not necessarily indicate either loss of faith or eternal alienation from the divine or from the earthly world. As a numinous experience, his journey is characterized not so much by loss of faith as by a loss of ego control; and while he is forced to wander the earth forever in the guise of Life-in-Death, his alienation from the divine has been overcome with his acknowledgement of the water snakes. Moreover, his alienation from humanity is not eternal either, since the Mariner interacts with others when he tells his tale. The Wedding Guest is not meant to be alienated from man or God, either. In the end, after hearing the Mariner's tale, he is meant to assimilate the moral of the story, rising the next morning a wiser man with a new outlook on life and a closer relationship with the divine.

The first step on the Mariner's spiritual journey takes place in the primitive mode of contact with the numinous and is characterized by a sense of alienation and isolation when the Mariner's perceptions of space, time, and human relationships are all called into question as he is thrust into an altered state of consciousness by the dreadful power of the *mysterium tremendum*. This alienation is suffered as isolation not only from his fellow men, but also from the divine itself. As the poem begins, the Ancient Mariner describes the beginning of his voyage; but when the kirk, the hill, and the lighthouse drop below the horizon, the Mariner and the rest of the crew suffer a kind of dissociation, leaving behind those things that orient them to their home country and, therefore, that signify what they perceive to be the reality of their world.

However, although they travel out into the disorienting space of the open sea, as sailors, their reality also includes life on board ship. Until they reach the equator, they continue to experience what they perceive to be normal life. The sun continues to rise and set when and where it should; and they have fair weather and a good wind to carry them southward. At this point, though, a storm rises which hurries them even further south into an unfamiliar region where they will experience a state of altered consciousness brought on by several dissociative phases, including the sublime conditions of physical isolation and sensory deprivation and, finally, dehydration. These conditions will lead the Ancient Mariner into a hallucinatory state in which he will encounter the vampire Life-in-Death.

The power of the sublime exists in the fear or dread felt at the possibility of danger or death and in the sense of helplessness this possibility evokes in the subject of the encounter. Although the sublime, like the numinous, is inexpressible in its essence, the feelings and the sense of helplessness can be described metaphorically. The Mariner's description of how "Storm and Wind" (line 45)[3] drive the ship and its crew "Like Chaff ... along" (line 48) signifies his sense of helplessness from the mysterious forces of nature and foreshadows the feelings he and the other sailors will share during their sublime experience in the Antarctic and what the Mariner will feel during and after his numinous experience with Life-in-Death.

The sublime seascape signals an entrance into an altered state both for crew and Mariner alike as the ship sails into a region of "Mist and Snow" (line 49), a place "wond'rous cauld" (line 50) and filled with towering icebergs. As the primary actor in the tale, the Ancient Mariner is at the threshold of what Gowan terms the primitive level of numinous experience where the sublime features of the Antarctic world prepare him for his later encounter with Life-in-Death. His perception is characterized by a loss of orientation in a bleak, white world in which spatial and temporal coordinates are no longer trustworthy. His loss of a sense of reality and, therefore, his sense of peril become deeper in the visually monotonous seascape formed by the vastness and magnitude of the ice flows in a region where no other living things, besides his fellow sailors, seem to exist. Here the Mariner has no way to orient himself or to define himself, and so he is in danger of losing his sense of self-awareness.

As their isolation increases, the sailors hear what can only be considered sublime noises, also. As the Mariner tells the Wedding Guest, huge chunks and flows of ice "crack'd and growl'd, and roar'd and howl'd,/ Like noises of a swound!" (lines 59–60). In *The Annotated Ancient Mariner*, Martin Gardner footnotes *swound* with the explanation that a person recovering their consciousness after a swoon or fainting fit "apparently experiences a sudden jarring onrush of sounds" (46). On a more historical note, in *Road to Xanadu*, Lowes discusses the terrifying sounds recorded by early sailors in the ice-bound regions of the globe, mentioning one particular account of sailors reporting how they felt "'a great swounding and dazeling in our [their] heads'" (135) after subjection to the cold and the sounds of the ice flows constantly cracking and grating against each other. Moreover, Edmund Burke's study of the sublime reveals that any sound which is excessively loud "is sufficient to overpower the soul, to suspend its action, and to fill it with terror" (82). Burke attributes the power of sound to the fact that the parts of the ear struck by sound vibrate under its influence and produce a tension in accordance with the "nature and species of the stroke" (*Sublime* 140). If the sound is loud, it strikes strongly upon the ear, creating a great degree of tension. If this loud sound is repeated often enough, "the repetition causes the expectation of another stroke ... and that expectation itself causes a tension" (140). As this tension builds each time the sound is repeated, the body's reactive tension produces in the mind a sublime situation which verges on physical pain. For the Mariner and the crew, the "repetitive and monotonous stimulation" (Gowan 99) caused by these noises would tend to block other sounds and place the sailors in a sublime situation as their individual psyches became overwhelmed by the intensity of the experience. This situation then would isolate them further, not only from their sense of reality shaped by their previous sailing experiences, but also from each other as they found it more and more difficult not only to communicate, but also to concentrate and think coherently.

Due to their physical isolation and the intensity of their experiences in this sublime world, the sailors are overjoyed when an albatross, a creature which they feel represents conventional reality, joins them. In "The Mariner's Nightmare," a chapter in Paul Magnuson's *Coleridge's Nightmare Poetry*, Magnuson relates Coleridge's "musing on the characteristics of dreams" (59) in 1805 to the "distempered dreams" (59) such as the Mariner has. Coleridge remarked in his journals how in this type of dream "all the realities about me lose their natural *healing* powers" (Coburn *Notebooks*, 2557). Magnuson states that the normal human sensations that ground us in reality are what Coleridge referred to as "the Sanctifiers, the Strengtheners" (Coburn *Notebooks*, 2543) of the will. For Magnuson, the albatross is a "sanctifier" (59) because it represents that "one recognizable reality in the unfamiliar world" (59). The sailors have not seen another living thing except each other for many days and have been inundated with sublime sights and sounds; under these circumstances, it is not difficult to understand their need for contact with something they perceive to be an ordinary part of their world. Therefore, engaging in an act of interpretation, they greet the albatross as if it were "a Christian soul" (line 63) and a good omen, even though its signification is ambiguous at best.

The bird has followed them for nine days when the Ancient Mariner kills it. According to most accepted interpretations, the Mariner kills the bird without reason. Gardner goes so far as to say that the Mariner commits the "ultimate ... crime of murder" (51) and calls it a "premeditated, wanton act of cruelty" (51) perpetrated on a friendly and harmless creature. Also, according to A. M. Buchan, in "The Sad Wisdom of the Mariner," the Mariner's act of killing the albatross imperils both "sanity ... and the moral law" (96) because it is an "irretrievable evil" (96). However, though the act of murder itself cannot be reversed, Otto finds that the sacred is not irretrievable; and, therefore, though the Mariner has sinned, his ritualistic telling of the tale is an atonement, reminding the listener of the sacred quality of life.

In the interpretation of the Ancient Mariner's experience as a numinous encounter, however, the Mariner's seemingly senseless act takes on another dimension. Violent action "is characteristic of ... ego excursion which deprives the subject of self-control, and superego excursion which deprives him of his judgemental capacities" (Gowan 52). Caught up in the sublime world of the Antarctic, the Mariner gives in to an "unconscious impulse" (27) and destroys the bird because his isolation and experience of the sublime have dissociated him from normal reality, separating him from the more controlling attributes of his ego and superego, so that the deeper, hidden impulses of his id take over. According to D. W. Harding's essay "The Theme of 'The Ancient Mariner,'" the Mariner experiences feelings of "depression and the sense of isolation and worthlessness" (53) that are almost pathological; and, as a result, he must "find a crime which, in its symbolic implications, is sufficient to merit even his suffering" (54). In shedding the blood of the albatross, the Mariner commits the ultimate cosmic crime, draining the energy of the divine world.

Having moved away from the traditional religious community of his home, the Mariner is now further isolated from the divine through his destruction of the one object that offered a connection to the rational reality of the sailors, a living thing which he has already designated as representative of Christian faith and of connection to God. Because of his murderous act, he is now destined to navigate the altered state of consciousness to its numinous conclusion. Suffering the sublime solitude of being "the first that ever burst/Into that silent Sea" (lines 101–2) the Mariner and the crew reach the Pacific; but once they are there, sublime nature evokes a sense of the suspension of space, time, and ego. The Mariner describes how the breeze subsides and the sails droop listlessly for want of air and calls up a vision of their immovable ship caught in the uniformity and vastness of the becalmed sea around them. At the equator with the sun directly overhead, the sailors do seem to be suspended in time eternal as:

> Day after day, day after day,
> We stuck, ne breath ne motion,
> As idle as a painted Ship
> Upon a painted Ocean [lines 111–14].

While the equator seems to be an illusory coordinate, it is representative of the threshold of consciousness that the Mariner has crossed in his journey. Caught in these doldrums, the men "speak only to break/The silence of the Sea" (lines 105–6). Tave interprets this passage to mean that the men now neglect their prayers and, therefore, further isolate themselves from God. However, they also are relating to each other as a community when they do speak; and their isolation has become almost complete now, as the illusion of social interaction is shattered.

Another factor now contributes to the weakening of the Mariner's self as he moves closer to the actual experience of the numinous. The sailors all suffer from dehydration. The Mariner informs the Wedding Guest that though they were surrounded by water, there was not a "drop to drink" (lines 117–18).[4] The men are all silent now from dehydration, with "every tongue ... wither'd at the root" (lines 131–32); yet they communicate their feelings about the Mariner's crime with "evil looks" (line 135) and by hanging the albatross around his neck.

Sensory deprivation often leads to paranormal effects such as dreams and both visual and auditory hallucinations as subjects of the experience lose their spatial and temporal referents and enter a trance-like state where they feel as if they are in a mist, then find themselves "in a world of [their] own internal imagery" (Gowan 101). According to Thomas De Quincey, Coleridge most likely had the germ of an idea sometime earlier than the composition of "The Ancient Mariner" for "a poem on delirium, confounding its own dream-scenery with eternal things, and connected with the imagery of high latitudes" (*Collected Writings* 145). It also has been well documented that "The Ancient Mariner" originated in the dream of Coleridge's friend John Cruikshank's, a dream of a "skeleton ship with figures on it" (Lowes 251). That there were other archetypal patterns that might have influenced Coleridge in the making of this poem, Lowes also establishes, including in his discussion the figures of Jonah, Cain, Falkenburg, and the Wandering Jew.

In the poem, the sailors have come through the mist and fog and are now in a world where they can no longer orient themselves in time and space; therefore, their own capacities for internal visualization and interpretation will take control. This level of their experience foreshadows a transition to the artistic level of numinous contact, where information is on a figural level, as some of the men "in dreams assured were/Of the Spirit that plagued us so" (lines 27–28). In these dreams they are told how the spirit has followed them nine fathoms below; and a sense of the sailors' peril is obvious in the choice of the word "plagued" (line 128) to describe the spirit's effect on their journey. They interpret their dreams as an affirmation of the existence of an invisible nature that somehow has control of their destiny; however, dreams are constructions and may be deceptive in terms of their interpretation of the meaning. It may very well be that their interpretation is a sublimated attempt to deny their collusion in the death of the albatross, by insisting that this fate is their destiny.

Dreams will become important later for the Mariner, also; however, at this point he still is caught up in a hallucinatory experience of the numinous. In the altered state of consciousness characterized by a hallucinatory episode, things appear real to the senses, but also exhibit a visionary quality in which "detailed fantasies" (Gowan 101), often involving archetypal or mythic figures which exist only in the person's mind, are manifested. Gowan maintains that under normal circumstances, the brain's "scanning of sensory input inhibits hallucinatory activity" (119). However, when, under circumstances of extreme isolation and sensory deprivation, the amount of sensory input is diminished greatly, "the organizing effect upon the screening and scanning mechanism then decreases" (119) and allows deeper memories stored in the brain to surface. In "On Popular Illusions," Ferriar summarizes *De Spectris* (1570) by Lavater, a Zurich theologian. Citing a particular example from *De Spectris* of how "unwary sailors" (76) were "deceived by spectres in Norwegian seas" (76), he maintains that "solitude and silence will always produce apparitions" (75). This argument holds true, as in the sky the Mariner sees what appears at first to be "a little speck" (line 141) and then seems to be a "mist" (line 142) of some sort and then a clearer form, the shape of a ship, as it grows nearer. Tave argues that "the precarious balance between the forces of the 'normal' universe and those of the demonological realm" (81) is shattered at this point in the Mariner's experience, and that the Mariner is "plunged deeper and deeper into a cosmos where the supernatural holds sway and the natural is helpless" (81). In her interpretation, the ship, as the albatross before it, is simply a glamour or magical spell produced by the demons that inhabit the region in order to mete out punishment to the Mariner. Glamour or spell notwithstanding, the Mariner's experience now becomes a frightening contact with Otto's *mysterium horrendum*, the horrifying negative numinous, in the form of both visual and auditory hallucinations. Still suffering from dehydration, the Mariner becomes absorbed in what he perceives is the reality of his experience.

Unable to speak because of his parched throat, the Ancient Mariner bites his arm and sucks his own blood in order to speak; and he recalls that the crew grinned at this act and "all at once their breath drew in/As they were drinking all" (lines 157–58). Gardner's critical interpretation is that "they drew in their breath as *if* they were drinking water" (62), but it may just as well be the blood of the Mariner they were drinking. This is the second blood the Mariner has spilled; and, although it seems to be the blood of self-sacrifice given in order to apprise the crew of the nearness of the other ship, with this act of feeding on his own blood, the Mariner becomes his own vampire, and, therefore, his own victim. Twitchell goes so far as to imply that the spilling of the Mariner's blood might be what brings the ship to them and that the Mariner might be "a willing participant in some weird process" (*Living Dead* 147). Since Twitchell has pointed this out, I feel it would not be too far off the track to suggest that the Mariner has invited this vampiric figure into his mind, also, as a form of hallucinatory apparition, by biting himself. If this is so, it is not demons who mete out his punishment, as Tave has suggested, but he himself who, as both instigator and agent of his crime, is also the agent of his own punishment. Having reached the primal underworld of the psyche, with his ego weakened to the point of non-existence, the Mariner is now conditioned to embrace the vampire nature that lies within him and to recognize his state of alienation from the divine.

The skeleton ship approaches and his horror intensifies as he is faced with the negatively numinous figures of the woman Life-in-Death and her mate Death, the ship's only inhabitants. The Mariner describes the vampire lady for the Wedding Guest, as he tells him,

> *Her* lips are red, *her* looks are free,
> *Her* locks are yellow as gold:
> Her skin is as white as leprosy,
> And she far liker Death than he;
> Her flesh makes the still air cold [lines 186–90].

At this point, the two are playing dice for the lives of the crew. Death wins the crew's lives, but the Ancient Mariner's life is forfeit to the lady. The Mariner once again is consumed with a sense of his own peril, the peril of a soul that is now under the control of the leprous lady. However, the archetypal character of the numinous comes to the surface as the Mariner faces the skeleton ship and the lady Life-in-Death. Through this encounter he will discover that cosmic laws prevail over mundane ones. Having already sucked his own blood, at this point, the Mariner's characterization as a vampire will be further strengthened as he gradually becomes like the lady Life-in-Death. It is through the taking of his own blood that the Mariner leaves himself vulnerable to a metamorphosis into the numen as he becomes the vampire; and it is through this transformation that he will understand his own isolation from God due to the murder of the albatross.

As the crew dies one by one, the Mariner is further isolated from the world, finding himself "alone, alone, all, all alone,/Alone on the wide wide Sea!" (lines 224–25). The kinesthetic impression of the two hundred crewmen's bodies hitting the deck one by one "With heavy thump" (line 210) and the Mariner's perception of each death as an auditory reminder of his sin as he connects the departing of each soul from its body to the "whizz of [his] Cross bow" (line 215) might be considered sublime sounds since they put his "soul in agony" (line 227) by underscoring the numinous quality of his experience and the magnitude of his sin. The Mariner's reflection that in life the dead men had been "beautiful" (line 228) juxtaposed against his awareness that only he and what he considers a "million million slimy things" (line 230) of the sea continue to live seems to indicate that he still values human contact and makes his isolation even less bearable. Unable to look at the creatures, he refuses the interaction that their existence provides and, in effect, denies a relationship with them. Moreover, when he looks at the deck, all he sees are the dead bodies of the crew, who can no longer provide a relationship that might connect him to the real world of the senses. The only place left to look is "to Heav'n" (line 236); but heaven offers no consolation, either. Even with his eyes closed, the Mariner can find no solace, for in his mind all he can see is the sublime horizon, the unending expanse of "the sky and the sea, and the sea and the sky" (line 242), signifying his continued isolation from both the visible and invisible worlds.

In *Romantic Horizons: Aspects of the Sublime in English Poetry and Painting, 1770–1850* (1983), Twitchell again discusses "The Ancient Mariner," this time in terms of the sublime. He sees the Mariner's experience of Burnet's *invisible natures* mentioned in the poem's epigraph as a sublime encounter, taking place on the horizon, between the sky and sea. For Twitchell, the epigraph expresses the purpose of the sublime, which is to enlighten and change humanity's view of itself and the universe. As "the visual icon of romantic liminality" (90), the sea "extends beyond the limits of the senses, ... ineffable, ... [and] boundless" (90); and the only spatial reference for the Mariner is the horizon, which Twitchell sees as the threshold dividing sea from sky, the earthly world from the world beyond. Since the "ordering of the cosmos is analogous to the ordering of the psyche" (93), the murder of the albatross "disrupts the harmony at the vortex between levels of consciousness" (91). For Twitchell, to experience "the world at the horizon" (100), with its hosts of angelic and ethereal spirits, is to experience the sublime. Until now the Mariner has been on a psychological journey involving a loss of the self; however, at this point in his journey, the Mariner will begin the religious part of his journey, his reintegration process, making meaning for himself out of his numinous experience.

Two • Surrendering the Self

"A Spring of Love": The Artistic Mode of the Mariner's Numinous Encounter

One makes contact with the numinous in the artistic mode through mediums such as dreams, archetypes, rituals, and works of art; and, therefore, the meaning of the numinous in this mode is both ambiguously personal and universal at once. However, this level involves more conscious control as the individual seeks to understand and articulate the experience of the numinous on a more intellectual level; and through a desire to make meaning comes a more clearly identifiable interpretation of the recognition of the isolated condition in which the person lives and of the need for a divine presence in human life.

In *Archetypal Patterns in Poetry: Psychological Studies of Imagination*, Maud Bodkin discusses "The Ancient Mariner" as an example of the rebirth archetype and includes a discussion of several archetypal features of the poem. Bodkin associates the rebirth theme with the archetypal night sea journey proposed in Jungian psychology. This archetypal pattern involves juxtaposed impressions of ascent and descent, movement and transfixion, as the hero descends into his own psychological hell and eventually rises up out of it a changed person. Based on a belief that "the physical wind, and the breath in man's nostrils, and the power of the Divine Spirit, were aspects hardly differentiated" (35), Bodkin sees the movement of the Mariner's ship during good weather as expressive of "happy surrender to the creative spirit" (35). However, for Bodkin, after the Mariner has shot the albatross, representations of the blood red sun and sea and the stagnation of the becalmed sea with its host of slimy inhabitants fill the tale. In these images, Bodkin finds feelings of terror and a sensation of drained energy. At this point in her interpretation, Bodkin calls on Freud's principle of the "death instinct" (69) to explain the poem. She likens the crime of the Mariner to those of Cain and the Wandering Jew and calls it "a crime against the sanctity of a guest" (57) and a refusal of "the Kingdom of Heaven" (58).

It is at this point, also, in the poem, as Tave interprets it, that the supernatural becomes "physical, tangible reality" (90) as the Mariner transforms into the supernatural figure Life-in-Death. In terms of the numinous, however, the Mariner does not contain the power of the archetypal figure of Life-in-Death quite yet. He is still in the process of evaluating his experience as the subject of the encounter and not as the numinous object to be feared by others. When he tries to pray, only a "wicked whisper" (line 238) comes out, making his "heart as dry as dust" (line 239). Rudolph Otto makes reference to the subject of an experience of the numinous feeling as though he or she is "dust and ashes" (*Idea* 9) before the power of the numinous; and at this point, the Mariner is realizing his lack of value and power and his insignificance in the universe. In response to his feelings of insignificance, he begins to feel a sense of personal responsibility for the deaths of the men, but not yet for the albatross.

This scene, however, is a turning point for him because as he watches the water snakes this time, he sees them with a different perspective. Where before all he saw was their difference from humanity and their grotesque nature, now he sees them as "happy living things" (line 274). In fact, because they are the only other living things within his world beside himself, he feels a greater connection to them, and through them a connection to the cosmos which he had denied when he killed the albatross earlier. Unable to articulate their beauty consciously, the Mariner does so unconsciously. He tells the Wedding Guest, "A spring of love gusht from my heart,/ And I bless'd them unaware!" (lines 276–77). In *The Philosophy of Literary Form*, Kenneth Burke interprets this passage as ambiguous, because the watersnakes themselves are ambiguous. Not taking the blessing at face value, he feels that the act of blessing is somehow connected to a kind of gap between one's desires and one's fate. However, this involuntary blessing is the Mariner's first attempt to represent his understanding of his connection with the universe; and just as a spring of water is a natural occurrence in the wilderness, the Mariner's spring of love is a natural phenomenon of his true feelings. Up to now, the Mariner has not been able to pray, but now he can. Though he attributes his ability to bless the snakes to the pity of his "kind saint" (line 278), I believe it is his intuitive blessing of the creatures which forms a psychic bond between his consciousness and the life force of the universe, giving him the ability to pray. This blessing is significant in that the Mariner's hidden impulses are now of a more benign nature, and he may now begin his journey of reintegration back to an ordinary state of consciousness in which the self has more control over reality and in which his dissociation from the cosmic pattern will be less as he interacts on some level with society in order to bring his message of cosmic unity to the community of man.

Two • Surrendering the Self

As the Mariner prays, the albatross drops off his neck into the sea; and at this point in his experience, his bodily discomfort is relieved in two ways, by sleep and re-hydration of the body. The Mariner's rest is more than normal sleep; it is the kind that heals his soul. In this sleep, Bodkin sees an almost reincarnative quality in that the Mariner "wakes renewed, as though by death" (69). This sleep also has archetypal overtones, as the Ancient Mariner dreams of dew; and when he awakens, it rains and his body is able to be re-hydrated, lessening the control of the altered state of consciousness on him. The rain storm, Bodkin argues, is a Jungian archetype of "pent-up energy" (48) released by prayer, signifying the Mariner's unconscious creativity and leading not only the Mariner, but the wider audience as well, to an understanding of the meaning behind the experience. On the artistic numinous level, the Mariner's dream of rain represents the wish-fulfillment of a tortured soul, who desires above all a moment of cleansing and baptismal blessing which will wash away his guilt.[5]

The Mariner now enters another altered state, one of lesser dread than his experience of Life-in-Death and the skeleton ship. Refreshed with rain, he seems to suffer a state bordering on a delirium trance, in which he feels disconnected from his own body. He recalls:

> I mov'd and could not feel my limbs:
> I was so light, almost
> I thought that I had died in sleep,
> And was a blessed Ghost [lines 297–300].

In this stanza, as Tave interprets it in her essay on Coleridge's demonological sources, the Ancient Mariner is caught up in another case of wish fulfillment, showing his desire to die as the others of the crew have done; but I would argue that this passage indicates that he is lost in a trance that will take him into the creative phase of contact. A feeling of lightness, common in an attack of delirium whether drug-induced or from the effects of illness, can signal the onset of a "mystical experience" (Gowan 85); and it must be remembered that the Mariner has been soaked through in the rain and, in his fatigued and overwrought state, may be physically ill.

The Mariner's hallucinatory experience continues as he becomes aware of a roaring sound that shakes the sails, and above him in the sky, the colors of the Aurora Australis or Southern Lights flow in whirling and spiraling patterns. It begins to rain again and the ship now moves under the impulse of what appears to be a supernatural wind. The dead men move also, groaning and rising from the deck in the throes of a primitive possession trance. In the involuntary state of a possession trance, the person affected is believed to be controlled by some supernatural means and, in his altered state of consciousness, may exhibit two phases of possession, one characterized by violent physical movement and the other by a catatonic condition which resembles a coma. The first outward sign of a possession trance is a convulsive movement of some part of the body or a sudden articulation of sound such as a hiss or groan, which signifies the inward loss of control in the subject.

Twitchell characterizes the crewmen as "revenants" or "still living dead" (*Living Dead* 149), whose bodies have been reanimated by spirits. Tave also establishes the possession of the dead bodies as possible, but she qualifies this possession. According to her interpretation, the possessed live body would retain all its normal physical abilities but must perform any action required by the possessing entity. The possessed dead body, however, would not retain any of the physical capabilities it had in life and, therefore, would only be able to perform the task required by the possessing spirit. For this reason, she writes, the crew's bodies do not speak or move their eyes and only work at their accustomed tasks. In terms of the Mariner's fate, however, one might read the reanimation of the crew as foreshadowing the Mariner's future isolation. Though the corpses of the crew, including the Mariner's nephew who works alongside him, pull at the ropes together, they do so with "limbs like lifeless tools" (line 331), and they do not speak or look at him. The Mariner, though once again part of the community of the crew, is still in isolation from the crew and even from family, as he will be when he is returned to his home country and begins to pay what may be the eternal part of his penance.

On the other hand, the Mariner is also the only one who is fully *alive* at this point, as he reassures the Wedding Guest that though the others died, he did not. He is also the only one, it seems, who has seen the illusions of time, space, the self, and human relationships shattered through his experiences, and who has seen beyond the veil into the cosmic reality of the world and survived; so, the actions of these *possessed* crewmen may indicate the way the inhabitants of the world should be viewed. The people who need to hear the Mariner's tale may be, in the final analysis, those who are so caught up in their everyday activities that they move through life like dead men walking, prisoners of the illusions of time, space, and the human relationships within a prescribed social system.

The quality of the Mariner's experience of the numinous is changing at this point in his journey, reaching toward a creative stage that might lead to his reintegration into society through communication of his experience to others. However, his experience of the numinous is not finished. At the higher level of numinous contact in the creative mode psychedelic experiences often are "accompanied by the hearing of celestial music, apparently played at a distance, and sweeter than any mortal music" (Gowan 125); and in the poem, at dawn, as the crew drops their arms and clusters around the mast, the Mariner hears sweet sounds emanating from their mouths. The sound of their voices seems to circle in the air and then dart upward toward the sun, returning again, each voice at times alone and sometimes mixed with others. First, the Mariner thinks he hears a skylark's song and then the songs of many birds together. Next, he thinks he hears the sounds of all the instruments, then a lone flute and "now ... an angel's song" (line 354). When this music ceases, the sails make their own sound, a noise that the Mariner likens to "a hidden brook" (line 358). This intense sensory experience of the Mariner's foreshadows his next hallucinatory encounter with the numinous.

The ship has moved on steadily at the impulse of the underwater spirit; however, at noon, the sails go slack and movement of the ship is arrested for the few moments that the sun is directly overhead at the equator. Then, "like a pawing horse let go" (line 394), the ship gallops away over the waves. The blood rushes to the Ancient Mariner's head with the sudden force of movement, and he faints, remaining unconscious for a time and then once more passing into an altered state of consciousness as the ship moves on at seemingly supernatural speeds. At this point, he has what can be interpreted as a mystical experience as he hears two voices speaking of his crime, his punishment, and his further "penance" (line 414). From this dialogue, he discerns what his fate will be.

In terms of contact with the numinous, as the Mariner's sense of time seems shattered by the fast movement of the ship bounding over the waves, his mental processes work to recover the material from his unconscious and to facilitate the creative organization of the ideas that the two voices speaking have put into his mind. As the Mariner now enters the creative phase of the numinous, both auditory hallucinations and transcendent, meditative experiences become important to his level of awareness. In this mode of communication, he represents the artist who must attempt to organize the insights of his experience into a coherent story. The Mariner hears voices talking of his sin and his penance, almost as if they were an "externalization of conscience" (Gowan 27), because of his sense of personal responsibility for the deaths of the albatross and the crew. Anne Williams, author of *Art of Darkness: A Poetics of Gothic*, interprets this passage as the "appearance of the superego, unconscious parental voice of 'right' and 'wrong'" (195). Incapacitated by his fainting fit or trance, the Mariner hears and, as he characterizes the experience, "in [his] soul discern'd" (line 401) two disembodied voices speaking of his punishment for killing the harmless albatross. The first voice indicates that the bird had "lov'd the man/ Who shot him with his bow" (line 410); and now added to the heinous nature of the Mariner's crime in his own mind is the perception that the bird had loved him. The voices then relate how he has done penance and will do more for his sin.

In his essay "The Ancient Mariner," Humphrey House sees the Mariner's plight as a "crisis of extreme isolation, with the frustrated desire for death" which eventually leads to "recovery and redemption" (61); in his article, "The Mariner and the Albatross," George Whalley further interprets the isolation of the Mariner as a "state of sin" (77) which both wanderers, Coleridge and the Mariner, suffered. However, the point is not the sin, but the atonement. The second volume of *Manchester Memoirs*, read by Coleridge, contains "An Essay on Crimes and Punishments," an article by Reverend William Turner that delineates the nature of punishments that fit the crimes perpetrated. Turner states that as the Deity is "of a spiritual or mental nature" (300) so the punishments inflicted for crimes against God also may be of a mental nature and quite possibly will continue "as long as their subject, the mind" (300). The punishment imposed by society might be as harsh as "*perpetual imprisonment, or exile, and death*" (300); however, Turner finds there are "those divines ... who contend, *that every sin, being an offence against an infinite being, is deserving of an infinite and eternal punishment*" (309). The Mariner's sin is a spiritual one against nature and the cosmic unity of all things in the universe, so he suffers the "infinite and eternal punishment" (309) of living death and isolation from society. Burke calls "the total and perpetual exclusion from all society ... as great a positive pain as can almost be conceived" (*Sublime* 43) and finds that the idea of death can hardly be more terrible; and indeed, the Ancient Mariner would clearly prefer death.

Once the spirits have finished speaking, the Mariner's trance begins to abate, he awakens from his trance, and the ship slows to normal speed. The dead men all stand together on the deck, fixing the Mariner with "their stony eyes" (line 441) which glitter in the light of the moon; and the Mariner is entranced by them. Once again, it seems, the Mariner's sense of personal responsibility for their deaths is underscored by his incapacitation. As he tells the Wedding Guest,

> The pang, the curse, with which they died,
> Had never pass'd away:
> I could not draw my een from theirs
> Ne turn them up to pray [lines 443–46].

In the face of this reminder of his sin, the Ancient Mariner is completely paralyzed, and his isolation from God and humanity is emphasized. However, the spell ends; and the only act that remains for the Mariner is to return to his own country.

Yet, now that he has returned to "living life" (line 400), an expression which Twitchell connects with vampirism by implying that any other kind of life would be the living death of the vampire, the Mariner is a changed man who,

> Like one, that on a lonesome road
> Doth walk in fear and dread,
> And having once turn'd round, walks on
> And turns no more his head:
> Because he knows, a frightful fiend
> Doth close behind him tread [lines 451–56].

In terms of a process of contact with the numinous, the Ancient Mariner has journeyed from the isolation of the primitive numinous through the artistic level of contact with the archetypal fiend, the vampire Life-in-Death, and now is back in what he feels is ordinary reality ready to communicate his awareness of the true reality of the cosmos.

Yet, the numinous is not finished with him. The Mariner sees the crew's bodies lying flat and lifeless on the deck, but with "a man all light, a seraph-man" (line 517) standing on each corpse to serve as signals to the community on land. Soon the Mariner hears the Hermit singing "godly hymns" (line 543) as the harbor Pilot rows him toward the ship. At this sound, he suddenly is filled with hope that the holy man will be able to absolve him of his sins. However, he is not to be forgiven for his sin so easily and not by human mediation. Having moved into the creative phase of numinous contact, he must communicate what he perceives to be the moral of his journey to an audience in order to fulfill the penance imposed by voices in his trance.

The Audience's Contact with the Numinous

The creative phase of numinous contact allows the communication of the experience to others and, therefore, is based in language. At this stage, the Mariner has encountered the primitive numinousness of the vampire Life-in-Death and has recognized his isolation from God. In his insight into his own alienation from the divine, he has discovered his need to reunite with all of nature, both visible and invisible. Having identified with the numinous object, he will affect others on all three levels of numinous contact as he passes this insight on to others through his ritual penance, the telling of the tale, and through his hypnotic influence upon his audiences. An examination of the audience's experience of the numinous must take into account the effects that the events in the poem and the Mariner himself have on two separate audiences. The Hermit, Pilot, Pilot's boy, and Wedding Guest become in the telling of the tale the primary internal audience. The external audience is comprised of those contemporaries of Coleridge who heard the poem recited by him or read the poem in the original or in one of its many revisions in *Lyrical Ballads* (1798 and 1800), *Sibylline Leaves* (1817), or Coleridge's *Poetical Works* (1834), and those later audiences who, not having the privilege of hearing Coleridge's rendition, have only read the poem. To understand the audience's reaction to the numinous on a primitive level of contact, one must look first at the direct influence that the Mariner has on the internal audience, which in the narrative of the tale involves the physical and mental reactions of the Pilot, Pilot's boy, and Hermit and the actual induction of a trance state in the Wedding Guest for the length of the tale. A discussion of the creative contact the audience has with the numinous covers the hypnotic effects of the Mariner and of the poem, this time as an indirect influence, introduced into the tale and poem itself by the artist's use of poetic techniques, which work not only on the Wedding Guest as he listens to the tale, but also on both reading and listening audiences from Coleridge's time onward. The last analysis concerning the audience deals with the creative numinous level and the communication of the moral of the story for internal and external audiences alike.

"I Mov'd My Lips": The Numinous Mariner Speaks

As the Pilot, Pilot's boy, and Hermit approach the side of the ship, a sound rumbles from deep in the ocean and is manifested as the waters of the bay open in a whirlpool, and the ship and dead bodies of the crew sink. The body of the Mariner stays afloat, however, and is taken into the Pilot's boat. At this point in the story, the Ancient Mariner has made a full transition to the creative level of numinous experience where he will be able to communicate his story to others. The Mariner has now become a representation of the numinous, metamorphosing into a likeness of Life-in-Death. According to Tave, "the sight of the Mariner is not enough to cause physical harm and mental disorientation to his fellows"; instead, for Tave, it is the "possessing demon" (127) that causes the harm. However, as he is the numinous object now, the sight of the Mariner *is* sufficient to cause harm at a primitive level of contact. He is a revelation of their own mortality as they sense their own powerlessness in relation to his numinous power. He moves his lips and the Pilot shrieks in fear and falls down in a fit. The Hermit raises his eyes to heaven and prays; and as the Mariner takes the oars, the Pilot's boy goes "crazy" (line 598). Because of their contact with him, the Pilot and the Pilot's boy, unprepared for the *mysterium horrendum* of the Mariner, fall victim to the primitive dread of the numinous and suffer a complete loss of the self. On shore, the Hermit can hardly stand, so enervated is he by his experience. His languor is a reaction to the *horrendum* that is a quality of the negatively numinous Mariner, as the Hermit's self is weakened but not lost completely. Tave characterizes the Hermit as balanced socially and religiously, because, while he sometimes seeks the company of mariners, he also lives in harmony with nature and the spiritual world. In addition, she feels he does not suffer the "horrible internal struggle which the Mariner faces as penance" (123). Twitchell, however, interprets this passage differently. He see the Hermit as somewhat corrupted because the "rotted old oak stump" (*Living Dead* 149) that he uses as a cushion is more suited as an "altar for a Druid" (149) than for one of God's representatives. The Hermit, he says, is too eager to reach the ship; and when he does, instead of absolving the Mariner, he makes the sign of the cross, which Twitchell reminds the reader is "anathema to a vampire" (149). In this regard, I tend to accept Twitchell's interpretation over Tave's, because if the Hermit is without sin, so to speak, why must he be the first one who needs to hear the tale?

The Mariner has become the vampire and, as such, can do harm; however, at this level, his vampirism also becomes the vehicle through which the community of man can reunite with the divine. Although he has become isolated from God through his killing of the albatross, the Ancient Mariner has not lost faith and, therefore, seeks redemption from the Hermit; but redemption is not to be. He must do full penance for his sin, and that penance is eternal excommunication because murder is considered a canonical sin and, therefore, requires a penance of equal weight like excommunication or death. However, the Mariner is allowed some sense of reconciliation. Through the creation of the tale and through its ritual telling, he can interact with society, if only for the time it takes to tell his story. As the Hermit then asks the Mariner "What manner man art thou?" (line 610), he invites the first telling of the tale, just as the victim invites the vampire to enter into his life. The Hermit's question is the catalyst for the Mariner's penance as he makes his confession for the first time; and the Mariner suffers "a woeful agony" (line 612) which forces him to begin his tale.

In *A Drug-taker's Notes*, R. H. Ward records that during the fourth drug experiment he had visions of himself as a man hanged for murder. Identifying with the murderer, he perceived that he had "*become the worst*" (143) of men; and in so identifying himself, he realized that there was "no difference between him and any man who commits murder" (143). He saw this realization as a positive interpretation of the vision because he was then no longer the murderer but the scapegoat, the sacrifice for atonement, carrying the guilt and accepting the punishment on behalf of other men. In some ways this is the fate of the Ancient Mariner. Though the crew does blame him at first, they soon change their minds and decide he was right to kill the bird, making them accomplices to his crime. For this they die, but as the murderer of the albatross, the Mariner carries the guilt for that crime and suffers the punishment for it. However, he also may carry the crew's guilt and suffer a degree of their punishment in his eternal penance, just as he later takes on the Hermit's and the Wedding Guest's guilt through the re-telling of his story.

However, the Mariner's transformation to numen not only means that he is the numinous object, but also that he is the message itself, artist and creative product both. The Hermit has initiated the ritual telling of the Mariner's tale; and the act has now become sacramental in character, a "doctrine of salvation" (Otto *Idea* 33) for himself and others. In telling his tale, the Mariner expresses his relationship to the numinous and brings order and unity to the empirical world. Since the result of the Mariner's numinous encounter is that he now exists in a more eternal time that embraces past, present, and future, there is a ritualistic, cyclic nature to the numinous experiences in the poem as the Mariner, who has had his encounter with Life-in-Death, tells his story to his various audiences. As the wave of his need to tell his story builds, vanishes, and builds again, the Mariner must continue his travels, a wandering disciple searching for the next audience who must hear his parable. In communication of the numinous, the sacramental quality of the tale acts as a buffer between humanity and the numinous, allowing enough of the numinous qualities through to teach the lesson to the listener, but not enough to cause the Hermit, or his later audience, the Wedding Guest, to react as the Pilot and the Pilot's boy had done.

"I Fear Thee": The Wedding Guest and the Mariner's Primitive Numinousness

Like the Mariner, the Wedding Guest must suffer a process of isolation and hopefully reintegration with society in order to gain insight into his loss of a divine relationship and to reestablish that relationship. His experience with the Mariner is his path to that relationship. The Wedding Guest first perceives him as a lunatic, branding his tale as untrustworthy. The Mariner clearly exists outside the Wedding Guest's range of normal personal relationships, despite his willingness to interact on some level with the Mariner, as he offers him an invitation to the celebration if he has a "laughsome tale" (line 11) to tell. In spite of his reaction to the Mariner, the Wedding Guest's brush with the numinous, as well as the numinous encounter for the larger reading audience, both then and now, is in the meeting with the Mariner and in the Mariner's strange tale. Because the Wedding Guest's experience of the numinous, like the Mariner's before him, involves a reorganization of the concepts on which the individual's view of reality is based, the Wedding Guest eventually must accept the reliability of the tale in order to gain insight into his own definition of reality and his own relationship with the cosmos. He must accept the Mariner at face value because the Mariner himself, in respect to both his appearance and his powers, represents the best evidence that the events of the tale actually took place. To gain insight into his separation from the divine, he must be isolated from society by the primitive numinousness of the vampire in the form of the Ancient Mariner. Once he has heard the tale of the Mariner, he can approach the numinous on the artistic level as he faces the archetypes of his own psyche which the Mariner and his tale bring to the surface; and through the insight into his own psyche he then can reintegrate with the divine on a creative level.

For the Wedding Guest, the hypnotic effect of the Mariner's tale and of the Mariner himself will draw him into the world of numinous contact. In "On the Voluntary Power which the Mind is able to exercise over Bodily Sensation" (1790), an article in volume two of *Manchester Memoirs*, Thomas Barnes states that "in general, whatever fixes the mind in INTENSE THOUGHT, or rouses it to STRONG PASSION, makes it less sensible to organical impression" (453). This is particularly true in the case of strong emotions such as fear, which bring about a "momentary pause of sensation" (454). The resultant trance state is a reorganization of reality in which the fixing of attention to the numinous experience isolates and reforms the mind of the subject and allows them to see reality differently. The Wedding Guest must go through his own process of isolation by being drained of energy as the Mariner was by the vampire Life-in-Death. When the Ancient Mariner arrests the attention of the Wedding Guest and directs it toward himself and his tale, he does so through a kind of hypnotic trance.

In the hypnotic trance, stimulus of the senses is restricted as the attention of the subject becomes fixed through the use of repetitious stimuli, and an emotional connection between the subject of the trance and the effecter of the trance is established. The Ancient Mariner acts much as a hypnotist would, decreasing the influence of the "external stimuli" (Gowan 71) of the wedding feast and its "merry din" (line 8) on the Wedding Guest in order to fix his attention. This, in turn, produces an emotional relationship between the two of them, which, in this case, involves both fear and fascination as the numinous power of the Mariner acts on the Wedding Guest.

As a supernatural agent, the vampire figure of the Mariner fixes the Wedding Guest's attention in three ways. In "On Popular Illusions" (1790), Ferriar discusses the supernatural powers of the eye, summarizing the treatise *De Fascinatione* by Sennertus, an early German philosopher and physician, who writes of the three ways witches were believed to be able to injure people, "*per visum, vocem, et contactum,*" (48) by sight, voice and touch. The Mariner's supernatural power to hold his audience involves all three: his eye, his voice, his touch.

First, he "holds him with his skinny hand" (line 13), attempting to share his vision with the Wedding Guest through his touch. The theories of Franz Anton Mesmer are of interest in relation to the Mariner's ability to calm the Wedding Guest with his touch. His research into the existence of a power he called *animal magnetism* during the last half of the eighteenth century caused him to argue that this power could be used to cure various illnesses that had never before been affected by medical procedures or medicines. His system of mesmerism involved a kind of laying on of the hands along with application of a magnetic force; however, his experiments showed that results also could be obtained at a distance by simply pointing and concentrating on a particular area of the body. He claimed that the power of this magnetic force could also be concentrated with the use of mirrors or sound. Mesmerism, as this power soon came to be called, is now referred to as hypnosis and is widely used in the management of various conditions.[6]

Then the Mariner affects the Wedding Guest "with his glittering eye" (line 17), a more powerful source of power for him. Coleridge makes the Mariner's hypnotic ability even more clear as the Wedding Guest tells the Mariner "For that, which comes out of thine eye, doth make/My body and soul to be still" (lines 364–65). Gowan records that a seer in a vision often displays catatonic traits—his "eyes are fixed, and the eye-lids sometimes reverted" (33), which may explain the power of the Mariner's gaze over his audience.

Last, the Mariner mesmerizes the Wedding Guest with his voice. In order to tell his tale, he is given "strange power of speech" (line 620), the power to speak in different tongues so he can communicate in the language of those who must hear the story. The Mariner's penance is to tell the story; and the telling of it is an attempt at unstressing or releasing the psychic tension built up by the mind's confrontation with the numinous element. This strange power of speech gives him the words to describe his experience, to release the psychic tension or energy built up through his numinous encounter by communicating his message to others. As a result of these three hypnotic means, "the Mariner hath his will" (line 20) and the Wedding Guest has no choice but to listen to his story. This fixing of attention decreases the amount of sensory stimuli for the Wedding Guest, just as the sublime features of the Mariner's journey limited his connection to reality, but does not block it altogether. Throughout the telling of his story, the Mariner renews his control of the Wedding Guest with a repetition of these hypnotic methods whenever the outside stimuli of the noise of the celebration or the fear of the Wedding Guest at this numinous encounter becomes too great and threatens to pull him back into normal sensuous reality.

At this point, also, the Wedding Guest, as the Hermit before him had done, entreats the Mariner with a question that triggers the Mariner's confession. "Why look'st thou so?" (line 79) is the same kind of query as the Hermit's "What manner man art thou?" (line 610) in that it asks the Mariner to explain himself and to do so he must repeat his story. His audiences, like those in The Fisher King legend, have to ask a question such as this in order to hear the rest of the tale and to heal the Mariner, if only until the next man who needs to hear the tale comes along. The Mariner once again must take responsibility for the sin he committed and confess he shot the albatross. Here, the Mariner seems to be in an agitated trance state, under the control of deeper impulses; and the sin he committed and the numinous event he experienced as a result of it are now what give him his identity, purpose, and the ability to communicate his tale. The confession becomes a reenactment of his sin, an acceptance of fault, and recognition of his alienation from society, from nature, from God, and from himself. However, it also becomes a vehicle for others to recognize their own crimes against the divine and their ensuing alienated condition. To gain this insight is to discover a need for a stronger relationship with the divine and a need to change one's life.

As the vampire Life-in-Death, the Mariner has the power to drain his audience's ego and transport him outside of conventional reality. Through the telling of the tale, as the Mariner recalls his experience, the Wedding Guest's rational state of consciousness is shattered, and, from this point on, he is thrust into an altered state of consciousness by the Ancient Mariner's tale. As the Mariner tells the Wedding Guest how the crew died one by one, the Wedding Guest articulates his fear; but the ancient man assures him he did not die. This, however, should not be reassuring at this point, since he has already told the Wedding Guest how the two spectres diced for the lives of the men and Life-in-Death won his. At this point in his personal experience of the numinous, the Mariner had entered the artistic level where the archetypal pattern of his experience could be visualized and organized into meaning; it is at this point in the tale that the Wedding Guest must enter the artistic mode of numinous contact also in order to find meaning in the Mariner's tale and the numinousness of the Mariner himself. As he signifies his fear of the Mariner, who he perceives as "long, and lank, and brown,/As is the ribb'd Sea-sand" (lines 218–19) he connects the Mariner to nature on an archetypal level by connecting him to the sea. As the archetype Life-in-Death, the Ancient Mariner has become a part of the cosmic pattern that for the Wedding Guest is still a mystery and, therefore, evokes fear.

"Of Sense Forlorn": The Creative Numinous, the Poem, and the Audience

Art is a way in which an individual gives a sense of validity and truth to the internal visions of his psyche; but archetypes have a fluid character and only obtain meaning in relation to the individual ego and its reaction to the numinous experience. The artistic numinous is necessarily more veiled than the primitive contact and is apprehended on a personal level through the character of the work itself. As the story-teller, the Mariner has reached the creative level where, having perceived his numinous experience in archetypal form, he can produce a structure which will make them available to the Wedding Guest and other audiences through the ritual telling of the tale. At the level of creative numinous contact, several influences are at work to put the audience in the right frame of mind to accept the numinous direction of the story; and, like the Wedding Guest before them, they are hypnotized and isolated from society for the time it takes to read or listen to the poem and to have the message communicated to them.

In *Hypnotic Poetry: A Study of Trance-Inducing Technique in Certain Poems and its Literary Significance* (1930), Edward D. Snyder proposes the idea that some poems, "The Ancient Mariner" among them, exert a psychological power over the audience through their ability to induce a light trance-like state. The audience's understanding of these poems happens on an affective, rather than an intellectual, level. Calling this particular species of poem "spellweaving" (1), Snyder sets out to establish what characteristics of these types of poems produce the hypnotic state in the both the reading and listening audiences. In order to produce a clinical hypnotic state, the subject must be a willing participant and the subject's attention must be fixed, most often through the use of rhythmic, monotonous sound such as a clock ticking or verbal suggestions in the form of "a simple phrase" (26) which is repeated in the same monotonous manner as the ticking of the clock. The "concealed artistry" (2) which makes these poems hypnotic involves "a technique which uses physical and psychical stimuli" (22), such as a hypnotist might use on a subject, to fix the attention and block other sensory input which might produce mental activity nonproductive of the emotions and thoughts that the poet desires to elicit from the audience. Though Snyder finds that, in regard to the spellbinding poem, a "strictly silent reader" (16) will gain much less hypnotic value from the reading of the poem because he does not hear the sounds of the words spoken, a "silent yet auditing" (35) reader, who hears the sounds in his head as he reads to himself or who perhaps reads aloud to himself in a low voice, can expect to self induce the hypnotic state, if on a lower frequency level than the audience who actually hears the poem recited by a reader with the full weight of artistic power in his voice and physical presence. Relative to the production of a hypnotic state, the artistic features of "The Ancient Mariner" include: a "vagueness of imagery" (42), or ambiguousness of vision, as Todorov would characterize it; the production of a state of fatigue or eye-strain; the form of the poem itself; a repetitious rhythm of meter, sound, and phrasing; and the power of suggestion.

The ambiguousness of vision that Snyder refers to as being conducive to the production of a trance state can be found in the poet's formation of characters that "have such soft, shadowy outlines that one may fill in the details to suit one's fancy" (42). The Mariner's descriptions of the dream-like state under which he hears the voices and, in fact, the entire prospect of the poem as hallucinatory produce a sense of ambiguousness that corresponds to Snyder's insistence that the imagery of hypnotic poetry must be vague (42). Even the figure of Life-in-Death, though described with the seemingly specific details of red lips and golden hair, is ambiguous until meaning is assigned to her because she is an archetypal vision from the Mariner's psyche. One might even say that the overall idea of the plot, of a ship sailing into unknown waters into an unknown experience, allows for a figurative use of language that is vague in its ambiguousness. The *unknown* in which the sailors find themselves, both in the Antarctic and in terms of the spiritual realm they seem to have been blown into by the storm, is sublime. For Burke, anything sublime is essentially vague and obscure; for Otto, the numinous is mysterious because of its obscurity. Therefore, in the poem, the obscurity of the seascape, where no one has sailed before, provides a mysterious quality that carries the audience along through the numinous events.

The second feature that Snyder argues is important in production of a poem's hypnotic quality is fatigue or eye strain. Edmund Burke's study of the sublime claims that a sound or sight is sublime as it acts on the ear or eye to cause fatigue; and this physical fatigue then causes the mental fatigue that Snyder feels places the subject in the proper mental situation to be hypnotized. In the case of "The Ancient Mariner,," Coleridge's use of ambiguous or archaic wording, the contemplation of which taxes the brain and eye, if one is reading, to the point of fatigue, help to produce a state in which hypnosis can take place. Snyder maintains that the use of words like "eftsones" (line 527) "gramercy" (line 156) and "swound" (line 60) and the overall archaic wording and spelling of such words as "cauld" (line 150) for cold and "ancyent" (line 1) for ancient and the use of specialized expressions such as the seafaring terminology "broad as a weft" (line 83) to describe the look of the sunset, fatigue the mind because the mind tires when it tries to figure out and assimilate the meanings in the short span of time it takes to read the line of poetry.

The Vampire as Numinous Experience

In terms of the organization of the poem itself, S. L. Varnado claims that a "frame structure, with its arrangement of a-tale-within-a-tale, dissipates the sustained building of numinous feeling" (40); but, in the case of "The Ancient Mariner," as narrator of the tale, the traditional structure of the ballad is a way of approaching the numinous events in order to gain more control in the artistic mode and, most importantly, a way of building the psychic tension that produces the hypnotic state. In organizing the poem with the Mariner's telling his tale to the Wedding Guest, Coleridge could build the tension between the audience and the poem by having the audience learn gradually of the Mariner's horrifying experiences with the numinous. By including in his tale the reactions of his earlier audiences, the Pilot, the boy, and the Hermit, the Mariner, as hypnotist, is able to plant suggestions in the mind of the Wedding Guest, and through him the external audience, as to what the reaction to the numinous should be and also to suggest what lesson the audience should learn to survive the numinous contact. In terms of the poem itself, in writing "The Ancient Mariner," Coleridge chose to appropriate and manipulate the ballad form, a narrative style that in earlier times was primarily oral and often used for the more supernatural and folk subjects. Gardner annotates the poem as containing repetitions of "the traditionally mystic numbers 3, 7, and 9" (38) and calls attention to the fact that in this regard the poem itself is mystical, having seven parts. In the ballad's meter and rhythm, rhyme, and refrains, Coleridge and, as surrogate artist, the Mariner found techniques that would create hypnotic influences on the audience. These techniques include the use of the iambic foot in alternating tetrameter and trimeter lines, of end-stopped lines with a primary stanzaic rhyme scheme of *abcb*, and repeated sounds, phrases, and refrains within the text.

Coleridge believed the audience should willingly give up their attention to the world around them for the course of the poem and should be carried along by the poem, not simply out of "curiosity, or by a restless desire to arrive at the final solution; but by the pleasureable activity of mind excited by the attractions of the journey itself" (*Biographia Literaria* 196). To carry the audience pleasurably along on its journey, Coleridge chose the iambic foot of one unstressed and one stressed syllable, respectively, as the poem's primary meter. Snyder finds the iambic meter to be most amenable to the stimulus of a hypnotic state since it most closely parallels the half-second time intervals of a metronome set to induce clinical hypnosis in a patient. Take, for example, the lines the Mariner speaks once he has the attention of the Wedding Guest. Having fixed the attention of his chosen audience with his touch and his eye, the Mariner seeks to hypnotize him with his voice and formally begins his tale with this iambic stanza:

> The Ship was cheer'd, the Harbour clear'd —
> Merrily did we drop
> Below the Kirk, below the Hill,
> Below the Lighthouse top [lines 25–28].

To establish even more strongly the hypnotic flow of the poem, Coleridge also manipulates the number of metric feet per line, employing tetrameter and trimeter in alternating lines. As the repetition of the alternating stressed and unstressed syllables creates an expectation in the listener, so does the repetition of the length of line in terms of metric feet; and Snyder finds the tetrameter line mimics "the stimulus of rhythm used by the hypnotist" (40) almost perfectly. In this regard, he writes that the "harmonious pattern of sound" (16) produced by the overall rhythm of iambic feet in alternating tetrameter/trimeter lines is like the human heartbeat and lulls the listener as hypnotically as the sea. However, in the use of a primarily iambic pattern of stresses, as well as in the alternating rhythm of the lines, the "balance or near balance between troughs and crests" (Shapiro and Beum 34) also provides an "intensity of expression" (34) characteristic of deep feelings, so that the audience is not only lulled into a hypnotic state by the rhythm, but is also open to the suggestion of the deeper feelings that the words of the poem words elicit, underscored as they are by the same iambic rhythms that lulled the audience into quiescence in the first place.

Order and pattern fix the attention of the audience; and, heightened by the emphasis drawn to the repetition of sounds by the end-stopped lines, the rhyme scheme of the ballad, in which the second and forth lines of the quatrain rhyme, gives Coleridge's poem another hypnotic rhythm, this time of sound. According to Edmund Burke, the sound of words can affect the soul of the listener without raising a vision in the listener's mind. Poetry might even "lose a very considerable part of its energy" (170), if specific representations "were the necessary result of all description" (170). Although Coleridge does alter the rhyme pattern occasionally to suit a particular emphasis or to accommodate a larger stanza, in terms of the creation of a hypnotic effect, his primary use of the *abcb* rhyme scheme focuses attention, much as the iambic foot repeats a rhythm of stressed and unstressed sound, by providing the audience with an alternating rhythm of repeated sounds, the repetitions of which are near enough to each other to build an expectation in the ear and eye. Part I of the poem shows how the Mariner produces a hypnotic state in the Wedding Guest; and in the telling of the tale, in order to fix the attention of the audience, Coleridge, and the Mariner, not only use the rhythm and rhyme techniques mentioned earlier, but also occasionally use internal rhyme and repetition of phrasing, as in the line "The Ship was cheer'd, the Harbour clear'd" (line 25), which lulls the audience by underscoring both the rhythm and rhyme and, therefore, increases the hypnotic hold on the audience.

As features of internal rhyme, the techniques of alliteration and assonance also focus the audience's attention. The repetitive character of these two techniques, involving consonant and vowel sounds, respectively, causes the audience to pause on the words and to feel the mood the poet is trying to create. As the expectations of the audience are awakened and then gratified, this internal rhythm of sound pulls the audience unconsciously and pleasurably further under the control of the poem. If one looks at the two stanza example below, in which the Wedding Guest is being hypnotized by the Mariner, one sees the use of alliteration and assonance which work together to create a melodic effect on the audience.

> He holds him with his skinny hand,
> Quoth he, there was a Ship —
> "Now get thee hence, thou grey-beard Loon!
> "Or my Staff shall make thee skip."
>
> He holds him with his glittering eye —
> The wedding-guest stood still
> And listens like a three year's child;
> The Marinere hath his will [lines 13–20].

The repetition of long consonantal sounds, as in the use of the letters *n* and *m* and the letter combinations of *ng* and *ds*, and *ns*, which create the longer *z* sound at the ends of words, give the stanzas a droning, humming quality akin to the quality of the hypnotist's voice as he induces a trance with the repetition of a particular phrase. The poet's repeated employment of such voiceless sounds as *s*, *sh*, *th*, and *ch*, along with liquid and sonorous sounds, as in *glittering* and in the repetition of the *w* and *m* sounds create a melodic, whispering, confessional atmosphere for the poem. Along with the sense of whispered confession, the repeated use of the *h* sound produces an almost breathless feelings of "fatigue ... [and] wonder" (Shapiro and Beum 11). The feeling of fatigue works directly on the audience as it places the listener or reader in a state conducive to the other hypnotic effects of the poem; the wonder, on the other hand, is part of the suggestiveness of the hypnotic poem itself, as part of the purpose of a spellbinding poem is to create a sense of wonder in the mind of the audience. Along with the alliteration, the assonance of the lines, in the repetition of the long and short vowels sounds adds to the melodic affect. The two stanzas previously quoted are representative of Coleridge's use of alliteration and assonance to create a melodic and hypnotic rhythm of sound that will fix the attention of future reading and listening audiences just as the Mariner's rendition of them in the tale fixes the Wedding Guest's attention and allows him to experience the numinousness of the Mariner and his story.

In Part II of the poem, the atmosphere of the confessional continues as the Mariner tells the Wedding Guest of the attitude of the crew over his killing of the albatross; but the alliterative rhythm changes as the ship is becalmed. In the sixth stanza, the explosive *d* sound emphasizes the abruptness with which the ship stalls on the ocean and the prevalent sibilant *s* sounds signify the breathlessness of the doldrums where no air fills the sails and where even the sailors themselves might find it hard to breath and, therefore, to speak, as the Mariner tells the Wedding Guest "we did speak only to break/ The silence of the Sea!" (lines 105–06).

Throughout Parts II and III, the Mariner has told the Wedding Guest of the sublime horror of being becalmed on the ocean, of his numinous experience with Life-in-Death, and his isolation from the crew because he cannot die. By Part IV, the Wedding Guest is fearful, and, if Coleridge has done his job correctly, so is the external audience for the poem, though on a lesser level than the Wedding Guest. In terms of the Wedding Guest's numinous experience with the Mariner, in this section of the poem, the repetitious sound of the Wedding Guest's refrain "I fear thee" (lines 216, 220) not only articulates his fear of the Mariner, but also acts like the hypnotist's repetition of words to suggest that emotion to the external audience. The incantory attributes of the refrain contribute to the poem's power of suggestion, the last property of importance to a discussion of the hypnotic value of poetry.

"A Sadder and a Wiser Man": The Power of Suggestion and the Moral of the Story

The hypnotic qualities of the poem act on the audience so that the listener's memory of the piece is enhanced and the poem continues to work on the mind long after the initial experience of it is over. As the Wedding Guest's refrain of fear works to suggest the same emotion to the audience, the power of suggestion is also important in making the meaning of the poem. The poet creates a mood in which the audience, once hypnotized, accepts without hesitation not only the most fantastic events and characters of the narrative, but also the moral of the tale; and the power of suggestion in the poem induces some action or thought on the part of the audience, some recognition of the message.

Passing on the message of unity from his numinous encounter, the Mariner tells the Wedding Guest of the loneliness of his experience: "So lonely 'twas, that God himself/Scarce seemed there to be" (lines 630–33). In the extreme isolation suffered by the Ancient Mariner, he has been separated from the divine and from mankind and now realizes that "sweeter than the marriage feast" (line 634) is the experience of community in God, walking to the church to pray with a company of fellow human beings, "Old men, and babes, and loving friends/And Youths, and Maidens gay" (lines 641–42). The Mariner would like to be part of the community of man again, but he exists in a state of suspended transcendence, caught at the edge of the mortal and spiritual worlds, an insider and outsider at once because of his sin against the cosmic community.

At best, by his own example and through the hypnotic nature of his tale, the Mariner can suggest this to others, and perhaps save them before it is too late. In the most obvious moral of the tale, he tells the Wedding Guest:

> He prayeth best, who loveth best,
> All things both great and small:

Two • Surrendering the Self

> For the dear God, who loveth us,
> He made and loveth all [lines 647–50].

Only through love of *all* his fellow creatures can he take part in the *communitas* of the cosmos, as well as the smaller community of man, and not be left lost and wandering in a nightmare land as the Ancient Mariner is. However, the moral is not as simplistic as the stanza implies. For the external audience, the moral of the story includes the questions asked by the Wedding Guest and the Hermit.

In the poem, the Wedding Guest, as the Mariner was before him, and as audiences have been after him, is drawn away from the temporal and spatial reality of everyday life and into an alternative reality where an encounter with the numinous will reveal not only the existence of the divine, but also humanity's place in the larger cosmic pattern of life represented by both the visible and invisible natures of the universe. However, on the level of what Gowan refers to as personality or human interactions with other people, the Wedding Guest, like the Hermit before him, must interact with the Mariner in order to learn his lesson. As the Hermit had done, the Wedding Guest asks the right question of the Mariner—what has made him the way he is. The importance of their respective questions to themselves, and to future audiences, as it should have been to the Mariner before he shot the albatross, is What manner of man are you? The Mariner's answer is to tell a tale of the kind of man who is caught up in the mundane, empirical realities of life and not aware of the invisible nature of the universe and his ultimate connection to it. Not governed by the fact that everything in the universe is connected, the Mariner sinned against nature and, therefore, against God without even thinking; and the audience understands that he pays the ultimate price for his sin.

The Mariner's answer to these questions changes the internal audience of his tale. The Wedding Guest leaves the bridegroom's door "like one that hath been stunn'd,/And is of sense forlorn" (lines 655–56). This sense that the Wedding Guest has lost is the same sense of the rational world that the Mariner lost earlier in his experience of the numinous on his journey. Now having had his numinous experience in the form of the Mariner and his strange tale, the Wedding Guest will wake the next day "a sadder and a wiser man" (line 657), aware that the empirical reality in which he lives is illusory, and that the only true reality is that of the cosmic community. In "The Sad Wisdom of the Mariner," A. M. Buchan argues that the Wedding Guest wakes the next morning "sadder and wiser" (96) because he has been "plunged into an utterly bewildering world..., a world of action without reason or justification" (96) and, therefore, is rightly terrified. Sadder and wiser does not necessarily equate with terror, unless one is dealing with the numinous and, therefore, with the possibility of death. Here R. H. Ward's *A Drug-taker's Notes* can be helpful in understanding what is happening to the Wedding Guest. In his book, he records that a feeling of sadness overcame him during his third experiment and connected this sadness with a perception that everything about him seemed "nondescript and dull" (116). In addition, he had visions, complete with olfactory hallucinations, of himself as a dead body in a charnel house. These visions of death he associated with the "sinful humour" (118) and negative emotions of self-pity he had felt earlier, attributing his sadness to the drug-induced cosmic realization that "everything's dead" (122). Sadness being akin to soberness and seriousness by definition, the Wedding Guest's realization on the next morning is the same as the Mariner's: everything on earth is mortal, everything dies. Monsignor Luigi Giussani calls this sense of sadness the "fundamental characteristic of a life lived with awareness" (51) of humanity's destiny. Having been given a vision of the consequences of his mundane existence, the Wedding Guest must attempt to balance his mortal reality with the spiritual by turning toward more sober, serious pursuits. The same is true of the external audience. If they have made the connection between the events and characters of the tale and the moral quatrain, they have, in their turn, asked the same questions as the Hermit and Wedding Guest; but they have asked these questions of themselves, since they have discovered in their hypnotic experience of the poem that they are both the Wedding Guest and the Mariner, subject and numinous object, audience and artist.

The Metaphoric Vampire as Numinous Experience

In "The Ancient Mariner," the numinous figure of the vampire not only demonstrates humanity's essential spiritual alienation, but also serves as a vehicle for the eventual reunion of human and divine. As the artist's primitive numinous experience produces representations of the numinous, these figures are interpreted artistically as part of his own psyche. Through his ritual approach to their numinous power, the archetypes are then translated on a more controlled, creative level into meaning and understanding for the subject and for the future audience; and through the creative work produced in this process, the artist gains energy from the audience's reaction and is restored or revitalized. The Mariner's separation from God becomes obvious as he encounters the numinous on the primitive level of contact. Having been isolated from empirical reality by the sublimeness of the seascape through which the ship sails, the Mariner suffers such a loss of self that he kills the one living thing that connects him not only with the ordinary world of the senses, but also with God. Isolated from the empirical realities of space and time and from relationships with other humans, and alienated from the spiritual world because of his crime against the cosmos, the Mariner only realizes his state of alienation through his numinous encounter with the vampire. As a psychic vampire, the numinous figure Life-in-Death drains the Mariner's energy without drawing a drop of real blood; but the Mariner himself has drawn blood literally on two occasions before he even meets the nightmare lady. In taking the albatross's blood and his own, he has become both vampire and victim, before Life-in-Death could ever effect the change in him. Because of these acts of blood-letting, he is thrust into a numinous experience in which his loss of energy to the vampire figure Life-in-Death will trap him in a state of suspended transcendence, isolated from both the physical world and the spiritual realm.

However, his eventual transformation into the numinous vampire through the taking of his own blood allows him to become part of the cosmos. The reestablishment of his relationship to the divine, which begins on the artistic level with his recognition of the meaning of the vampire archetype, depends upon his creative use of that figure to communicate the cosmic message to the world. His telling of the tale is a way to gain energy, and, in gaining it, to regain control of his own ego and to establish contact with the divine on a higher creative level of understanding. As he does this, he not only reactualizes himself as human, but also pushes back for a moment the sense of meaninglessness in his life by serving as a communicator of the divine message of unity.

The energy transfer between artist and audience through the artifact does more than just give the Mariner energy, however. The energy loss keeps the audience in a state of weakened ego where they can encounter the vampire figures of both the female Life-in-Death and the Mariner on the artistic level of numinous contact. One hopes that in perceiving both figures as representations of their own alienated state, the audience can approach creatively the truth of their existence; and although neither the Pilot nor the Pilot's boy is able to rise above the primitive numinous experience of their meeting with the Mariner in order to bring that knowledge to the conscious level so that they might change their lives, the Wedding Guest and the Hermit do rise to a higher understanding of their encounters. Both experience the primitive level of the numinous in the vampire figure of Life-in-Death and in the form of the Mariner as he stands before them telling his tale. At this level, as audiences, both lose energy to the Mariner's artist; but both gain energy in the form of truth from the encounter, also. As vampires, both the figure of the Mariner and that of Life-in-Death represent the condition of living death and remind the Hermit and the Wedding Guest that life lived completely in the contemplative world or in the illusory world of the senses is only a living death. The Mariner's penance for the crime of earlier alienation will help to repair the rift between the cosmos and the community of man, as for the audience his tale underscores the sense of alienation and meaninglessness in all people who have not managed to balance the personal and the cosmic and allows them to recognize their need and reactualize their connection to the divine.

In terms of the reunion of human and divine, though, the energy exchange of which Twitchell speaks is more complicated than simply the relationship of artist and audience. That the artist needs replenishing should tell the reader that there are other vampires somewhere in the mix. Not only is the artist a vampire, but the artistic product and the audience take on vampire characteristics, as well. To discuss imagination in Coleridge, Sharon Jones Schellinger appropriates Nietzsche's representation of the veiled dancer as the truth that is hidden, but that the artist continually seeks despite the veils that fall away in the dance (Preface xi). This representation works just as well for the audience, too, since every artist is at first an audience of the mystery of the numinous. Like the vampire, the artist cannot relate the feelings of a primitive numinous experience directly because by nature it is inexpressible, but also because the audience would be overwhelmed by it, as the fates of the Pilot and the Pilot's boy show so well. In order to achieve creative understanding of his work, the artist first clothes the mysteries he has seen in his imagination in metaphysical veils like dreams, archetypes, and rituals, sending his creation out to dance and reveal the mystery slowly. In the process of revelation, the psychic energy builds, and, as parts of the truth are revealed, the audience is first mesmerized and then enervated by the experience, "caught up and embraced by the enchantment" (Preface x) of the mystery before them.

However, the tale itself can also drain the audience in its own way as the audience recreates the numinous encounter in their own psyches through the hypnotic qualities of the work. In reading or listening to the poem, the external audience reactualizes the numinous and the vampire in themselves as well, by recreating the text and the Mariner in their minds. In this way, the vampire is born again in the audience, as both text and artist; but this vampire, like the Mariner, who has shown a consciousness of his fault in the telling of the tale, has a potential for good in reminding the audience that reality lies in the connection with all things. The audience receives something in return for their loss of energy. Through the artistic numinous and the same hypnotic techniques which the artist has used to give life to his creative work, the external audience, like the Wedding Guest, moves to the creative level of numinous contact, becoming a numen/vampire through identification with Life-in-Death and the Mariner, gaining energy from an understanding of the meaning of the tale and poem, and through that understanding also gaining insight into the human need to maintain a relationship with the divine. Through identification with the artist and the text, as well as with the internal audience represented by the Wedding Guest, the external audience receives knowledge, truth, understanding of the world and their role within it, and a renewed energy based on their reunion with the divine.

• THREE •

Recreating the World
The Sacred and the Profane in Bram Stoker's Dracula

In her book *Dracula: Between Tradition and Modernism* (1998), Carol A. Senf characterizes Victorian citizens as looking "Janus-like ... in two opposing directions" (6). While many people looked forward to the new century and to further progress, Senf writes that others looked "nostalgically to the past, a period that they *believed* (my italics) contained a clear synthesis of moral, religious, artistic, political, and social thought" (6). For many individuals, faith became a secular matter of production, consumption, and profit margins; and nature, once an example of God's rational design for the world, seemed more of an arena "red in tooth and claw" (Tennyson, "In Memoriam" 176) in which humans competed with each other for the Darwinian glory of survival of the fittest. As many late nineteenth-century individuals came to understand how so many other species had lived and died out during the past millennia, they also had to accept their own mortality as a species; this realization called into question traditional religious promises of redemption through Christ, leaving many individuals in a condition of spiritual poverty characterized by doubt. However, the fact that men were divided over whether the alleged progress of the present time or the simpler ways of the past were best for society both morally and religiously seems to show that Victorian Britons were struggling to find some spiritual quality in their lives.

During the last decades of the nineteenth century, some Victorians sought reunion with divine mystery in study of the occult. Many turned to metaphysical organizations like the Hermetic Order of the Golden Dawn, a secret society formed by William Wynn Westcott, a Rosicrucian

Freemason. Their mandate was to establish connection between the divine within man and the divine within the cosmos through the practice of magic, ritual, and the occult sciences.[1] The Society for Psychical Research, whose search for a numinous connection with the divine took place on a scientific level with the study of occult phenomena in nineteenth-century culture, also evolved during this period. Created in 1882 by a group of scholars from Cambridge University, London, and other nearby cities, the Society's purpose was to discover "whether some of the strange and unacceptable events— telepathy, clairvoyance, foreknowledge — had any basis in fact" (Sidgwick *Foreword* v). As nearly as possible a systematic and scientific method of collection, authentication, and analysis was followed; and in 1886 the information gathered by Edmund Gurney, Frank Podmore, and Frederic W. H. Myers was published in two volumes as *Phantasms of the Living*.

While Stoker would not have been aware of the numinous as such, since Otto had not yet coined the word when Stoker was living and writing, his family history seems to indicate that he would have understood the feeling. Charlotte Stoker, Bram Stoker's Irish mother, regaled the sickly child with tales of ghosts and of the Irish banshee, whose keening cry, it was said, "presaged imminent death" (Roth 2) in the family. With this oral tradition as part of his early upbringing, Stoker would have been well versed in the qualities of non-rational experience. However, as an adult Stoker also would have been aware of the mystical side of pagan religious belief through his acquaintance with several people who practiced the art of magic.

In her biography of Stoker, Barbara Belford notes the unsubstantiated rumor that Stoker was a member of the Hermetic Order of the Golden Dawn. However, she also notes that he did have many friends who belonged to the organization and might have learned the secrets of the society from them, despite their pledge of silence on the subject. Further evidence of Stoker's awareness of the effect an experience of the numinous might be found in his personal reaction to Henry Irving, whose reading of Thomas Hood's "The Dream of Eugene Aram" Stoker described in terms reminiscent of the hypnotic power of the Ancient Mariner, saying "so great was the magnetism of his genius, so profound was the sense of his dominancy that I sat spellbound" (Belford 73). At the end of the reading, Stoker reportedly collapsed in apparent hysterics in the face of Irving's spellbinding power; and it is this power to hypnotize that becomes an integral part of the vampire's arsenal of supernatural weapons in Stoker's novel.

Published in 1897, *Dracula* reflects the attitudes and ideas of the late Victorian period in regard to several important issues of the day, including the importance of professional and social advancement, the significance of their own culture in the minds of nineteenth-century Britons, and the concern over what the influx of foreign influences might do to that culture and to the competition for place in society. Juxtaposed against these attitudes is the sense that in *Dracula* faith has taken second place to the professional advancement of many of the characters. As the men and women of the novel are confronted by the numinousness of the vampire, the search for salvation becomes more important; however, they approach their spiritual quest more as a community, or even a committee, than as individuals. Perpetuating the sacredness of their own cultural world view, when that view is threatened, they seek to fortify its crumbling foundations through the reestablishment of its secular sacredness, rather than through an actual reunion with the divine on a higher level of spiritual awakening that might be signified by a change in their world view.

Transforming the epistolary style of earlier, realistic novels, such as *Pamela* (1740–42) and *Clarissa* (1747–48) by Samuel Richardson, Stoker's work transcribes a Gothic nightmare whose multiple versions might raise doubt as to the reliability of any of the versions, despite his use of realism. However, when Jonathan Harker finally realizes what the women of castle Dracula and Dracula himself represent, he feels the weight of the truth of the events that have transpired. Later, also, when Mina Harker compiles all of the characters' individual stories into one, acceptance of the situation as real must follow. Once the various events are put in perspective, the fears of the individuals become the fears of society. If society is to be protected, the individuals must form a community and use their combined powers to destroy Dracula and his women. Their more secular search and destroy mission against the vampires becomes a spiritual journey that requires them to call on their faith, imagining themselves to be crusaders upholding the sacredness of British society.

Instead of forming a relationship with God and remaking the world in a more cosmic context on an individual level, as the Ancient Mariner has done, the group in *Dracula* works in a more communal, almost corporate, fashion, forming a small committee of dedicated men (and one woman) banded together for the good of the larger British community. Although Dracula is, like the Mariner, a figure of the numinous condemned to wander eternally, unlike the Mariner, he is not allowed to tell his story and can take no active part in the healing of society. In Stoker's novel, the human characters are in power, despite Dracula's divine status, because they control the narrative. While the Mariner is constrained to serve the divine by becoming a vehicle for reconnection with it, the humans in *Dracula* make a decision to serve themselves and their larger society as protectors of the already established cultural system. For them, Dracula is not a vehicle of revelation or transformation, but a threat to the conservative, established order of British Victorian society that must be destroyed. Although the group calls on God in times of danger, by denying the sacred, though negative, aspects of the vampire, they deny the divine a place in their secularized world; and while the Mariner answers the question of the human place in the world by positing the unity of all things under God, the humans who destroy Dracula answer the same question by choosing to believe in the righteousness of their own established secular power, which they perceive as sacred.

In *Haunted Presence: The Numinous in Gothic Fiction*, S. L. Varnado utilizes Rudolf Otto's philosophy of the non-rational to argue that "the *mysterium tremendum et fascinans*, with its associated categories of the sacred and the profane" (1) is at the heart of Gothic literature. Applying Otto's theory of the negative numinous, in his chapter "The Daemonic in *Dracula*," Varnado argues that Bram Stoker's novel "dramatizes the cosmic struggle between the opposing forces of darkness and light, of the sacred and profane..., sweeping racial, geographical, even ontological counters in its wake" (97–98). In accordance with his interpretation of the opposition of good and evil in Otto's definition of the negative numinous, Varnado reads the sacred in *Dracula* as "benign" (108) and the profane as evil. While his analysis has much merit, due to the perceived evil of the vampire characters in the text, he does not explain what universal principles are behind the cosmic conflict in the novel. However, employing religious historian Mircea Eliade's critical studies of the sacred and profane helps illuminate the mythic patterns in the text and demonstrates why it is important that Dracula be destroyed.

Also drawing on Otto's investigation of the non-rational, Eliade defines the numinous as threshold or journey experience, a "boundary situation ... man discovers in becoming conscious of his place in the universe" (*Images and Symbols* 34) and describes the polarities of sacred and profane as "two existential situations assumed by man" (17) in relation to the cosmos. Impelled by dread, Eliade argues, the subject of an encounter with the numinous feels a sense of "profound nothingness" (*Sacred and Profane* 10) and acknowledges the non-reality of his earthly existence as a feeling of profaneness that is in opposition to the sense of absolute reality that surrounds the sacred. This feeling of powerlessness causes many individuals to seek ways to resacralize the world. Eliade defines two ways in which the religious person might recreate the world as a sacred cosmos: spatially, by projecting four horizons from a central point or forming a symbolic vertical axis through a central point to above and below earth; and temporally, by ritual repetition in imitation of the gods creating the world from the body of a primordial being most often characterized as a serpent or dragon. In Eliade's study of world religions, this being defines metaphorically the chaos which existed at the beginning of time when the world was formed, and which exists again each time the world loses its sacredness. For the proponents of the primitive religions Eliade studied, this primordial chaos often is experienced as a condition that must be vanquished so that order may be instituted in or restored to a society. For Eliade, a feeling of the numinous and a resultant yearning to be close to the divine are evoked thematically through the opposition of the sacred and profane, divine order and primordial chaos. In *Dracula* this theme is carried out on several levels as the conflict between vampire and living human becomes a reenactment of a mythic ritual in order to preserve the sacredness of the British world.

My examination of the novel mainly deals with the various representations of sacred and profane space and time within the text. However, inherent in the numinous experience is a wish to believe in God and the possibility of reunion with the sacred, leading the characters to engage in mythic rituals in order to establish their relationship with the divine. As the characters in the text confront the numinousness of Dracula, they must also confront their own apathetic faith in God; therefore, this analysis leads eventually into a discussion of faith and belief and why it is important to the late Victorian culture that the vampire be destroyed.

Three • Recreating the World

"Transylvania Is Not England": Sacred and Profane Space

According to Eliade, all "space is not homogeneous" (*Sacred and Profane* 20) but is perceived as either sacred or profane, order or chaos. Manifestation of the sacred reveals a fixed point or center where a person experiences absolute reality directly; all spaces outside this center are profane, "without structure or consistency, amorphous" (20). To transform profane into sacred space, individuals recreate the habitations of their immediate world, from their countries and cities to their houses and even their bodies, by visualizing a sacred center; however, this point then becomes a threshold point where the profane may also reveal itself. In *Dracula*, sacred and profane spaces, in opposition and intruding upon one another, are represented by England and Transylvania and the individual habitations and characters associated with them, so that both sacred and profane seem fluid and change qualities depending upon the influence of Dracula.

Sacred and profane spaces are represented initially by the polarity of West and East, England and Transylvania. Jonathan Harker's first diary entry records the impression that he is "leaving the West and entering the East" (Stoker 1)[2] as he travels to Transylvania. Although England is considered the "polar opposite of Transylvania" (Varnado 105) and the "rational center of the novel" (105), Victorian Britain may represent more than rationality in its opposition to Transylvania. If, as Eliade writes, every primitive religious individual considers his or her own world consecrated space with the world outside it unconsecrated, and if, as he also states, colonization is a method of consecration of profane space, then one might see Britain's exploration and colonization of other more primitive countries as a consecration of profane space by a country that considers itself in possession of a stronger sense of the sacred.

In his speech at the second reading of the Australian Colonies Bill before the House of Commons on February 18, 1850, Charles Adderley spoke of colonization as the "destiny" (32) of the English people. The former motives of war and commerce, which once had been behind the English proclivity toward imperialism, had been replaced by "a motive higher than either" (32). From this motive, which Adderley articulated as "the desire of spreading throughout the habitable globe all the characteristics of Englishmen — their energy, their civilization, their religion and their freedom" (32), it is not difficult to infer that, through the belief of most Englishmen in the superiority of their culture and in their right and duty to expand their world, the country of England itself acquires a higher dimension of meaning and can be interpreted as the sacred center of the British Empire.

Representing the East, Transylvania also incorporates both sacred and profane space. For people belonging to many of the early religious systems analyzed by Eliade, a belief existed that at the limits of any sacred microcosm lies profane space, a "dangerous region of the demons, the ghosts, the dead and of foreigners—in a word, chaos or death or night" (*Images and Symbols* 38), which threatens the sacred cosmos with destruction, regression, and chaos. In *Horror and the Holy: Wisdom-Teachings of the Monster Tale*, Kirk J. Schneider does examine the sacred aspects of several horror tales in spatial terms, as either "*constrictive* [or] *expansive*" (7). However, although arguing that *Dracula* is hyperconstrictive due to Harker's feelings of fear and the representations of imprisonment in the text, he fails to account for the representations of chaos that are an important cause of Harker's fear.

In *Dracula*, the chaos of profane space is represented in several ways; however, writing in *Our Ladies of Darkness: Feminine Daemonology in Male Gothic Fiction*, Joseph Andriano argues that the "circle is ... the most pervasive archetypal symbol in *Dracula*" (113) with the sacred circles formed by the heroes of the novel in opposition to the unholy circles of the vampires represented by the "whirlpools, vortices, and circles within circles" (114). As Harker begins his journey, he describes Transylvania in terms of watery chaos, as the "centre of some sort of imaginative whirlpool" (Stoker 2) of superstition; and later Dracula characterizes it as "the whirlpool of European races" (28). In Emily Gerard's *The Land Beyond the Forest*, which Stoker read while researching Transylvania, her discussion of Roumanian superstition includes a reference to the whirlpool as a place to be avoided because it is considered the residence of a water spirit "the cruel waterman who lies in wait for human victims" (200).[3]

Further representations of the circle also show up repeatedly during Harker's confusing journey from Borgo Pass to Dracula's castle. A "living ring of terror" (Stoker 13) surrounds him as the wolves gather about the coach and menace him while the driver is off searching for the blue flames he and Harker have seen flickering in the darkness. Later in the novel, the chaos of the vampire is juxtaposed against the order of the sacred as Professor Van Helsing and his band of men work to save Mina. When Mina has been partially turned to a vampire by Dracula and wears the circular imprint of the Sacred Wafer on her forehead as a sign of her profaneness, Professor Van Helsing places a "Holy circle" (369) of the blessed wafers about Mina to protect her from the female vampires. Furthermore, at the climax of the novel, it is a "ring of men" (376), Jonathan Harker, Quincey Morris, Arthur Holmwood, and Dr. John Seward, who do their sacred duty by ridding the world of Dracula.

In addition to the circular images, the chaos of storm and wildness is also important in engendering Harker's fear. He records in his diary that on crossing the mountains through the Borgo Pass it "seemed as though the mountain range had separated two atmospheres, and that now we had got into the thunderous one" (Stoker 9). In *The Essential Dracula*, Leonard Wolf annotates this passage, noting that Stoker is informing the reader "that Harker is passing from the civilized to the primordial" (14). This is Harker's threshold experience at the edge of the numinous, as he crosses over from the order of his familiar world to the chaos and danger of the unknown land beyond the forest.

For Otto, the power of the numinous lies in the subject's realization of the possibility of death and his fear of the mystery of existence beyond that death; and as Dracula will later remind Harker, "Transylvania is not England" (Stoker 21). As a wildly primitive and largely unknown part of the world, Transylvania is a nether world of superstition and death, a place which Harker will later characterize as a "cursed land where the devil and his children still walk with earthly feet!" (53). In Transylvania, Harker will be confronted with the destructiveness of profane space in the form of the living dead and their habitations. Language fails him as he journeys into a world where the Babel of "queer words" (6) spoken by the various nationalities disconcerts him. The odd behavior of the peasants protecting themselves from the evil eye and their insistent offerings of various superstitious and religious objects of the Catholic faith also leave the Protestant Harker uneasy, hesitant and wondering, open to the eventual experience of the numinous in the form of the vampire. Having ventured into the chaotic zone of Transylvania, he must recognize that beneath his rational, empirical façade he stands powerless in relation to Dracula.

Harker's journey has embodied the chaos of the East as opposed to the order of the West. However, Stoker also develops the Transylvanian landscape as a model of sacred and profane space within itself. According to Eliade, the cosmos may be recreated by projection of an imaginary axis that extends vertically above and below the horizon point. The central point of this *axis mundi* is considered the communication point between heaven, earth and the underworld; and Eliade suggests that an extremely common representation of the abode of the gods is "a Mountain ... situated at the Centre of the World" (*Images and Symbols* 42). In Harker's description of Transylvania, one can see the representation of an *axis mundi*. The road which he and his fellow passengers travel winds in and out of "the green swelling hills of the Mittel Land" (Stoker 7) which rise toward the Carpathian Mountains. This middle land takes on the aspect of earthly paradise as Harker describes its "forests and woods" and "a bewildering mass of fruit blossom — apple, plum, pear, cherry" (6), all carpeting the green grass with their petals. Suddenly, one of his companions, crossing himself in reverence, directs Harker's eye to a mountain peak looming above them. He refers to this mountain as "'Isten szek!' [or] 'God's seat!'" (7).

In these passages, it is clear that the peasants operate in this earthly middle ground in touch with a God whose abode is the peak of this lofty mountain and with the underworld in the form of Dracula's castle, and Dracula himself, to whom they show a particular aversion. Although Dracula's castle is not technically under ground as one might expect a representation of the underworld to be, and although the coach and its passenger must ascend to reach it, the castle signifies the underworld because the burial crypts far below the earth are Dracula's resting place. It is, however, in its representation as a threshold or horizon that Transylvania itself becomes important as a site of the numinous. From the middle land of earthly existence Harker must cross the threshold into the hell of Dracula's castle and face the probability of physical death without hope for a spiritual afterlife.

Chaos at the Center: Ruins and Madhouses

According to Eliade, many religious people recreate the *imago mundi* by settling a country or establishing a city and also construct their homes

Three • Recreating the World

by imitating the patterns of the cosmos; therefore, "cosmic symbolism [can be] found in the very structure of habitation" (*Sacred and Profane* 53). As the sacred can be represented in a house, the profane may be, also; and Dracula's castle "stands as a symbol of the *mysterium tremendum*" (Varnado 101). However, the castle itself produces only feelings of uneasiness in Harker, not the level of fear or dread that the *mysterium tremendum* is capable of evoking. Although the uneasiness Harker feels when confronted with the mystery of Transylvania and its people does grow stronger once he is in the castle and has met Dracula, it only becomes the full blown dread of the *mysterium tremendum* once he is assured of the horrible existence and the mysterious power of the vampire.

If Transylvania represents profane space, Dracula's castle represents the vortex of chaos. The castle is a maze of corridors, rooms, and locked doors, which for Harker come to illustrate his lack of knowledge and, therefore, his powerlessness in the presence of Dracula. As the guest of Dracula, Harker lives a "strange night existence" (Stoker 25) in which his imagination runs wild, producing even more anxiety. Within this realm of chaos, Harker attempts and fails to find some kind of order and safety. Although he feels safe upon first entering the one forbidden room that he finds unlocked in the castle, his feeling, based upon what he imagines about the former occupants of the room, is illusory. Then, after he has experienced the horror of the female vampires, he looks upon his own room in the castle as a refuge from danger; however, at the center of chaos, true sanctuary does not exist. At the mercy of these "devils of the Pit" (53), Harker lives in fear of death, wondering how he can escape from the danger.

Up to this point, Harker's experience in Dracula's castle has been one of an uneasy sense of danger; however, once he has met the vampire women, he suffers the horror that characterizes Otto's definition of the numinous in its negative aspect. This feeling causes him to fall to his knees in prayer, insisting that, if he dies at the hands of the vampire women, he will be spiritually ready. At this point, he apprehends the sacred in its positive character. As it rises, the sun strikes the highest point of the gate to Dracula's castle which Harker can see from his window; and it seems to him "as if the dove of the ark had lighted there" (46), pointing the way to safety. Like Noah in his ark, Harker is delivered from his "sea of wonders" (18) to a new birth, a second creation of the world from watery chaos.

The Vampire as Numinous Experience

After the cataclysmic events of the previous days, Harker's fear dissipates, and he realizes that he must take action to save himself. He must risk death by imitating Dracula, climbing out over the precipice of the castle to escape. Although, like many men, he dreads the unknown "Hereafter" (46), Harker's dilemma is more urgent than most. Fear of being turned into one of the Un-dead makes the choice of possible death a necessity for Harker. In the end, it seems, he prefers the unknown and hope for a spiritual life to the decidedly purgatorial existence of vampirism, as he risks his mortal life climbing down the wall and escaping the female vampires.

In the primitive systems of religion studied by Eliade, profane space is commonly represented as having no fixed point of reference; and this amorphous and neutral space will erupt in the heart of seemingly sacred space when Dracula lands at Whitby, England, bringing with him a chaos that will threaten an already shaky English order. The sun will set with a vengeance on the British Empire when he arrives. As Dracula arrives in England aboard the *Demeter*, however, Stoker reminds the reader of Dracula's connection to Coleridge's wandering Mariner. The wind dies and the stormy seas are replaced by a dead calm; and Mina remarks, quoting Coleridge's Mariner, that the only ship visible, a foreign ship, seems "as idle as a painted ship upon a painted ocean" (Stoker 76; Gardner line 113). This is the dead calm before the true storm of Dracula's presence is felt in England.

If discovery or projection of a sacred center is equivalent to the creation of the world, as Eliade posits, then Dracula's invasion of England becomes a de-creation of the sacred, extending chaos to the religious institutions and habitations of the British population. Just as houses are considered as forms of the *imago mundi*, holy sites and sanctuaries are considered even more so because they are sanctified religious structures and, as such, are supposed to be "proof against all earthly corruption" (Eliade *Sacred and Profane* 59); however, in the potentially profane world of England, holy sites and sanctuaries are no proof against Dracula. Since, as Eliade argues, no place exists exclusively as sacred or profane, Dracula has always had his own privileged places, sanctuaries as it were, to which he can retreat. For centuries, his *sanctum sanctorum* has been his Transylvanian castle and the tomb deep beneath it in the old chapel; however, when he decides to travel to England, he must make use of more portable sanctuaries. Harker records his understanding that the vampire can "only rest in sacred earth" (Stoker 297), information which he has learned from Professor Van Helsing's reference to the belief that the graves of Dracula's heroic ancestors have sanctified the soil for Dracula's sanctuaries. Although Wolf notes that he finds no evidence in either folklore or history to support Professor Van Helsing's observation, the precedent does exist in Eliade's research of primitive religions. Eliade argues that many primitive people felt a sacred connection to the earth because they believed their original ancestors came from it; and Dracula also partakes in a more profane way in what Eliade describes as the "religious experience of autochthony" (*Sacred and Profane* 140), which is "the feeling ... of *belonging to a place*" (140), of having a connection with the native soil of one's own land. Dracula's autochthonic connection with the earth of his native land is represented by the fifty boxes of "friendly soil" (Stoker 31) which he has shipped to England to serve as sanctuaries for him.

However, in Britain, Whitby Abbey, the estate of Carfax, the insane asylum, and Hampstead Heath also represent types of sanctuary, which have been rendered profane and, therefore, provide other privileged places for Dracula and for Lucy once she becomes a vampire. In his chapter "Sacred and Desecrated Space: The Cathedral and the Ruin in the Gothic Novel," in *The Cartographers of Hell: Essays on the Gothic Novel and the Social History of England*, Alok Bhalla argues that the foundation of the "religion and religious institutions" (72) represented in Gothic novels lies in the "economic, political and cultural conditions of a given society" (72). Although he concedes to Eliade's finding that the cathedral is sacred space and, quoting Eliade's *Sacred and Profane*, agrees his assertion that the sacredness of the cathedral allows the worshipper to "make a 'religious valorization of the world'" (Bhalla 74; Eliade 23), he makes a more pessimistic argument that the cathedral produces only the realization of human inability to restore the sacred relationship of primordial times. He describes the Gothic ruin as a amorphous place which holds no promise of a "return to a divine origin" (74) and characterizes the Gothic ruin as "a region of moral and spiritual desolation, a desecrated space tainted with sin and corruption" (79). As such, these places represent a world devoid of "spiritual meaning or purpose" (80) which for the characters in *Dracula* may be indicative of the time in which they live. However, Bhalla has missed an extremely important point. For both Eliade and Otto, spiritual value is not irretrievable; the feelings of unworthiness felt by the person who has encountered the sacred, in either its negative or positive guise, cause the person to recognize his longing to reclaim the sacred and to seek out ways to do so. The Gothic ruin only indicates that mankind has failed in his responsibility to maintain and renew the sacredness of his world; it does not represent the sacred as irredeemable. In *Dracula*, the ruins in England are a sign that humanity must change or be caught up in the chaos of a profane life, which is perceived by many religious people to be a living death with no promise of spiritual release.

Whitby Abbey, once a religious sanctuary, has been in ruins since its sacking by the Danes in 867 (Wolf 84) and is purportedly now only fit to house ghosts.[4] Even the parish church standing between Whitby Abbey and the town of Whitby itself is surrounded by a ruined graveyard. According to Mr. Swales, the gravestones are "simply tumblin' down with the weight o' the lies wrote on them"; and "nigh half of them" (65) have no body in them at all since the men were lost at sea. The old man tells Mina Murray that not only the graves, but also the memories of the dead themselves are not held sacred by the living. One grave in particular belongs to a suicide; and it is here that Dracula takes shelter when he arrives in Whitby. This grave is a privileged place for him, since, according to the research of both Montague Summers and Leonard Wolf, in vampire folklore a person who committed suicide was considered susceptible to becoming a vampire. However, the suicide's grave is also a logical hiding place for Dracula because the disrepair of the graves and the lies that have been written on them suggest the absence of true sanctity in British society.

In Whitby, there exists the same polarity of West and East that Harker had noticed on his travels to Transylvania. The suicide's grave and the death seat above it are on the East cliff, while the town and the hotel where Mina and Lucy are staying are on the West cliff. Once Dracula has brought Lucy under his influence, he can invade the town and her rooms at the Crescent and eventually move even further west to her home at Hillingham, near London. When the novel's action moves on to Purfleet, outside London, the intrusion of profane into sacred space becomes even more apparent. Since in primitive religious belief structures may take the cosmos as a "paradigmatic model" (Eliade *Sacred and Profane* 45), Carfax may be considered an *imago mundi*. The estate purchased by Dracula represents the world in two ways, as a structure of habitation and as a representation of intersection. Harker's description of the estate to Dracula refers to the derivation of the name Carfax from "*Quatre Face*, as the house is four-sided agreeing with the cardinal points of the compass" (Stoker 23). Moreover, in Eliade's study, an intersection is considered a sacred representation of the world. As the human universe stretches out from the sacred center "toward the four cardinal points, the village comes into existence around an intersection" (*Sacred and Profane* 45). Carfax can be perceived as an *imago mundi* because it is situated at a crossroads in Purfleet. Although Harker only describes the house as being on a side road, the structure aligns with the four compass points by virtue of its name. In *The Essential Dracula*, Wolf employs *The Oxford Dictionary of* Etymology definition of Carfax as "a place where four roads meet, especially as a proper name" (31); he also makes an interesting point that Carfax is a perfect choice for Dracula's English lair because suicides were traditionally buried at crossroads.

Regardless of its sacred orientation, this estate is now a model of chaos, abandoned and in ruins. Harker tells Dracula that Carfax is comprised of an ancient keep and church (Stoker 23) and several additions made haphazardly over the generations. The high wall surrounding the property has long been in disrepair and the iron parts of the gate are exceedingly rusted. These descriptions of Carfax not only suggest a lack of order, but also a lack of the responsibility that the English society should have taken for the sacredness of its habitations. The fact that Dracula will now inhabit this place shows that the profane has invaded the symbolic center of the Victorian world; yet this center is empty and in ruins because the British people have neglected the sanctity of their own space.

At this place of intersection, however, Carfax is not the only sight of profane activity. Here is another residence, an insane asylum owned by Dr. John Seward. Although by the late nineteenth century the stereotypical madhouse had evolved into a hospital atmosphere with a more humane approach to the care and cure of patients, the insane asylum in *Dracula* should still be considered more a center of chaos than of order. According to Andrew T. Scull's *Museums of Madness: The Social Organization of Insanity in Nineteenth-Century England*, both strait waistcoats and chaining were methods used in the early eighteen hundreds to restrain patients. Dr. Seward's reference to the use of the strait waistcoat and to the chaining of the inmate Renfield in order to restrain him indicate that Seward is still making use of earlier methods and mechanics for keeping the asylum's patients in a condition more like prisoners than sick people.

As a privately owned "lunatic asylum" (Stoker 23), Seward's establishment also may be associated with the profane side of existence in the economically oriented British culture. Private asylums arose as business ventures in the eighteenth and nineteenth centuries and had to make a profit in order to survive; therefore, the doctors in charge not only became the "arbiters of mental normalcy" (McCandless 341), but also had a monetary stake in diagnosing someone as insane. Furthermore, the opposition of sacred and profane space is seen in the isolation of the asylum from the so-called normal community. By locating the asylums outside the city, the foreignness or "'otherness' of the insane was emphasised by their geographical separation from 'normalcy'" (Mellett 46); and in *Dracula*, Harker assures the Count that the asylum cannot be seen from the grounds of Carfax Abbey. This isolation will give Dracula access to the lunatic Renfield and, later, to Mina (Murray) Harker when she is left in the asylum by her husband and the other men, ostensibly to protect her as they all go in search of Dracula.[5] Like Harker in Dracula's castle, Mina is isolated from the outside world and from the additional knowledge that the men are gathering on the danger Dracula poses to them all. Her isolation and ignorance of this knowledge indicates a lack of control in chaotic space; Mina has been placed in a vulnerable and profane position in relation to Dracula's great power. The asylum offers her no sanctuary, no safety; and while the men are out searching for his hiding places, there is no one to stop Dracula from making Mina one of his vampire women.

Another place of chaos within the sacredness of Britain is Hampstead Heath. In *Literary England*, David E. Scherman and Richard Wilcox refer to Hampstead Heath as "an expanse of wasteland" (plate 48) within the confines of the London suburbs. According to data in Henry Mayhew's *London Labour and the London Poor*, prostitution was prevalent there (Mayhew 266).[6] For Lucy, once she is a vampire, the graveyard near Hampstead Heath becomes a place of sanctuary. From there the demon Lucy, her vampire body now representative of the chaos brought to England by Dracula, roams the lonely domain of Hampstead Heath preying on children.

Good Women and Great Men, Demons and Lunatics

Eliade maintains that when primitive individuals perceive the world as a creation of the gods, they apprehend themselves as a part of that creation and discover within themselves "the same sanctity ... [apparent] in the cosmos" (*Sacred and Profane* 165). This discovery, he argues, causes them to assimilate the cosmic patterns of the world into individual life and reproduce the cosmos on a human scale. Therefore, for Eliade's primitive individual, the human body can be considered as either sacred or profane; and "passing beyond the human condition finds figural expression in the destruction of ... the personal cosmos" (177). In *Dracula*, the characters represent the opposition of sacred and profane space on a personal level. However, as a group, a large part of what they come to represent is the sacred order of the cosmos, at least the British cosmos.

Good Women

The main female characters in the novel, Lucy Westenra and Mina Murray, represent the sacredness of such institutions as society and family; yet both women have the potential to become profane. As a representative of British womanhood, Lucy rather typifies the fears of many British men in regards to the Victorian New Woman.[7] She is a woman who wants to marry three men; and this sexually rebellious attitude places her squarely on the side of the profane, making her susceptible to Dracula. Lucy's surname Westenra also allies her with both the sacred and the profane. Most interpretations, according to Wolf, call attention to the displaced "r" to give the reading "Western" to Lucy last name, identifying her name "symbolically as 'Light of the West'" (Wolf 71). He also notes that her name has been interpreted as a derivative of 'Lucifer' and mentions Mark M. Hennelley's suggestion in his article "*Dracula*: The Gnostic Quest and Victorian Wasteland," that her name stands for "'the principle of right light'" (71). However, there is a further interpretation to be explored. According to Christopher Frayling's *Vampires: Lord Byron to Count Dracula*, Stoker had E. A. Wallis Budge's *The Mummy: Chapters in Egyptian Funereal Archeology* (1893 edition) in his library at the time of his writing of Dracula, and Frayling lists this book as "relevant to the writing" (346) of the text. In light of the information in this book, one might interpret Lucy's last name as divided into the syllables West-en-Ra, 'en-Ra' most often translated in the Budge book as 'of the Sun'. Her name might then be interpreted as 'Light of the Western Sun' which would associate it with sunset, thereby identifying her even more strongly with the vampire who can only rise from the grave at that time.

Unlike Lucy, Mina Harker is considered "practical and ambitious" (Varnado 105) and dreams of helping her husband with his work. This description may align Mina with the rational; however, she demonstrates even more strongly that she is allied with both the sacred and profane. Mina is characterized as wife, mother, and sister in relation to the men in the story, all sacred familial relationships. In addition, she is described in religious terms. Professor Van Helsing's description of her as "one of God's women" (Stoker 188) resembles the standard description of a nun's relationship to God; and, after she has exchanged blood with Dracula, she is described as a "martyr" (290) when she vows to die before she would hurt any of the others. However, Mina also is allied with Eve when she gives Professor Van Helsing a shorthand copy of her diary to read, excusing her wish to astonish and puzzle him by laying the blame on "some of the taste of the original apple that remains still in our [women's] mouths" (183). In identifying herself with Eve, she has characterized herself as transgressor and so is a suitable victim for Dracula, as Lucy was for different reasons.

After the exchange of blood, however, Mina recognizes herself as "unclean" (Stoker 296) and profane; but she has no power to recreate herself again as sacred. Soon she begins to feel a strange sense of freedom and becomes more affectionate with Harker than usual. Although Lucy and Mina may represent the rational and the sacredness of English society, Dracula's penetration of them both with his fangs may be interpreted as a penetration of chaos into heart of the personal cosmos and, through them, into the center of the sacred British cosmos. It will be up to Mina's husband and the others to resacralize the bodies of both Mina and Lucy and the world of England with the death of Dracula.

Great Men

If one looks at the relationships between the men, one can see the beginnings of the group structure that will be brought against Dracula. Dr. Seward, Morris, and Holmwood have formed strong ties of friendship through sharing adventures in the Marquesas, South America, and Korea; Seward, Holmwood, and Professor Van Helsing, in their turn, share the same kind of connection, and more so, because Dr. Seward saved the life of Professor Van Helsing by sucking the poison from his wound after Holmwood accidentally injured him. As comrades in danger, these men have already formed a community within the larger social structure, participating in a relationship which honors the sacredness of life, friendship, and duty, among other things; and these are the men who become the foundation of the forces of the sacred to which later will be added Jonathan and Mina (Murray) Harker.

Arthur Holmwood's name also aligns him with the sacred in two important ways. First, the surname Holmwood establishes his connection with the sacred. Holmwood is another name for the holm-oak, a bush often defined as the holly because of a resemblance in the foliage; and the holly is a sacred plant signifying "death and regeneration" (Walker 406). In relation to the meanings of holly, in his study *The Golden Bough*, Sir James Frazer found the mistletoe plant to be connected with divinity as it was considered supernatural, growing on oak trees as it does without benefit of roots in soil. Then, the name *Arthur* brings up the obvious connection with King Arthur, a fifth-century British hero of both historical and mythic proportions, whose leadership consolidated the tribes of Britain to repel its enemy, the Saxons. Furthermore, the connection between Arthur Holmwood and King Arthur takes on a tripartite pattern if one takes into account the association of Irish hero Finn MacCumhal and King Arthur.

Finn was the leader of a band of men called the Fianna, who, according to historical and folklore research, were most often characterized in early texts as social outcasts who survived by "hunting and warring" (Nagy 18). As outlaws, these men functioned "outside or on the margins of the tribal territory or community" (18). However, through time and the telling of the tale, as so often happens, the character of Finn and his band was transformed; they came to be perceived as the champions and protectors of Ireland. Many experts in Celtic literature find a bond between King Arthur and Finn, considered in their respective folklores to be heroic, cultural figures and leaders of bands of men who protect their respective lands from enemies again; and Finn is often described in later tales as the "'Irish Arthur'" (MacKillop 63).

A particular tale of Finn may be relevant here. In *Gods and Fighting Men: the Story of the Tuatha De Danaan and of the Fianna of Ireland*, Lady Augusta Gregory retells the tale "The Hospitality of Cuanna's House" which Stoker quite possibly was familiar with from the stories his mother told during his Irish childhood. While hunting with his band one day, Finn MacCumhal and his friends see a giant carrying a pig on his back. A

The Vampire as Numinous Experience

heavy mist rises suddenly, hiding the road and the giant; and when it clears, they discover a house with two wells near it. On the edge of one well is an iron vessel; on the other is a copper vessel. The occupants of the house welcome them; and soon Finn becomes thirsty. Caoilte, one of Finn's band, is sent by the owner of the house to bring water from either well. He brings water in the copper vessel. This water tastes like honey while Finn is drinking it, but it turns to gall in his stomach, causing "fierce windy pains and signs of death" (264). Caoilte is sent out again and this time brings water in the iron vessel. When Finn drinks this water, it tastes of "bitterness" (264); but afterward, he feels better. The old man explains that the two wells represent "Lying and Truth; for it is sweet to people to be telling a lie, but it is bitter in the end" (266). By the same token, though the truth may taste bitter when first heard, in the end it is sweet. It may be this idea that Stoker is trying to impart when he has Professor Van Helsing tell Arthur that they all "will have to pass through the bitter water to reach the sweet" (Stoker 170), especially since he reiterates this sentiment two more times in the course of the novel (202 and 213).

For Holmwood, as for all of them, the truth of Lucy's existence as a vampire may be bitter in the beginning, but later, after the men have returned her to a more blessed state in death, memory of her can be sweet again. In light of the connection between these legendary heroes, Arthur and Finn, it seems probable that Stoker combined them in the character of Holmwood, both by naming him after King Arthur and by incorporating the story of Finn in the repeated references to bitter and sweet water. As the only aristocrat in the group, Arthur Holmwood represents something of the divine himself in his connection to the heroic nobility of the legendary king Arthur. He also represents the more chaotic polarity through Finn the Irish outlaw hero. In addition, it is foretold in the tales of both noble and outlaw that they will be resurrected when their respective countries are in desperate need of them; and, in his act of staking Lucy, Arthur Holmwood becomes the sacred agent of death and resurrection for her.

The group's connection with the sacred is apparent in other characters as well. As a newly made solicitor, Harker is now a member of the middle class, serious about his new duties. In the rational world these attributes are admirable; but in the non-rational world they will avail him little. Once Harker crosses over into Transylvania, his journey becomes a rite of passage, and he becomes the initiate. When subjected to the mysterious actions and words of the peasants, he is ignorant of their true meaning and so is only uneasy; but as he gathers knowledge of Dracula and the three women, the horror of both his own and society's fate nearly paralyzes him. After his escape from the castle and the female vampires, he suffers from brain fever, his hair turns white overnight, and he is reported to be raving "the secrets of God" (Stoker 103). To some extent, although he seeks to deny his knowledge, once he survives his ordeal in Transylvania, he is a wise old man figure because he has immediate experience of the vampire, which Professor Van Helsing, for all his knowledge, does not have; and his foreign journal, in turn, becomes for the others a narrative of initiation into the numinous.

However, despite the fact that he has no direct experience of the vampire, Professor Van Helsing's role in the group seems the most important. As the oldest of all the men, Professor Van Helsing represents a kind of father figure to the younger men. His experiences of the world are far greater than those of the other men; and he has his Catholic faith and his knowledge of medicine and of folklore as weapons to combat Dracula. As a metaphysician and the leader of the band of men who will destroy Dracula, Professor Van Helsing represents the sacred in the role of warrior priest, as a St. George, leading the fight against the evil dragon—chaos. Dr. Seward, Holmwood, and Morris join Professor Van Helsing, as they had in earlier years, eventually drawing Jonathan and Mina Harker into their ranks, to become a force in service of the sacred.

Demons

If Professor Van Helsing is the good father figure, leading his band of children in a sacred ritual, Dracula is the evil father who has some of the same characteristics as Professor Van Helsing but who has turned them to the service of evil. As a representation of the negatively numinous, Dracula embodies both sacred and profane space. Dracula embodies some of the aura of the sacred hero; he is, as he tells Harker, the "heart's blood" (Stoker 29) of his people. It is widely believed that Stoker at least partially patterned Dracula after Vlad Tepes, a ruler of Wallachia in the 1400s, who, according to historic documents, used impalement as a form of punishment, and sometimes as a source of entertainment. If accounts of Tepes are true, one might rather interpret the connection of Dracula to him as a signification of the profane; but, despite these reports, Tepes was not and is not considered a monster in his own country. To this day, he is considered a hero for driving the Turks from the borders. According to research done for their book *Dracula, Prince of Many Faces: His Life and Times*, Radu R. Florescu and Raymond T. McNally, history professors and Dracula experts with several books on the subject to their credit, found that through Romanian folklore Vlad Tepes became a national hero on the order of America's George Washington. The Romanian oral tradition characterizes him as "a law-upholding statesman who is implacable in punishing thieves, liars, idlers, or people who otherwise cheated the state" (216). As a "rational despot" (216) he attempted to "centralize his government by killing unpatriotic anarchical boyars" (216), and his exploits were believed by the people to be socially and morally right. It is this interpretation of history that connects Tepes and Dracula as heroes and allows Dracula to represent sacred space.

Dracula also has at his control what appear to be divine powers—to control the animals and the weather, to turn to motes of dust or bats, and to read minds. Although these powers would seem to ally him with the sacred, they represent Eliade's description of profane space in several ways. Dracula reacts with horror both to religious objects and to the natural, folk remedies of garlic, mountain ash or rowan and wild rose given to Harker by his fellow coach passengers. These represent a more superstitious approach toward danger and are meant to protect the intended victim or dispatch the vampire. Emily Gerard writes that Roumanian superstition calls for the mouth of a suspected vampire to be filled with garlic, in addition to the cutting off of the head as a precaution against vampirism (185). As an agent against plague and various supernatural evils, in Romania garlic is used both to detect the vampire and to prevent attack. On both St. Andrew's and St. George's Eves windows and doors are anointed with garlic to keep vampires away. In addition, Gerard also found that it was "usual to lay the thorny branch of a wild-rose bush across the body to prevent it leaving the coffin" (186). Montague Summers also records that in Saxon superstition in Transylvania on St. George's Day it was customary to place branches of the wild rose bush on the gates of the yard to keep out witches (309). Moreover, the mountain ash or rowan, a member of the rose family, was customarily planted in churchyards and at door of houses and barns to protect people and animals from evil spirits (Melton).

Three • Recreating the World

Dracula's abilities to shape-change, become invisible, and read thoughts also demonstrate his profane nature because they are not ultimate powers. His shape-changing and invisibility are limited to night time and noon; and his ability to read thoughts is contingent upon his first having a blood link with the person through an act of vampirism. Furthermore, as the living dead, Dracula represents a man whose *personal cosmos* has been destroyed, who has passed "beyond the human condition" (Eliade, *Sacred and Profane* 177). He is and is not human at the same time — both a man and a "monster" (Stoker 51), a hero of the wars against the Turks and a "criminal, and of criminal type" (342), according, as Mina Harker says, to Nordau and Lombroso, nineteenth-century physician and criminologist, respectively, whose theories argued that criminal behavior was degenerate and a reversion to the primitive.[8] Dracula, although he was once a living, breathing human and a hero, is now a daemonic corpse; still of human form, he now is characterized by Harker as having a "marked physiognomy" (Stoker 17). As Harker and his fellow vampire hunters come to know Dracula more fully, they find in him a physical, rather than spiritual, immortality, prodigious strength, and uncanny powers of metamorphosis and control of animals and people. These aberrations link him to the primitive and, therefore, to the criminal type.

These are not the only qualities of Dracula that make him profane, however. He is foreign; and, according to the analysis done by Carol A. Senf and Stephen D. Arata, as a foreigner, Dracula may represent the British fears of colonization by other countries and/or cultures.[9] Moreover, in many of the more primitive religions that Eliade researched, colonization is considered a form of creation of the world and, as such, is always considered a consecration (*Sacred and Profane* 32); therefore, as the creator of a "new order of beings" (Stoker 302), Dracula will, in effect, colonize and consecrate England to the profane. Dracula penetrates to the sacred center of the British Empire and brings chaos into an already partially desacralized world characterized by industrialism and profit making, but because Dracula is a vampire, his destructive power also means desacralization of the human body. Although the vampire cannot procreate in a normal human fashion, he creates by destroying, taking over an already existing body and turning it into the living dead and an already existing universe and returning it to primordial chaos. His creations all have the same attributes and desires; and all are parasites living off the blood of a human host, just as Dracula does. In light of the parasite/host relationship between vampires and humans, the forces of the sacred fear Dracula's ability to create more beings like himself because his way will lead to a profane, parasitic existence for all of them. It is this fear that produces the sense of extreme powerlessness and dread in the human subjects as they realize death as a vampire will result only in an amorphous and perverse version of mortal life.

The images of chaos are even stronger when applied directly to the body of the vampire. In England, in her memorandum to Professor Van Helsing and the others, Lucy Westenra tells of the visit of Dracula that precipitates her mother's death through descriptions of chaos resembling those Harker had used earlier to portray Transylvania. Dracula arrives as cloud of "little specks" (Stoker 143) which seem to blow in through the window broken by the wolf; then, these specks are further described as "wheeling and circling round like the pillar of dust that travelers describe when there is a simoom in the desert" (143). A simoom is a dust storm — hot, dry, heavy with sand, and dangerous to travelers as it sweeps across the deserts of Africa and Arabia during the spring and summer months. Of Arabic derivation, from the word *samm*, which means *to poison*, the word is particularly apt to describe the entrance of Dracula, especially in light of the earlier revelation to Mina by Sister Agatha about Harker's almost premonitory ravings of "wolves and poison and blood" in the throes of the "violent brain fever" (99) induced by his stay at Castle Dracula. The pillar of dust that Lucy describes also has implications of the danger Dracula poses. In *The Land Beyond the Forest*, Gerard makes reference to the whirlwind as denoting "that the devil is dancing with a witch, and whoever approaches too near to the dangerous circle may be carried off bodily to hell" (197). This description of the whirlwind has dangerous implications for Lucy. Struck with fear, she cannot avoid the phenomenon that is Dracula. Like the whirlwind in Gerard's example of Roumanian superstition, the destructive and chaotic space that is Dracula will eventually carry Lucy off to the underworld of vampirism.

Figures of chaos prevalent in the description of Transylvania as profane space extend to the characterization of the vampire women as well. At the castle, the second time Harker is confronted by the vampire women they are described first as dispersed matter, "quaint little specks floating in the rays of moonlight" (Stoker 44). Then, taking more solid shape, they seem to organize "in clusters in a nebulous sort of way" (44). Later, near the end of the novel, Professor Van Helsing and Mina see the vampire women form out of the "whirling mist and snow" (368) of the Transylvanian landscape. In *Our Ladies of Darkness: Feminine Daemonology in Male Gothic Fiction*, Joseph Andriano discusses the ability of the female vampires or lamiae of *Dracula* to shape-change from solid form to the chaos of dust and swirling snow and vice versa. In an analysis of the numinous qualities of the vampire, the ability to shape change shows its divine, as well as profane, character. The numinous object is dangerous in and of itself, as an objective reality, because of its perceived power. However, its transformation at will into a chaos of whirling, floating obscurity — amorphous, undetectable, and dangerous — only adds to the mystery and creates the sense of shuddering horror which Otto feels characterizes the negatively numinous. In addition, these descriptions of whirling, wheeling, circling substance taking form or dispersing also indicate that the fate of those who are transformed into vampires will be dissolution into the primitive state of chaos.

Renfield, the Lunatic

Perhaps the most complicated character in the novel, Renfield, the lunatic, evokes both the sacred and the profane in various ways. In his desire for immortality, Renfield seems to suffer from a form of religious mania in which, as Dr. Seward puts it, "he will soon think that he himself is God" (Stoker 100). In Book II of *Degeneration*, Max Nordau argues that mysticism is a form of "religious delirium" (45) and a "principal characteristic of degeneration" (45). Mysticism is, he writes,

> A state of mind in which the subject imagines that he perceives or divines unknown and inexplicable relations amongst phenomena, discerns in things hints at mysteries, and regards them as symbols, by which a darker power seeks to unveil or, at least, to indicate all sorts of marvels which he endeavors to guess, though generally in vain [Nordau 45].

Renfield's preoccupation with blood as the symbol of life and with the coming of the "Master" (Stoker 100), who will bestow upon him immortal life, seems to echo Nordau's definition of mysticism as a degenerative mania.

The Vampire as Numinous Experience

Within the text, however, the evidence for diagnosis of Renfield as a religious maniac comes because he does not distinguish between Dr. Seward and the attendant, treating them both with a somewhat arrogant indifference and disregard. Because Renfield does not differentiate between the rank of doctor and attendant, Dr. Seward feels the lack of proper respect for his station and draws the analogy that the "real God taketh heed lest a sparrow fall; but the God created from human vanity sees no difference between an eagle and a sparrow" (110). However, Renfield's own analogy of the bride and bridesmaids shows that he recognizes the difference in importance of people. He tells Seward that "the bride-maidens rejoice the eyes that wait the coming of the bride; but when the bride draweth nigh, then the maidens shine not to the eyes that are filled" (111). In *The Essential Dracula*, Wolf notes that the spiders are comparable to the bridesmaids overshadowed by the appearance of the bride. If Dracula is to be the bride, Renfield is cast in the role of groom, according to Wolf; and "Dracula's murderous visit to Renfield takes on the meaning of a macabre consummation of a monstrous wedding night" (133). Certainly, the bride-maiden-spider analogy works; however, I believe that the bride-maidens are also Dr. Seward and the attendant, both of whom Renfield feels are unimportant now that Dracula has arrived.

Eliade describes the profane individual as one for whom "the universe does not properly constitute a cosmos—that is, a living and articulated unity; it is simply the sum of the material reserves and physical energies of the planet" (*Sacred and Profane* 93–4); and this description seems to have implications in the novel. As Dracula feeds on the blood of living humans, Renfield feeds on insects, spiders, and birds, totting up their numbers in his little book as if the sum of them will give him a greater and longer life. He even goes so far as to stab Dr. Seward in the wrist with a dinner-knife and then lap up his blood from the floor. However, Eliade also proposes that most primitive humans had an obsession with recovering the world as it was in the beginning. This obsession is characterized by a thirst for sacredness; and in light of this, Renfield's mental problem could also be interpreted as allying him in some respects with the sacred.

In *Will Therapy and Truth and Reality*, psychoanalyst Otto Rank argues that, while "the more normal, healthy, and happy" (250) person willfully accepts the empirical world as reality, the neurotic suffers "not from a painful reality but from painful truth" (251) because, spiritually, the neurotic sees "through the deception of the world of sense, the falsity of reality" (251). In Rank's understanding of the psyche, the individual cannot survive without illusions, "not only outer illusions such as art, religion, philosophy, science and love afford, but inner illusions which first condition the outer" (250). If the average person has adapted the individual will to accept the truth which society sets forth as reality, the neurotic person's focus on self-consciousness is a denial of that will and a refusal to accept what society deems reality. The moment an individual begins see through the false reality created by society, the willfully created reality is destroyed; and the person's relationship to the world of the senses changes. In refusing to accept a willfully created reality, the neurotic shares a deeper sense of the world with Eliade's religious individual, who sees the earthly world as illusory and the mystical world of the gods as the true reality. If one considers Renfield's insanity as a denial of his own will in response to the more powerful will of the numinous object Dracula, then one might also read his mental state as a spiritually true perception of the world. His preoccupation with blood then might be examined as an attempt to reproduce the sacred reality of the world.

According to Eliade's exploration of early religions, "ritual cannibalism ... is the consequence of a tragic religious conception" (*Sacred and Profane* 106), in which sustenance is "not given in nature," but is "the product of a slaying" (103), and in which blood sacrifice helps religious individuals re-actualize their relationship with the cosmos. In *Voyage of the Beagle* (1839), Charles Darwin, nineteenth-century proponent of the survival of the fittest evolution theory, comments on the primitive land of New Zealand being "the centre of the land of cannibalism, murder, and all atrocious crimes!" (313). This description reminds one of Jonathan Harker's description of Transylvania. In *Dracula*, cannibalism takes place each time the vampire feeds, whether it is Lucy or the other female vampires feeding on the children, or Dracula himself feasting on the sailors, Lucy, or Mina. Participation in this kind of cannibalism seems to be entered into for the most obvious of motives—the sustenance gained allows the vampires to survive. Even one of the humans, Dr. Seward, has partaken of blood when he sucked the wound of Professor Van Helsing to save his life.

However, the most insistent ritual of cannibalism is demonstrated in Renfield's zoöphagous behavior. His connection with the world, his sense of being, depends upon blood; and he even goes so far as to try to convince

Dr. Seward that his redemption hangs upon his getting a cat or even a kitten. According to Sir James Frazer's studies of early cultures in *The Golden Bough,"* many primitive individuals believed that ingesting the flesh of animal or human gave them the attributes of that entity. If the entity happened to be divine, the individual believed he or she would acquire some part of those divine powers as a result of the act. For Renfield, "the blood is the life" (Stoker 234); and he is counting increments of life with every fly, spider and bird, hoping through this blood sacrifice to gain immortality. Wolf notes that the expression *for the blood is the life* is part of a proscriptive Old Testament passage (Leviticus 17: 11–13) that forbids the eating of the blood in order for the Israelites to distinguish their religion from those who practiced human sacrifice (181). It is not in that sense, however, that we should view Renfield's cannibalism as profane. Renfield's cannibalism is in search of salvation — a state of grace with the cosmos, represented by the divine aspects of Dracula. However, the potentiality for evil inherent in Dracula stains Renfield's attempt at salvation, because his salvation will be only physical, if he receives the immortality the vampire is prepared to give.

"Truly There Is No Such Thing as Finality": Sacred and Profane Time

Eliade's study proposes that, in the perception of various worldviews, time, "like space, is neither homogeneous nor continuous" (*Sacred and Profane* 68) and, as such, encompasses the sacred and profane as existential situations for humans. Sacred time is posited as *"primordial, mythical time made present"* (68) through periodic repetition of sacred rituals and myths, and is, therefore, eternally recoverable, and effectively non-temporal, outside human time. Profane time, on the other hand, is believed to be "continuous and irreversible" (*Images and Symbols* 57) and of finite "temporal duration" (*Sacred and Profane* 68). While Eliade considers the non-religious person to be aware of his or her existence only within the profane time of a life circumscribed by birth and death, he believes religious individuals perceive themselves as living within both sacred and profane time, aware of their existence in finite time but returning periodically to sacred through reenactments of sacred rituals. For Eliade's religious individual, the eternal present of the mythical event makes possible the profane duration of time; and the year is the temporal dimension of the cosmos, circular in nature with a beginning and end, yet infinitely renewable each year with the cosmic rhythms of seasons, days, and nights.

"In This Matter Dates Are Everything"

As Mina Harker attempts to put together the entries of all the participants into a comprehensive narrative in *Dracula*, she records in her own journal her feeling that "in this matter dates are everything" (Stoker 224); therefore, chronological order must guide her transcription of events. In the novel, the sacred calendar is of first importance. The action begins on May first and ends November sixth. May first is an important date on the sacred calendar. A celebration of regeneration of the land, it is also a day honoring Saint Walpurgis. According to canonical history, St. Walpurgis, an 8th century English nun and abbess at Heidenheim, Germany (Cooper 299), became confused in legend with the pagan fertility goddess Waldbourg. Through this mix-up, Walpurgis Night became associated with the activity of witches and even vampires. Although the date of celebration in honor of St Walpurga was changed to February to discourage her celebration being confused with the pagan one, Walpurgis Night remains the primary festival night of witchcraft.

This night also is associated with Goethe's *Faust*, in which the aged scholar makes a deal with Mephistopheles in order to gain all knowledge and experience. In part one of the play, Goethe uses the Walpurgis Night celebrations of the witches to illuminate the chaos that characterizes Mephistopheles and his dwelling place in the underworld; and in part two, as Faust searches for Helen of Troy, Goethe sets the action against a Walpurgis Night festival from classical Greece. Stoker's *Dracula*, influenced as it must have been by his close association with actor Henry Irving, who played Mephistopheles innumerable times, originally opened with a chapter, later published under the title "Dracula's Guest," that takes place on Walpurgis Night.

This night is significant to a discussion of *Dracula*, since it is a night, as Sir James Frazer maintains in *The Golden Bough*, when witches and all evil spirits are said to have great power. It is also the time of Beltine

(Beltane) in Ireland, the beginning of summer and renewal. November, particularly the first week, is important as Hallowtide, the season of All Saints; and November first is All Saints' Day, the Christianized version of Samhain, which in Irish legend, is the "beginning of the dark season..., especially associated with the dead and the underworld" (Ó hÓgáin 403). Samhain celebration was held on October 31, All Hallows' or All Saints' Eve, and was considered a propitiatory gesture in response to the "threatening and warlike ... powers of destruction" (Sjoestedt 69) which characterized the intrusion of the spirits into the earthly world.

The idea behind the pagan celebration of these days seems to be "that crucial joints between the seasons opened cracks in the fabric of space-time, allowing contact between the ghostworld and the mortal one" (Walker 372). In pre–Christian Celtic belief, a retaliatory relationship existed between the mortal and immortal worlds, which not only allowed the spirits to threaten mankind at this time, but also allowed humans to enter their world and "to attack in their turn those mysterious dwellings which for one night lay open and accessible" (Sjoestedt 72). According to research by folklorist Dáithí Ó hÓgáin, in Irish folklore and myth "many of the supernatural adventures of heroes ... are said to have taken place at this time" (403). Whether one uses pagan feast days or their Christianized counterparts as a time frame in which to map the events in the novel, it is clear that the plot of *Dracula* takes place within a cyclic, sacred calendar of summer and winter, birth and death, with the possibility of a cosmic rebirth for the forces of the sacred and their society when Dracula is killed. Harker ventures into Transylvania as the fabric of time and space is rent in May and helps Dracula to take up residence in the world of men. Once loosed upon the world, Dracula cannot be driven back across that border between the two worlds until the next tear in the fabric is effected during Hallowtide or Samhain.

The cyclic nature of days and nights also is important in a discussion of sacred and profane time. While the human characters live their day from sunrise to sunset, Dracula's daily span is inverted. His earthly life has been profaned by his vampirism and is now a perversion of human life. Many humans perceive death to be a return to the womb of the earth (Eliade *Sacred and Profane* 140); however, Dracula is profane so he can not rest peacefully. Although, he is seen a few times during daylight, he is generally constrained to rising at sunset and returning to his bed at sunrise.

Three • Recreating the World

In Transylvania Dracula manages to invert Harker's time schedule. He keeps Harker talking all night, manipulating him into conforming to his own more profane time schedule; and soon Harker's lack of sleep wears on him, increasing his uneasiness. Harker records how his diary seems like the tales of the "'Arabian Nights' [where] everything has to break off at cockcrow— or like the ghost of Hamlet's father" (30). Like Shahrazad, Harker is given a reprieve from a sure sentence of death each morning; like Hamlet, Harker cannot know if his experience is real or not. Once he is in Transylvania, he is plunged into the abyss that separates sacred and profane time, where primitive evil haunts the night and daylight is the only sanctuary.

For Eliade, the temporality of the human condition is defined as a "'historical situation'" (*Images and Symbols* 58). As a representative of the rational West, Harker lives in historical time and tries to place his destination Transylvania in an historical context. To this end, he searches for information on the area in that icon of historical artifacts, the British Museum, but can find no map pinpointing the exact location of Dracula's home. However, he does gain some information on the history of the area and on the traditions and superstitions of the inhabitants. Time, though, becomes much more urgent and more personal as Harker begins his journey. As he travels to Transylvania, he seems to move back in time, to travel outside of time. However, here the clock time of Great Britain is irrelevant; the cycles of seasons and of sunrises and sunsets dictate the actions of the people. Transylvania is a place of late trains and early coaches, as the driver of the public conveyance hurries through Borgo Pass, hoping to miss meeting Dracula's coach. Once Harker has exchanged the public coach for Dracula's private one, his journey is confusing as time seems to repeat itself. The coach seems to cover the same ground repeatedly; and the driver seems to stop repeatedly, going off into the darkness where they have seen blue flames flickering.

When Dracula and Harker finally arrive at the castle, Harker notices that time and the elements have taken a great toll on the carved stones of the edifice. However, time within Castle Dracula seems to stand still. The furniture and bed hangings, though clearly ancient, are in excellent condition; and Harker records that similar ones he saw in England's Hampton Court were in a much more dilapidated condition. Later, as Harker tells Dracula that Carfax has existed in one form or another since "medieval times" (23), the audience is given its first clue about Dracula's great age.

The Vampire as Numinous Experience

He replies to Harker that he is "of an old family," (23) and used to old houses. A house, he maintains, "cannot be made habitable in a day; and, after all, how few days go to make up a century" (23). In the case of the vampire's immortality, the number of days it takes to make a century are not many in relation to the endless nights spent in the service of survival.

The next night, as Harker questions Dracula about the history of Transylvania, the conversation leaves Harker feeling as though Dracula had experienced it all personally. Dracula explains this away by calling it pride of house and name which a boyar feels. His is a history both sacred and profane, including, as it does, tales of how the Szekelys and Dracula himself were born out of blood-drenched colonizations by Icelandic tribes and by the Huns and of the heroism of rulers who continually drove back the Turks and shook loose the oppressive grasp of Hungarian rule. Dracula's history has lost its significance, however. His legendary and historical associations, and his heroism, though once great, are far in the past.

By May 15th, Harker's fear has increased greatly; he knows himself to be a prisoner and has seen the Count's lizard-like descent from a window of the castle. Harker's empirical mind calls for facts and exploration and he finds himself in a room he romantically imagines was the part of the castle occupied in much earlier times. Here he juxtaposes against the history of the long dead occupants of the room the fact that he is sitting at their writing table, using shorthand, a method of transcription which "is nineteenth century up-to-date with a vengeance" (Stoker 36). Yet, the incongruity of his actions in this old place makes him aware of living in both sacred and profane time as he writes "unless my senses deceive me, the old centuries had, and have, powers of their own which mere 'modernity' cannot kill" (36). On first entering this room in Dracula's castle, Harker had felt a sense of the history of the place and a closeness to the inhabitants of the castle because of the history he imagined for the woman who once might have used the writing desk in the room; however, this sense of the past soon turns profane as he encounters the vampire women. The historical time, which he perceives in his imagination, does not exist; it is not recoverable.

Later, Harker awakens in his own bed; and the next day's journal entry recaps his experience with the vampire ladies, an experience that he cannot identify as dream or reality. However, evidence supports his belief that the experience was reality when he discovers his watch is not wound as he is "rigorously accustomed" (Stoker 40) to doing before bed. A few days later, the urgency of time is brought home to Harker with a finality that is horrifying. Dracula requests that he write three letters post-dated for June 12, 19, and 29, each indicating his progress toward home. At this request, Harker records "I know now the span of my life" (41). Harker is to be left at the mercy of the vampire women when Dracula leaves for England.

"Time Is on My Side"

At this point the novel's action moves on to England. Dracula lands at Whitby where Mina Murray and Lucy Westenra are on holiday. He has done his homework, having discovered much more about England than Harker did about Transylvania, from English magazines, newspapers, and books on all subjects "relating to England and English life and customs and manners" (Stoker 19). Dracula's history and the profaneness of the time that delineates his existence can now include England.

Here the ruins of Whitby Abbey and later Carfax represent profane time, historical and irrecoverable, both places dating from far in the past. However, it is here that the span of a lifetime is brought to the forefront again. In Whitby, Mr. Swales, the old man whom Mina and Lucy meet at the seat where a suicide is buried, sensing his death is imminent, talks to Mina of how long he has lived. Indicating that "a hundred years is too much for any man to expect" (74) to live, he tells Mina that he smells death on the wind and that if the "Angel of Death" (74) were to come that very night, he would be ready to go. Mr. Swales is allied with the forces of the sacred in his belief in the immortality of spirit; however, the death he has sensed on the wind from the sea is Dracula.

Unlike the mortal Swales, Dracula has lived centuries beyond the lifespan that Swales feels is beyond human expectation, and because of his extended existence, he is a representative of profane time. Eliade claims that the profane individual has a *"pessimistic vision of existence"* (*Sacred and Profane* 107) because the end of linear time is death. For this person, Eliade posits, repetition has no religious meaning. When repetition is no longer "a vehicle for reintegrating a primordial situation, and hence for recovering the mysterious presence of the gods, that is, *when it is desacralized*, cyclic time becomes terrifying" (107). In its terrifying aspect, cyclic time is perceived as "a circle forever turning on itself, repeating itself to infinity" (107), as the references to the whirlpool and the nebulous shapes of the vampire in the novel demonstrate. Dracula's life goes on year upon long year as he is resurrected only bodily within historical time frames. As a figure of the negatively numinous type, Dracula seems outside of time in a way, because he lives forever. However, he is caught in history and cannot recover sacred time. For Dracula, there is no renewal because there is no death. Therefore, time means nothing to Dracula; true death is not for him. As he tells Professor Van Helsing and the others, time is on his side, and his revenge upon them can meted out eternally.

Eliade claims that for a non-religious person time constitutes the deepest existential dimension linking life from beginning to end, but a religious individual refuses to live solely in the historical present. For him or her, the cosmos is a model for other kinds of doing and creation; and repair of the cosmos through ritual is a religious act, an *"imitatio dei"* (*Sacred and Profane* 88) in which the object repaired becomes a "mythical archetype" (88). With each original act associated with the creation of the cosmos, according to Eliade, religious individuals believe they have the opportunity to transfigure their existence and renew their connection to the sacred and their place in the cosmos. By virtue of this eternal return to sources of the sacred, human existence appears to be saved from nothingness and death. The important point here is that modern secular individuals live within a sense of empirical, linear time that is considered by many religious men to be profane. However, traditional, more religious people claim to live within a sense of sacred time that is cyclical, recurring periodically to reconstitute the cosmos.

Sacred time is demonstrated near the beginning of the novel, when on his journey Harker sees the people worshipping at the shrine by the side of the road. They cross themselves in a "self-surrender of devotion" (Stoker 8), seemingly detached from the earthly world around them. Harker seems to be a profane man because he lives in profane time and space as represented by Victorian Britain's seeming concentration on profit and promotion; but later, after Harker learns the truth about Dracula's castle, he attempts to connect to sacred time as he surrenders to a need for spiritual intervention. Having seen the vampire women for the second time and realized that Dracula means to leave him to them, he throws himself on his knees in prayer; and the next morning, rising for what he feels is his last day, he again sinks to his knees resolved to be spiritually ready if death, in the form of the vampire women, should come for him.

Once the action of the novel moves to England, the idea of spiritual surrender is suggested by Mr. Swales who indicates his readiness to face Death by raising up "his arms devoutly" (Stoker 74), his lips moving as if in prayer. Also, as Lucy Westenra is dispatched to the spiritual world, Professor Van Helsing reads the prayer for the dead over her; and later, once Mina Harker is turning into a vampire, she asks for this same prayer to be read, as if her funeral were taking place at that moment. Sacred time is also manifested in the novel when Professor Van Helsing states of Mina that "good women tell all their lives, and by day and by hour and by minute, such things that angels can read" (184). The humans in the text, however, fear profane time. Time presses upon Harker who focuses on the "minutes and seconds so [preciously] laden with Mina's life and happiness" (292) that are passing so quickly while he and the other men discuss what to do about Dracula. Bitten by the vampire for the third time, Mina is in eternal danger because her soul is at risk.

Eliade claims that "in the experience of sacred time" (*Sacred and Profane* 65), a religious person can apprehend the cosmos "as it was *in principio*, that is, at the mythical moment of Creation" (65). In rituals, as in the myths that generate them, the individual attempts to make contact with what is perceived as the absolute reality of the sacred and, in so doing, the individual hopes to transcend the profane condition of a historically oriented existence, reuniting with cyclical time and returning to an originating moment in the renewal of the cosmos out of chaos. The historical reality of the human characters in *Dracula* is superseded over time and through knowledge of what Dracula represents by a sacred reality; and the human characters become a force for the sacred, recreating their world with the death of the vampires. However, as a force of the sacred, they perceive their duty to God as a duty to protect British social values.

"A Duty to Do": Reenacting the Ritual

In *Dracula: Between Tradition and Modernism*, Carol A. Senf describes Harker's diary as a chronicle of "underlying prejudice against practically everything foreign" and sees in it a growing sense that what Harker finds "exotic" at the beginning of the journey soon becomes "suspect and ultimately evil, as Harker changes from tourist to patriot" (36). According to her reading, Dracula is a foreigner whose invasion is feared by the men of England "during a period in which England was intent on preserving her colonial holdings and may even suggest the fear of reverse colonization" (37); and Harker's patriotic reaction against helping him to colonize England, when echoed by the others, becomes a communal pledge to "destroy all that threatens their beliefs" (37). However, Harker's reaction to Dracula's monstrosity is patriotic only in so far as he wishes to preserve *his* England. While patriotism is a sacred duty on a nationalistic level, if one looks at the composition of the band of men who destroy Dracula, patriotism is too narrow a concept for what these men are doing. Although England is the sacred center of Harker's world, one must not forget that Morris is an American, a frontiersman in the tradition of Jim Bowie. Since, during the Victorian period, England and America were two of the most important countries in the Western world, linked through a common language and an industrialized economy, they might both be considered sacred in the eyes of their citizens, and the pledge which Harker and the others make to destroy Dracula is a pledge to save not just England, but also the world, from chaos.

As representatives of cosmic sacredness, Professor Van Helsing and the others have become aware of the non-rational or numinous, and through that awareness they have come to recognize the more profane side of themselves and to understand their obligation to society. In the novel, the Victorian sense of duty takes on both profane and sacred natures, acquiring a sacred dimension of meaning when duty to business becomes the higher duty to "rid the world of such a monster" (Stoker 51) as Dracula. In Transylvania, both Dracula and Harker tend only to business. For Harker "duty [is] imperative" (5); as a newly made solicitor sent to Transylvania to complete the sale of property in England to Count Dracula, Harker's responsibility is the business of his firm. However, duty takes on a sacred character in England, when Professor Van Helsing must convince the others of their responsibility to return the Un-dead Lucy to the proper condition of bodily death and spiritual life and to rid the world of Dracula. It is at this point that the second method Eliade posits for transforming the profane world into a sacred one becomes important in the novel, as the forces of the sacred set out to destroy the transformed Lucy.

Three • Recreating the World

Eliade argues that most primitive religions believed that the gods had to slay and dismember the marine monster or primordial being to create the world from it; and to recreate the human world as sacred space, the individual must imitate this ritual. Many primitive, religious societies believed in imitating the gods even when the act "verged on madness, depravity, or crime" (*Sacred and Profane* 104). In *Dracula*, although the desecration of graves and bodies, and even the crime of house-breaking which the men must commit in order to fulfill their purpose, may seem like "unhallowed work" (Stoker 200) to them, yet it is holy work in defense of the sacredness of human life and English society. For Professor Van Helsing, he and the other men are like medieval Crusaders, who should look upon themselves as instruments of God's will. The crusade of the forces of the sacred is likened to Christ's bearing of his cross for world sanctification. However, Eliade argues that, although of a sacred nature, Christianity is also a religion "sanctified by the incarnation of the Son of God" (*Sacred and Profane* 72) and, therefore, "historically conditioned" (111). As such, Christianity may be seen to demonstrate a new dimension of the presence of God in the world, which Eliade terms salvation history; and the sacred and profane meet at this point. In *Dracula*, the forces of the sacred must imagine themselves to be crusaders for the holy cause of their own historically-based religion in order to validate their actions in resanctifying the world within their more modern value system; and they call upon God to defend a social view of the cosmos predicated on duty and profit. However, regardless of the fact that they must imagine themselves as soldiers of God acting out of a sense of solemn and sacred duty, they are still repeating an age old pattern of recreation of the world in order to beat back chaos from the borders of their world.

To reconsecrate their world, the men must first kill and dismember Lucy Westenra. Professor Van Helsing tells Holmwood that he has "a duty to do, a duty to others, a duty to you, a duty to the dead" (Stoker 206–207); and that obligation is to stake her through the heart, cut off her head, and fill her mouth with garlic. At the tomb of Lucy, as Professor Van Helsing reads the prayer for the dead over her undead body, he counsels Holmwood to "strike in God's name" (216), in order that Lucy's soul might be redeemed from Dracula's power and that she might find the peace he has promised. After Lucy's true death is accomplished, the men will take on another sacred duty: saving Mina Harker from the same terrible fate.

However, when Dracula's existence in England is threatened, as his sanctuaries are found out and his boxes of earth are purified with blessed wafer, he retreats to the safety of his own country; but the forces of the sacred are not to be stopped. They follow Dracula back to the origin of chaos in Transylvania.

Devils, Dragons, and Dragon-slayers in the "Heart of the Enemy's Country"

Since whatever space the religious person inhabits is considered a sacred cosmos, according to Eliade's study, attack from outside the cosmos threatens to desacralize it, to turn it to chaos. Attacks are, therefore, in his estimation, equivalent to "ruin, disintegration, and death" (*Images and Symbols* 39); and, in many world views, enemies are considered to be "demons, and especially ... the archdemon, the primordial dragon conquered by the gods at the beginning of time" (*Sacred and Profane* 47). In *Dracula*, the foreign chaos of Dracula has invaded England, attacking the human characters and turning their cosmos to chaos, and the only way to restore the sanctity of their world is to destroy the vampire. To this end, the forces of the sacred become dragon slayers, risking all to penetrate to the "heart of the enemy's country" (Stoker 354) and kill the primordial dragon, Dracula.

Devils and Dragons

In *Vampires in the Carpathians: Magical Acts, Rites, and Beliefs in Subcarpathian Rus'*, Pëtr Bogatyrëv, Russian folklorist and ethnographer, argues that "belief in sorcerers, vampires, and forest spirits is reinforced by the fact that the Church also teaches about the existence of the Evil Spirit, the Devil" (137), causing people to meld their notions of folk spirits with their concept of evil. Eliade maintains that "the conception of the enemy as a demonic being, a veritable incarnation of the powers of evil" (*Images and Symbols* 38) is an idea which has survived through time; and Otto connects the feeling of horror inherent in an experience of the negative numinousness of demons to the fury of Lucifer and his status as a fallen angel. "The devilish" (*Idea of the Holy* 106), he maintains, has some part of the divine in it, yet is opposed to it by having a "potentiality of evil" (106) in its divine wrath. If one looks at Dracula's history, as he tells it to Jonathan Harker, one can see that he is connected to the devil through the history of his blood ties with the Szekelys who are said to have come from Scythian witches mated with devils and with the blood of the Berserkers brought into his land by the marauding Ugric tribes of Iceland (Stoker 28).

However, Dracula is represented as both a dragon and devil in other ways. He is affiliated with both, first when Harker has reached the eastern side of Borgo Pass and records their passage into the "thunderous" (Stoker 9) zone. This affiliation becomes clear if one looks at Emily Gerard's work in reference to local superstitions about weather. In her recording of local Roumanian superstitions, she finds a connection between thunderstorms and the legend of the "*scholomance*, or school, supposed to exist somewhere in the heart of the mountains and where the secrets of nature, the language of animals, and all magic spells are taught by the devil in person" (198). According to legend, at the end of the course of study, one of the ten students would be required to remain with the devil as an assistant to help him "in 'making the weather'—that is, preparing the thunderbolts" (198). Gerard also records how the peasants believe that "a small lake immeasurably deep, and lying high in the mountains to the south of Hermanstadt, is supposed to be the caldron where is brewed the thunder, under whose water the dragon lies sleeping," (198) in fair weather. To wake the dragon is to invite the storm. In the novel, Professor Van Helsing relates some of the history of Dracula to the others, including his connection with the Scholomance and the dealings which Dracula's family had with "the Evil One" (Stoker 241) who taught the dark arts there.

Moreover, the last leg of Harker's journey to castle Dracula begins from the hotel in Bistritz on May fourth, "the eve of St. George's Day" (Stoker 4), a day on which, as Montague Summers writes, "the power of vampires, witches and every evil thing" (*Vampire in Europe* 312) is strongest, a day celebrated in honor of St. George, heroic "soldier-martyr" (Baring-Gould 93) and legendary dragon slayer. The Eastern legends of St. George, both Christian and Muslim, refer mostly to his suffering for religion; however, reminiscent of the myth of Perseus and Andromeda, the Western myth incorporates a fight with a dragon whose depredations were destroying the town of Silene in Lybia. Tribute was first paid in animals, then in human lives as the supply of animals was depleted. Finally, the king's daughter was chosen as tribute, taken to the lake, and offered up to the beast. As George passed by the lake, he saw her weeping. Discovering what had caused her fear and sadness, he vowed to save her. As the dragon rose from the water, George made the sign of the cross, recommended himself to God, and went to fight the beast. His prowess with the sword so mesmerized the dragon that George was able to tie the princess's girdle about its neck and lead it into town. Through this miraculous feat, George converted and baptized thousands of men, women, and children; then he cut off the head of the dragon (Baring-Gould *Curious Myths of the Middle Ages*).

In *The Essential Dracula*, Wolf notes that in the legend of this saint "the dragon represents Satan" (8), as it does in *Dracula*, since in the Roumanian tongue "*Dracul* ... means both 'dragon' and 'devil'" (8). Some of the names bandied about by the peasants on the coach with Harker are "'Ordog'— Satan" and "'vrolok' and 'vlkoslak'" (Stoker 6), which Wolf, referencing Montague Summers' research, annotates as having the same meaning as "*vârcolac*" (Wolf 10). Summers describes the *vârcolac* as "a third type of vampire ... thought to be an extraordinary creature which eats the sun and moon and thus causes eclipses" (306). In addition, in her article "The Vampire in Roumania," Agnes Murgoci connects Eastern European belief in the vârcolaci with the moral that "God orders the vârcolaci to eat the moon, so that men may repent and turn from evil" (25).

Wolf also draws attention to folklore's connection of buried treasure with dragons; the source of this connection, he feels, can be found in the ancient practice of burying heroes in caves or barrows along with treasures for the afterlife and the fact that snakes find burial caves and barrows suitable habitations. Though, in *Dracula*, the sites of buried treasure are easily located because of the blue flames, the treasure is not so easily obtained because of the powers of evil that roam the land on St. George's eve. However, it is clear that Dracula has the ability to find the valuables cached underground. Upon his arrival at the castle, Harker first notices treasure of immense value as he assesses the furniture, curtains, bed hangings, and table service. Later, when Harker climbs into Dracula's room looking for a key to help him escape, he finds a hoard of jewels and gold from many countries and periods. As the dragon guarding the treasure, Dracula also has an advantage in finding and appropriating it for his own purposes.

Moreover, from Dracula, Harker learns not only of the monetary treasures, but also of the soil being "enriched by the blood of men, patriots or invaders" (Stoker 22). In the early history of the region, Dracula's ancestors led the fight for freedom; but now those heroic times are over and "blood is too precious a thing in these days of dishonourable peace" (30). For Dracula, the days of honor are over, and blood is precious to him now only as it can continue his own life. He has lost his cosmic connection and become profane. Only his battle fury is left, turned into a struggle for survival instead of dedicated to a larger more sacred cause for society. Again, later, in England, the characters representing the sacred learn that blood is precious through Renfield's preoccupation with the food chain and his repeated assertion that "the blood is the life" (141). Then, as Lucy Westenra suffers from the bite of the vampire, it is the blood of brave men that she needs. To save her, Holmwood "would give the last drop of blood" (121) in his body; and Professor Van Helsing, Morris, and Dr. Seward eventually are called upon to sacrifice their blood for her, also; however, it is Dracula who gets all of this blood in the end when he finally makes Lucy Westenra a vampire. Moreover, Morris gives his life's blood in the destruction of Dracula, sacrificing himself to regenerate society and save Mina Harker's from a vampire's existence. The dragon Dracula guards the treasure of monetary riches which English society values so much for the power which it provides; but the forces of the sacred find that they also must value the treasure of more spiritual forces. A victory over the primordial dragon is a victory over chaos, a victory over the material profane life ruled by the value of riches by the forces of the spirit.

Dragon-slayers

According to Eliade, "struggles, conflicts, and wars for the most part have a ritual cause and function," where repetition of the conflict is in "imitation of an archetypal model" (*The Myth of Eternal Return* 29) for creating the cosmos through violent means. Sacrifice is made in order to sanctify the world anew as an *imago mundi*; and a ritual death is required for the resacralization of society. The forces of Western sacredness imitate the gods when they kill and dismember the profane Lucy Westenra in a bloody ritual, impaling her in her coffin with a sharpened stake, then cutting off her head, and filling her mouth with garlic. The female vampires at the castle all are dispatched in the same way, as a primordial dragon should be; however, Dracula is destroyed differently. Harker cuts Dracula's throat with his Kukri knife while simultaneously Morris penetrates Dracula's heart with his Bowie knife. Although there has been at lot of literary speculation over the decades as to whether Dracula truly died at the hands of Jonathan Harker and Quincey Morris, one must believe he did. While the classic tools for dispatching the vampire were not used in Dracula's case, the Kukri knife which Harker uses on Dracula is a ferocious instrument of death, much like a machete in its size and form with a curved double-edged blade, known for its ability to shear through small tree trunks with ease. With some degree of force behind it, the Kukri knife would shear the head from the body in one stroke. Moreover, the Bowie knife that Morris carries is almost as formidable a weapon as the Kukri. With a length of fifteen inches from end to end and a double-edged blade, it would be a suitable weapon with which to stake the vampire.

However, regardless of how the vampire is dispatched, it would seem that the effect is the same; the cosmos is again restored to sacredness. Eliade writes that "the true sin is forgetting" (*Sacred and Profane* 101) what happened in the beginning of time; and the story of Mina's courage which at the end the men vow to tell young Quincey Harker when he is old enough to understand is a sign that they will not forget, but will pass that knowledge on to him, making him capable of recovering sacred time for future generations.

"In Dread ... Is Some Need of Belief": *Faith and the Numinous*

Eliade argues that "death is often only the result of ... indifference to immortality" (*Images and Symbols* 56), indifference to the sacred. In *Dracula*, the vampire is a threat to the other characters on both a physical and spiritual level because they are indifferent to his sacred qualities. He represents what humanity can become if its faith in God and sacred duty to the cosmos are not taken seriously and periodically maintained. However, since the foundations of religious faith had been called into doubt over the decades of the nineteenth century, many people of the late Victorian period could not confidently turn to traditional religious beliefs for relief from their spiritual crisis. This is true of the characters in *Dracula*, who create their own brand of sacredness based on social, economic, and political values and draw on the occult only to reestablish that world in the face of the vampire's threat to their society and to themselves.

Eliade's study of early religions argues that "it is the experience of death that renders intelligible the notion of *spirit* and of *spiritual beings*" (*Occultism, Witchcraft, and Cultural Fashions* 34); and for many religious individuals, he maintains, death is not the end of life, only the beginning of another mode of existence. Drifting into the unknown darkness, the person seeks to conquer death by transforming it into a rite of passage, the beginning of a new spiritual existence. In initiatory contexts, death signifies passing beyond the profane, unsanctified condition to an experience of the sacred and the responsibility of being human. Numinous dread is felt in anticipation of death and is, therefore, an initiation into the human condition. Through death, it is supposed, a person changes from body to spirit; and, likewise, in the experience of possible death "man becomes aware of his own mortality" (35), the reality of his physical presence in the universe. In confronting the numinous, a person is confronting himself or herself; the profane side of the person's personality with all its worldly desires comes under scrutiny in its conflict with a spiritual yearning for eternal life. The value of the numinous experience is sacred truth, a higher understanding of the human relationship with the gods and of an innate yearning for faith in an afterlife.

The humans in *Dracula* struggle with the mystery of vampirism and the ontological truth it reveals; and it is faith that in end gets them through their ordeal, regardless of the fact that what they are protecting is a historically-structured sacredness. The dread that the forces of the sacred feel at the numinous experience of the vampires reaffirms their need for faith in a spiritual existence. As they all strive to understand the meaning behind the mystery of Dracula, the "mystery of life and death" (Stoker 192), Professor Van Helsing tells Mina that despite the facts of the case which she has transcribed from Harker's journals, she "will need all [her] faith" (218) to deal with the situation before them. Then, on the way back to Transylvania in pursuit of Dracula, his former journal showing the way for the others, Harker writes "it is in trial and trouble that our faith is tested — that we must keep on trusting; and that God will aid us up to the end" (289). They put their fates in God's hands, as "drifting reefwards ... faith is our [their] only anchor" (310) in the chaos of a sea of troubles. Their modern belief in science and the industrialized world must give way to a reliance on older traditions. Professor Van Helsing tells the other men that when they catch up to Dracula they must trust "to superstition ... at the first; it was man's faith in the early, and it have its roots in faith still" (328). Belief in their own God gives them the courage they require to face the negative numinousness of Dracula; trust in the traditions and superstitions of earlier times, when there was no doubt of a divine presence in the world, gives them the tools and the power to recreate their world in imitation of the gods.

Eliade argues that to experience sacred space and time is to reveal a longing to reactualize the primordial situation of creating the world. In his analysis of early religions, Eliade found that many people believed that sacred space and time was renewed each year with the rebirth of the land; and when each new year began, chaos had to be overcome once more. So, too, would this be true on a larger scale at the end of a century or a millennium. Humanity's terror of each new century or new millennium may be perceived as a terror of chaos and the possibility of death without renewal. The longing to live in the presence of the gods then may be expressed as an unquenchable thirst for being, a need to exist as a spiritual entity as well as a physical one. This thirst for being may be manifested as the individual's will to take responsibility for the sacredness of his or her own society, as Professor Van Helsing and the others do when they seek out Dracula, risking possible nonexistence and dissolution into chaos and death to imitate the gods and return their profane world to sacred space. As numinous fiction, *Dracula* is a story of salvation, of initiation into the sacred, despite the fact that their sacredness has a secular slant. In their confrontation with the negatively numinous vampire, the humans evaluate their own evil potential and their longing for reaffirmation of a spiritual future because the chaos of the unknown, the chaos of living death, is too frightening.

• FOUR •

Eros and the Thanatotic Hero
Anne Rice's Vampire Chronicles

> There are only three great puzzles in the world, the puzzle of love, the puzzle of death, and, between each of these and part of both of them, the puzzle of God. God is the greatest puzzle of all [Niall Williams, *As It Is in Heaven* 3].

In *The Culture of Narcissism*, cultural historian Christopher Lasch maintains that during the nineteen-sixties and seventies America suffered a "crisis of confidence" (Preface xiii). Distrust in "American institutions of authority—school, church, government, the family itself" (Magistrale and Morrison 2) was thought to have produced a society of despairing individuals "haunted not by guilt but by anxiety" (Lasch xvi). Lasch argues that this anxiety characterizes a spiritual alienation caused by a loss of faith in society's ability to construct a system that could "confront the difficulties that threaten to overwhelm it" (xiii). Psychologist James B. McCarthy, author of *Death Anxiety*, further defines this spiritual alienation as an anxiety characterized by a fear of death that "often takes the form of scientific misgivings about the reality of God's existence or a disbelief in the possibility of life after death" (1). In response to this spiritual anxiety, Lasch maintains that, as many sixties and seventies-decade individuals questioned what it means to transcend death, they seemed to have been searching not only for a reconnection with God, but also for reassurance that He exists at all.

In the afterword of his book's first paperback edition, Lasch updated his evaluation of twentieth-century culture, arguing that the eighties saw little change in American society's response to the breakdown of its social structures, and finding that many people still approached the world in a selfish and self-absorbed fashion. The nineties, however, according to Lasch's argument, were a time of change. Although the presumption of asserting change for the entire decade of the nineties from the perspective of the beginning of the decade makes his assertion more of a prediction, it is his change of focus in his own definition of narcissism that is important to this discussion. Earlier he had focused his thesis on the secondary narcissistic tendencies characterized by disappointment of desires, defining the twentieth-century individual as suffering from "a feeling of inauthenticity and inner emptiness" (239), and as having trouble connecting in the world. However, after continued research on the subject, he found that Sigmund Freud had defined the concept of narcissism in two ways: primarily, as a longing for Nirvana or eternal life; and secondarily, as self-love. In primary narcissism, Lasch saw "the pain of separation" (241) which he described as the foundation of the human fear of death from birth onward; and his new definition of the term took on a more spiritual tone with his new definition of it as "a longing to be free from longing" (241) and a seeking for "everlasting life" (240). Characteristically, this longing takes the form of such extreme spiritual alienation that the alienated person not only doubts the existence of God, but also feels that if God does not exist, then the afterlife may not either. Furthermore, *if* an afterlife does, indeed, exist, Lasch maintains that the alienated person perceives it as a further extension of existence here on earth and, therefore, an eternal alienation from God. In reaction to this fear that neither God nor the afterlife truly exists, the dilemma of much of twentieth-century society became how to invest a transitory life with meaning. Lasch felt that the nineties-decade desire for everlasting life was distinguished by "a revival of ancient superstitions, a belief in reincarnation, a growing fascination with the occult, and the bizarre forms of spirituality associated with the New Age movement" (245); and his characterization seems to have been born out.

Writing at the end of the nineties, in "The Future of Faith," an article for *New Yorker*, John Updike also argued that twentieth-century society was searching for a spiritual path. Despite his statement that, in America, "God and the afterlife were doing well in polls, clocking affirmative ratings of around ninety per cent for belief in God and eighty per cent for the afterlife" (84), he cites a study by University of Arizona sociologist

Four • Eros and the Thanatotic Hero

Mark Chaves that shows church attendance rates dropping. Updike attributed the drop in church attendance to the religious person's easy access to "home study and the Sunday-morning religious shows" (84), as well as to the wide variety of religious books and New Age mystical texts available at the local bookstore. However, in the nineties, whether one adhered to the traditional religious practices of their church or experimented with some type of New Age spirituality, and despite living in a culture characterized as self-absorbed and consumptive, many people seemed to be searching for an inspired and spiritual path toward meaning in their world. Psychologically, these quests for personal spirituality might be perceived as attempts to control the anxiety of spiritual alienation and to repress the fear of death that alienation exacerbates.

For cultural anthropologist Ernest Becker, author of *The Denial of Death*, our innate fear of death is a "biological and evolutionary problem" (Becker 16) with a foundation in our animal "instinct of self-preservation" (16). The main focus of this kind of survival is an insistence on the primary value of one's own existence. For humans to function in any way normally in the everyday world and to keep their identity intact, Becker feels that they must repress their fear of death by denying an awareness of their dependent situation and of their true human fate. One denies death by constructing a reality that defends against the fear, allowing for a "creation of meaning" (7) that will provide the significance craved by the individual. Since a given society usually controls how its people perceive transcendence of death through the structure of its predominant religious beliefs, if those beliefs are questioned, that particular social system no longer has the power to confront its existential problems or to defend its constituents against their fear of death. Questioning the existence of God or the possibility of eternal life brings the natural human fear of death to the surface in the individual; and as a result, the breakdown of the social system of religion is often accompanied by a disintegration of other social systems.

Becker defines the urge toward death or Thanatos as an urge toward the truth of human destiny. To deny that destiny, a person counters his thanatotic impulses with Eros, an urge toward life, meaningfulness, and creativity. As Becker interprets this psychological problem, the human mind, caught between the two urges, Thanatos and Eros, creates a fiction of heroic authority to give meaning to life and, thereby, to deny the death-urge. These systems of authority include structures such as family, society, religion, myth, and even history. According to Becker, human beings deny death by creating a "manageable world" (23) through organization of these authorities, which function much like psychological defense mechanisms to protect them from fully realizing their mortal condition. Lasch and Becker both argue that twentieth-century society questioned the structures of cultural authority; however, the heroic systems of authority seemed to have failed twentieth-century humans with a frequency not experienced in earlier centuries. The reason for this, according to Becker's analysis, is that in the last half of the twentieth century, young people no longer perceived any chance for heroic action in the structures that their culture provided for them (Becker 6). Without the traditional heroic avenues, humans must either look for other ways to create meaning or re-create the old ways within the new social structure.

Of the human urge toward life through heroism, William James writes in *Varieties of Religious Experience* that "pain and wrong and death must be fairly met and overcome in [the] higher excitement" of "wild and heroic" (363) deeds. The human "instinct for reality ... has always held the world to be essentially a theatre for heroism" (364); and it is in heroism that James feels human beings perceive "life's supreme mystery" (364) to be hidden. The heroic individual, then, might be defined as one who, by facing his fear of annihilation and making meaning from it, devotes his life to a search for "higher meaning" (Becker 268), both socially and cosmically.

The "metaphysical mystery" (James 364) of which James writes may be found in our relationship with death. When the defense mechanisms used by a person to suppress anxieties of annihilation fall short of their intended purpose, reality may intrude and overwhelm everyday thought and action. It is at this moment of overwhelming anxiety, where "fear of death emerges in pure essence" (Becker 23), that we encounter Rudolf Otto's numinous. A fundamental part of the experience of the numinous is the confrontation with death. As Otto argues, in an encounter with the absolute power of the numinous we gain an immediate sense of our creatureliness and dependence. The dread or fear we feel helps us to see the true reality of our existence, our limited power and our place in the universe. As one experiences fear in the face of the supernaturally powerful numinous object, one must recognize mortality on a personal level and face the inevitability of death in the possibility of physical annihilation due to the force of the numen. Just as the human characters in both *Dracula* and "The Ancient Mariner," discussed in earlier chapters, must face the objective reality of the vampire, so must Lestat face the truth, not only of the vampire Magnus, but also of himself as vampire.

In the numinous encounter, the subject is caught between the urges of Eros and Thanatos. Fascinated and excited by the urge toward death, which draws one toward numinous contact, yet dreading the idea of death, the subject counters fascination with a fear of annihilation and an urge toward life and meaning. It is in the ambiguousness of a position between dread and fascination that the subject of the numinous encounter finds the capacity to create meaning from fear. In an attempt to survive the reality of the numinous encounter, to master or control the mystery and dread of the numen, the person searches for ways to create moral meaning out of the experience, and, thereby, to deny the promise of death which life holds. Therefore, terror of death can be understood to lead to heroic action, as the reaction to the numinous encounter for the healthy mind is to create systems of action that will help to repress the fear that threatens to overwhelm it. To repress the fear of death is to deny it and, therefore, to deny the power of the numinous in order to function in the world. As a vampire, Lestat is caught in this ambiguous position, representing the numinous as Thanatotic hero-vampire, yet striving for Eros because he needs more than simple survival. He needs to have his life stand for something more than the evil he perceives the vampire to be.

Vampires Are Us

Maintaining that her vampire novels are "not just about vampires" ("A Message from Anne Rice"), Anne Rice sees the vampire as representative of the human condition in all its physical and spiritual implications. For her, vampires are a "natural metaphor for us, for our affluence, our powers..." (King Interview). The vampires in Rice's novels are "outsiders, creatures outside of the human sphere who can therefore speak about it — the way Mephistopheles could speak about it to Faust" (Ramsland "Let the Flesh" 61). Rice admits her own obsession "with the idea of whether or not we have a God ... [or] a personal Devil" (King Interview) or an afterlife and sees her characters, as surrogate humans, exploring such troubling issues as "the mystical relationship in our lives between life and death and the larger moral definitions of good and evil" (Hoppenstand and Browne 5). She characterizes her writing as a "mystical experience" (Rose Interview) and feels that her work allows her to come to a higher understanding of the world and what it is to be human in it. Her characters speak to us because they suffer the same feelings of ambiguity that we do in terms of these issues.

Rice herself speaks of feelings of ambiguity fostered in her own childhood. Raised in the Catholic faith in New Orleans, Anne was confronted by evidence of the numinous every day as she went to mass before school. At church the images of saints and stories of miracles, as well as the ever-present miracle of transubstantiation, surrounded her and influenced her young mind. In addition, Anne recalls how she was raised by a mother who gave her a "sense of limitless power" (Ramsland *Prisms* 46). However, Anne says she also had an extreme fear of death from early in life; and when her mother died, and then later her young daughter Michelle, and she could do nothing to save either one, she lost her faith and began to wonder if there were even an afterlife. Her vampire books were the way back to some kind of belief in a higher power and an afterlife. They speak of a personal journey that is at the same time universally human — the apocalyptic journey of life itself.

As late twentieth-century society looked toward the millennium, the questions Rice's characters ask also became important in an apocalyptic sense. As her vampires search for reassurance that there is a God and an afterlife and good in the world, so, too, it seems, did the humans of the last three decades of the last century. In having her characters question the existence of God, the Devil, and the afterlife, Rice says she is asking questions that concern her in her own life and, hopefully, in the lives of her readers. She sees her writing as a "deep ... search for truth" (King Interview) and wants her readers to "soul search" (Gumbel Interview). Rice is of the opinion that, over and above the entertainment value of her fiction, this soul searching is what her readers want from her books.

In an interview with Bryant Gumbel on the publication of *Memnoch the Devil*, Rice admitted that there is a "heavy religious tone and a very serious one" to her work and called Lestat's story "a spiritual journey" (Gumbel Interview). For her, "vampires ... have always been spiritual explorers" (King Interview); and, as such, "the vampire represents somebody who's transcended time and transformed himself into an immortal and becomes like a dark saint ... with all the powers that transcend the corruptible" (Ramsland "Let the Flesh" 65).[1] As the transcendent object, the vampire represents the negatively numinous; and, therefore, the vampire is inherently, ambiguously indifferent, filled with both good and evil potential. For this reason, Rice's vampires can serve as the heroes of her tales, heroes whose search for a higher meaning makes them vehicles for a discussion of both the universal issue of human transcendence and its concomitant problem of the ever-changing definitions of good and evil. While representing the numinous, Anne Rice's vampires also represent human beings, with all the questions we have about what it is to be human. They are the heroes of their stories and work in the same ways as other heroic individuals to deny their own deaths and to make meaning of their lives. The question that the numinous leaves Rice's protagonists with is the same one we are confronted with: how do we balance our awareness and acceptance of the absoluteness of death with an urge toward life and meaning?

In her novels, Rice employs the autobiographical technique to convey an individual experience of the human condition through the eyes of the vampire. These purportedly *true* histories of her vampire's life take a different approach to the telling of the tale than either Coleridge's poem or Stoker's novel; the ambivalence of her main character is focused more on the questions Lestat asks about his role as vampire and his spiritual fate. Lestat is clearly more of a hero than the vampires of the earlier texts discussed; it is his search for divine truth with which the audience identifies. As the numinous hero, Lestat is all too human, as he tries to create a world like the one he has been banished from wherever possible. Unlike the Mariner and the main characters of *Dracula*, who fall back on a wavering belief in God in response to the vampire, Lestat is an avowed atheist. His experience of the vampire, and of the vampire's *life*, causes him to question whether the divine exists and whether he is now alienated from it.

Rice's vampire shares many similarities with the vampires of Samuel Taylor Coleridge's "The Rime of the Ancient Mariner" and Bram Stoker's *Dracula*. In "The Rime of the Ancient Mariner," Coleridge's structure involves a tale that must be told and the main characters include the teller of the tale, the Mariner, and his audience, the Wedding Guest. In Rice's novel, Lestat takes on the role of the eternal wanderer, telling his stories via the print media rather than orally. As a rock star Lestat uses music to transcend and to hypnotize listeners, much like the Ancient Mariner and his poetic tale. The theme is also much the same, since Lestat the vampire kills without thinking of the consequences. When he is finally faced with his crimes, in the form of his victims' souls, he must change his moral outlook and conclude that human life should be respected.

In *Anne Rice: A Critical Companion*, Jennifer Smith considers that the similarities between Stoker's *Dracula* and Rice's vampire novels include the fact that both authors play with the concept of free will in the vampire's "choice of evil" (13), thus making the vampire figure more human. In addition, drawing on Nina Auerbach's writings on vampire literature, Smith finds that Rice's vampire also shares an "aversion to closeness with living" (13) with Dracula because they turn those to whom they feel close into vampires. However, I consider Lestat different from Dracula for precisely this reason: his need to understand his place in both the earthly and spiritual world results in a desire for a meaningful life. This desire draws him into situations where closeness with the living, both his own loved ones and mortals in general, is not only unavoidable, but also necessary for his continued existence as a meaningful individual.[2]

Lasch defined his seventies narcissistic individual much as one might a vampire: "acquisitive in the sense that his cravings have no limits" (xvi). Although "he does not accumulate goods and provisions against the future, in the manner of the acquisitive individualist of nineteenth-century political economy, ... [he] demands immediate gratification and lives in a state of restless, perpetually unsatisfied desire" (xvi). However, by the dawn of the nineties his definition of narcissism came to include the individual's desire for immortality on a spiritual level. Like Lasch's twentieth-century individual, Rice's vampire Lestat does not desire "to inflict his own certainties on others but to find a meaning in life" (Lasch xvi). The character of Lestat in Rice's *Vampire Chronicles*[3] may become a numinous hero as a vampire; but since he also represents the human condition, his questions about the existence of God, the afterlife, and good and evil follow him from his human life into his vampire existence. Caught between his fear of death and his numinousness as a representation of Death, he copes with both conditions by searching for meaning in his life. The purpose of this chapter is to discuss the spiritual journey of Lestat: his confrontations with the numinous; how the various established cultural authorities have failed him, both as a human and as a numinous figure; and how he tries to resolve the question of his existence by reconstructing these cultural authorities within his new existence and remaking meaning in his eternal afterlife as a vampire.

Lestat's Spiritual Journey

In "Toward an Adult Spirituality," an article for *America*, theologian William J. O'Malley delineates five stages that characterize a spiritual journey. They are: a "sense of the numinous" (342); the need to understand the numinous experience; the desire to become an "honorable human being" (342) in the face of that understanding; "the hunger ... to reach beyond the limits of time and space" (342) to the higher reality of the soul; and the "drive to expend what little life" (342) one has in a transitory world in the service of both humanity and the divine. Once Lestat's social and cultural structures have broken down, he experiences the numinous as the first step on his spiritual journey. Then, as he attempts to understand the nature of his experience, he wrestles with the question of good and evil — in effect, asking himself what kind of honorable person he possibly could be as a vampire. When the questions grow more complicated, delving into whether God and the Devil exist, and whether there is an afterlife, Lestat attempts to discover whether as a vampire he still can experience the higher transcendence of the soul. Lestat's quest takes him not only around the physical world, but also into the realm of mythology and ancient religious worship. In *Memnoch the Devil*, the last of the tales dealing primarily with the character of Lestat, one can see an "apocalyptic spirituality" (Strozier and Flynn 74) at work as Lestat travels into heaven for a revelation of the "secrets of the celestial realms and their inhabitants" and "of the course of history" (74); at the end, Lestat does resolve to live his life without drinking human blood, which is to say, in an honorable fashion and in service of other human beings.

In order to understand how an experience of the numinous affects the life of the vampire Lestat, one must begin with some background on his mortal life and how the cultural authorities that should have helped him repress his innate fear of death have failed him, leaving him dissatisfied, in despair, and, therefore, vulnerable to the numinous contact with the vampire. Lestat's cultural authorities include family and religion, which might be designated in his case more as an overall belief in God rather than in any organized religion. These two structures, that would normally provide meaning for a human being, are intertwined in his life and the one, belief in God, fails him because the other, his family, did. In response to their failure, Lestat creates his own structure based on an aesthetic of goodness that he hopes can produce the meaning he craves.

Lestat's mortal history begins before the French Revolution; and in his recounting of childhood, one sees a young boy who seeks to invest his life with meaning and goodness and whose family denies him that opportunity at almost every turn. Sent to school at the local monastery when he is twelve years old, Lestat discovers that he loves the monastic life — the rituals, the many books in the library, the hymns, the constant work, and the belief that he can be a good person. In comparison to the monastic life, Lestat sees his home life as chaotic. The family is poor and hungry much of the time; and everywhere about them is "dirt and decay" (Rice *Vampire Lestat* 32), while the monastery is "clean and orderly" (32).

Lestat is a young man who wants life to stand for something. To simply exist for a moment and then be forgotten is not an option for him. He needs to affect the present and the future of the world around him; but his home life will not provide him that opportunity. When his father refuses his request to enter the monastic life, his mother gives him two mastiff puppies and his first musket and horse. As he breeds and trains his dogs, he also becomes the hunter of the family; and with this new purpose in his life, he gains more confidence in himself. Soon, he wants to make changes, to revive the crumbling fortunes of his family's estate; but no one else is interested. The possibilities for heroic action that Becker has argued are absent in the late twentieth-century seem lost to Lestat, also.[4] Still, he continues to search for meaning in his life; and when he is sixteen years old he runs away to become an actor. On stage with the other players, Lestat feels "ecstasy" (Rice *Vampire Lestat* 34); but his brothers find him and bring him home once again. The male members of his family feel that Lestat's desire to become a monk at twelve was "excusable" (35) but his desire to become an actor has "the taint of the devil" (35) about it. Already, by the age of sixteen, Lestat is caught between God and

Four • Eros and the Thanatotic Hero

the Devil in his desire for some meaning in his life other than the chaos of his family. Once again, his mother buys him a rifle and a new horse, but he is still bitter and discouraged.

Overseeing the estate does give him satisfaction and some meaning in his life; however, it is an unproductive path for him and can only exacerbate his sense of despair. Since he is the youngest son of the Marquis, Lestat has no hope of inheriting the estate. As far as he can see, since the family has thwarted him in his bid for the church and for the stage, he has no way to order his life. He has no desire to make meaning by conforming to any particular path his family might chose for him; having been "born restless—the dreamer, the angry one, the complainer" (Rice *Vampire Lestat* 23), he is the one who refuses to accept life as it is presented to him. Finding no meaning in history, Lestat feels that talk of the past is useless. As it was for Dracula, so it is for Lestat. The old heroic days are gone; and the hero must learn to survive in the new order, the new society. At twenty-one years of age, however, Lestat has a chance at grandly heroic action as he goes in search of a wolf pack that has been attacking the family's sheep. However, the pack turns out to larger than he expected. The starving wolves have no fear of him; but at the first sound of howling, Lestat feels terror. Although he destroys some of the wolves in the first minutes of the ensuing battle, the remaining ones soon dispatch Lestat's dogs and horse. When he sees them die, Lestat realizes the danger of the task he has taken on and the possible consequences for himself if he fails.

Lestat's experience with the wolves is a sublime one. In his treatise on the sublime, Burke argues that the "angry tones of wild beasts are ... capable of causing a great and awful sensation" (Burke *Sublime* 84). This sensation, the naturally human "fear at the apprehension of pain or death" (57), is cause enough for a sublime experience. However, that fear is brought about, as Otto suggests in his discussion of the numinous, by a sense of powerlessness in the face of some overwhelming power with the force or will to annihilate. As a sublime experience, Lestat's battle with the wolves is also his first hint of the numinous, as his confrontation with the wolves becomes a confrontation with a power quite probably stronger than him, at least in numbers and ferocity; in facing the possibility of his own death, he must face the reality that he is mortal. The wolves might be taken as an early sign of Lestat's destiny, a journey of heroic proportions that will lead him to a higher reality of the soul.

The Vampire as Numinous Experience

Although Lestat triumphs, killing the rest of the wolves, and gaining the nickname Wolfkiller, this heroic act only isolates him further from his family. With his dogs and horse dead, and his brothers both disbelieving and jealous of his act, he closets himself in his room for days, suffering from despair and hatred, and dreaming of killing all his family. This was the way he felt on the mountain with the wolves, and now he does not know if he is Lestat or a killer. His identity is being called into question by his brush with death; however, his mother counsels him that he does not have to shoulder "the burden of murder or madness" (Rice *Vampire Lestat* 38) to be free. Lestat is overcome by the implications of what his mother has told him. Until that moment Lestat had felt that goodness only existed in what his family sanctioned as acceptable behavior; and that kind of goodness was not acceptable to him. With his mother's words, he realizes that he might find some other ideal of goodness on which to hang his identity.

Lestat's philosophy of goodness is articulated in more detail when he becomes a friend of Nicolas de Lenfent. During one of their conversations, he confesses that none of his family had ever truly believed in God, although they attended mass out of a sense of duty. Even at the monastery, he had not believed in God, only in the monks. Lestat's belief lies in the existence of goodness, not Godness. For Lestat, goodness lies in action, in "sacrifice" (Rice *Vampire Lestat* 52), in making something better of oneself. "There's sanctity" (52) in that, "and God or no God, there is goodness in it" (52), he tells Nicholas. For Lestat, daily existence without meaning is chaos, and acting holds that chaos at bay. He is afraid, however, that even death does not hold the answer to why he was put on earth; if the meaninglessness of life goes on forever, so will the despair one feels at the recognition of his own meaninglessness.[5] He begins to question everyone around him as to whether they believe in God or not; and even nature holds no beauty for him because it can decay and die. Lestat tells Nicholas that for him belief in goodness is more important than a belief in God or in an afterlife. With this realization, he chooses the rational and aesthetic concepts that underlie religious belief to form what Eliade defines as a fixed point of orientation in his chaotic world, a sacred center in a "desacralized cosmos" (*Sacred and Profane* 17).

Lestat's early life has been spent in turmoil. The family structure which should have supported his search for meaning as a youth failed him: first, by not providing a religious structure or a belief in God; and second,

Four • Eros and the Thanatotic Hero

by not allowing him to enter the monastery or act on the stage. His need for some doctrine in which to place his faith and his need for meaning have caused him to produce his own value system, a doctrine of goodness, in which he sees himself in opposition to the men of his family. Not allowed the outlets he desires, he is left with only his family life to provide the significance he craves. However, the middle ground of family life, taking care of the estate and protecting the family's assets, is barren ground for him, also. His encounter with the wolves, though heroic and meaningful on a personal level, leaves him in despair and questioning not only his identity, but also the existence of God. Lestat is now at the threshold of an experience of the numinous with all its spiritual implications; but the dilemma of how to invest his life with meaning will continue to challenge him.

A Sense of the Numinous

Eliade writes that "life is not possible without an opening toward the transcendent" (*Sacred and Profane* 34). It is through Otto's numinous, with all its attributes of mystery, dread, and fascination, that one finds the transcendence that makes life, as opposed to mere existence, possible. O'Malley defines the numinous much like the sublime, describing it as the awe one feels in the presence of God. He characterizes this sense of awe as "an intuitional insight into the largeness and richness of our context" (*God* 45). For him, awareness of the numinous involves a journey toward higher understanding and "vulnerability is the absolute prerequisite" (44) for that journey, the same vulnerability that Otto describes as a sense of profaneness and creatureliness in the presence of a more divine power. Like Otto's definition of the numinous, O'Malley's also includes the idea of death. Death is the only reality humans can count on for the future; and so, confrontation with the idea of death results in the feeling that "there's *got* to be more than this!" ("Toward" 343) to life. At the point where death is not only contemplated, but also is an imminent possibility, particularly if that possibility is embodied in an entity that is as negatively numinous as the vampire, we find the soul and the physical body in grave jeopardy. While the attitudes of Lestat as a human makes him susceptible to a numinous encounter with the vampire, because they show a chink in the armor of faith and belief, his vulnerability is increased greatly when he faces death. The fear and despair Lestat feels during and after his brush with death in the battle with the wolves causes him to question his identity and his ability to be good. He will now face death at the fangs of a more powerful entity, and the questions of existence he asks will cause him to embark on his spiritual journey.

Lestat's experience of the numinous begins when he travels to Paris with his friend Nicholas to make his way in life by acting on the stage. To Lestat, acting on the stage is good; and this is how he resolves to make meaning in his mortal life, which he feels he must live without belief in God or in an afterlife. However, once on stage in Paris, Lestat begins to see a ghostly face in the crowd; this presence knows about Lestat killing the wolves and about the cloak lined with wolf fur that Lestat wears. Then, one night, Lestat hears the name Wolfkiller and is filled with fear. During the night the figure comes into his room and spirits Lestat away to a tower in the country. This tower might be said to represent the *axis mundi* of which Eliade writes, the center point at which heaven, hell, and the earthly world connect, where matters spiritual may be investigated. Appropriately, it is outside of Paris, a city, much as London was for the characters in *Dracula*, which seems imbued with the sacred for Lestat because it is where the sainted actors ply their trade.

Calling on God for help when he recognizes the figure as a vampire, he fights for his life to no avail and is bitten anyway. Lestat is in a position of helplessness, much like Freud describes in "The Uncanny" or Kristeva defines as abjection in *Powers of Horror*. Like the primitive religious man, the non-believer, the child, Lestat is in the position of dependence brought on by "'daemonic dread'" (Otto *Idea* 14). Powerless in the arms of the vampire, Lestat cannot reject or deny the threat the creature poses, and he calls on God to aid him. As a cultural figure of great mystical power, God might have the power to save him; however, since Lestat has never truly believed in God's existence, God is not there to answer his prayers. In this situation, also, Lestat's doctrine of goodness does not help him any more than it helped him with the human adversaries that he felt his brothers and father to be.

Describing the element of fascination as "the Dionysiac-element in the numen" (*Idea* 31), Otto writes that though the numinous object engenders dread and a sense of profaneness in the subject of the encounter, it

Four • Eros and the Thanatotic Hero

also is "something that allures with a potent charm" (31) as, in *the mysterium tremendum*, the subject finds "something that entrances him ... that captivates and transports him with a strange ravishment, rising often enough to the pitch of dizzy intoxication" (31). His confrontation with the vampire gives Lestat feelings of both the ecstasy of fascination and the fear of *tremendum*; however, these feelings are much more intense than the rapture he felt on stage, the fear he felt as a child, when he sensed the ghosts of witches at the burning place, or the fear he felt in his battle with the wolves. At this moment of ecstasy, Lestat is caught up in the mystery of the numinous, in that moment of Todorovian hesitation, between the fascination and terror of the numinous encounter; in this position, he is powerless before the divine will of Magnus, the vampire. The fear he feels now is a spiritual terror. On the second meeting with the vampire, he fights again, aware now he is battling for his very soul, and is overcome again. In a dreamlike vision, he sees the vampire Magnus, a mortal and powerful alchemist who had captured a sleeping vampire and was drinking its blood. To Lestat, Magnus is "a dark Prometheus" (Rice *Vampire Lestat* 89); and Lestat, drained to the point of death, must ask Magnus for that fire of immortality, his vampire blood. Unlike the dragon images of *Dracula*, the images of alchemist and Prometheus seem almost heroic, with their connotations of transmutation and of cure for human problems.

Eliade's studies show that religious man recreates sacred time and space through acts in imitation of the gods. Magnus' words make Lestat's experience like a religious ritual. While Dracula looked upon Mina as his "bountiful wine-press" (Stoker 288), a vessel only, holding the substance of his survival, Magnus mimics Jesus' words to the disciples at the Last Supper, calling Lestat's blood "the wine of all wines" (Rice *Vampire Lestat* 89) and ritualizing Lestat's conversion with Biblical words of communion. When Magnus takes Lestat into his arms and exchanges blood with him, Lestat feels overwhelmed by love. God has no meaning now, if he ever did for Lestat. The rapture of this new vampire's sense of the world is all that matters to Lestat.

Lestat feels he has found the meaning of life. His eyes have been opened by his experience of the numinous; however, this epiphany is not a spiritual one, only an aesthetic one. In the first moments of his vampire existence, Lestat finds his spiritual need fed not by the presence of a God he never believed in anyway, but by a sense of love that he feels from

Magnus. For him, this is all there is; this is all there needs to be. This is the mystery of the world. Lestat now has an aesthetic of love to bolster his aesthetic of goodness as a way to place value on his experiences; love has conquered his fear of death for the moment. However, aesthetics are based on feelings and not on moral attitudes. It is through his desire to understand, to find moral meaning in his experience, that Lestat will move onward in his quest. Since Lestat represents the human condition, he will bring the human, moral dilemma about the meaning of his life into his vampire existence.

The Desire to Understand the Numinous Experience

In his study of the spiritual journey, O'Malley argues that humans have the capacity to make their world better rather than to accept their world as it is. As Otto explains this potential, it involves a desire to pierce the mystery of the divine and to find true meaning in relation to that mystery. Beneath the overwhelming nature of the numinous experience lies the deeper matter of surviving the encounter without spiritual despair through the creation of value and meaning in life. In *God: The Oldest Question*, O'Malley maintains that "to be fully human is to seek" (2) for the meaning, purpose, motive behind our existence. To question is, in essence, our quest; and to quest we must cross the threshold between the known and the unknown. Lestat's psychological problem is this threshold experience as a vampire.

When Lestat becomes a vampire, "immediate reality is transmuted into a supernatural reality" (Eliade *Sacred and Profane* 12). As a vampire, he is both sacred and profane, a new and powerful entity and yet still himself, the human with so many questions. Lestat feels that beyond the rapture and mystery of his newly acquired vampire existence there must be some deeper meaning and value. To discover this deeper context, he looks to his maker for answers to his questions about life as a vampire and the meaning of his existence; however, he is soon abandoned by this father figure. When Magnus does not provide the answers Lestat seeks and, then, commits a kind of vampire suicide by leaping into the fire, Lestat must find his own answers; so, his quest begins as he attempts to impose his own values on the situation. Eliade argues that man creates or recreates a meaningful world by "imitating the paradigmatic creation of the gods, the cosmogony" (*Sacred and Profane* 56–7). Without a father figure to teach him, and having abandoned God in his own way, Lestat is left to form his own new world. To impose meaning on his vampire existence, Lestat reverts to his earlier aesthetic of goodness and combines it with an aesthetic of the love he felt when Magnus created him. With these rational concepts to order his relationship with the sacred, he proceeds to answer the questions of who and what he is according to a personal code of value.

In Otto's theory of the numinous, meaning often is predicated on what we lack; and the lack is often characterized through the dynamics of power and powerlessness. Lestat is now the powerful numinous entity, yet he is still himself, the powerless human. What makes him feel powerless is his lack of knowledge about what the experience of being a vampire should be for him. Sensing that vampirism is full of "some deeper lesson" (Rice *Vampire Lestat* 92), Lestat is disappointed when all that Magnus teaches him before he commits vampire suicide is to stop feeding before the heartbeat stops and that sun and fire can kill a vampire. Never having felt close to his mortal family, and having ignored the possibility of God's existence, now Lestat is left alone again, overwhelmed by fear and a need to know what this experience means. First, much like the Ancient Mariner, Lestat is overcome by that fear of death that characterizes the element of *tremendum* in the numinous encounter. O'Malley argues that the "greatest obstacle in the search for God is indifference" (*God* 4), a self-absorbed and egotistical life. When this narcissistic approach to the world is shattered by a numinous experience, one cannot maintain indifference to the divine. Perspective changes everything. Danger, pain, and death are inescapable and hard to bear if there is no higher purpose behind their existence. The terror of the numinous is "the terror of nothingness" (Eliade *Sacred and Profane* 64), of non-existence. In *Dracula*, Dr. Van Helsing reminded his friend Seward that in "dread ... is some need of belief" (Stoker 194); and this is also true for Lestat. As a self-proclaimed nonbeliever confronted suddenly by the numinous, Lestat suddenly feels his fall from grace and calls on God, or any higher power in the cosmos, for help. He prays until his words become "those inarticulate pleas we make to all that is powerful, all that is holy, all that may or may not exist by any and all names" (Rice *Vampire Lestat* 97). However, Lestat's prayers are not answered, just as they were not on the first night of his experience of the vampire, because, as he had told Nicholas earlier, he never truly believed in God or any spiritual entity in the first place. Lestat always believed in the power of good and, now, he would believe in the power of love. The personal morality of these two aesthetics becomes his salvation. However, he must also learn some lessons about what it means to be the numinous one — the one who has the power and the will to destroy or to save depending on his whim.

As he sleeps at sunrise, he is reminded that there is some deeper meaning to his new existence. In response to his dream, he enters a church and handles the ciborium. As a result of this experiment, his disbelief in God is reiterated, because he, Lestat, seems to be the only powerful entity in the church. Since there seems to be no higher power, he must depend on his own will power to survive. The thought of his own power fills him with pleasure. Unfortunately, there is no meaning in feelings themselves, whether of fear or pleasure, love or goodness; so, he still has the problem of finding some meaning in his new life. In response to this need, he reverts to his mortal belief in goodness and his new belief in love as codes by which to live.

Eliade maintains that although in times of extreme crisis people turned to a supreme divinity, most often, in their daily lives, the supreme deity seemed remote and inaccessible. For Eliade, that "divine remoteness actually expresses man's increasing interest in his own religious, cultural, and economic discoveries" (*Sacred and Profane* 125). These discoveries are seen as more "intimately connected with life" (126) and become holy acts of a "private universe" (24), as man uses what is part of his daily life to access the seemingly inaccessible sacred. This attitude and its concomitant restructuring of the sacred exist not only for primitives, but also for more modern religious people. Since Lestat had no understanding of God's existence before he became a vampire, and since his present experience seems to reiterate for him the non-existence of God, the solution to his existential dilemma must be more personal and private. He must make his aesthetics of goodness and love sacred. He must be loved, and he must feel he is a good person. That he kills to survive is simply a fact of life to him. Beyond that he is sure he can attain the goodness that he sought in his mortal existence. Not able to connect with God in the hour of his greatest need, and isolated from his family and friends, Lestat must make his own choices in order to live with his new status as vampire. He finally is in a position to do whatever he wants with his time and resources; and he decides to continue to move among mortals and to experience everything he can with his newfound power. Then, as an extension of that choice, he realizes that if he can interact with mortals, he can live among them as if he were still human, also. Carrying his desire for goodness and love into his vampire life, Lestat determines to keep his human contacts with family and friends intact through the act of doing good for them with the riches he has acquired as Magnus' vampire heir. For Lestat, this is acceptable behavior for a vampire because it is what he wants to do. In the long run, however, this system of meaning will not be enough to lay his questions of existence to rest; he must know what he is, also.

Living as an Honorable Man

In the human search for life's meaning, O'Malley argues, one must take the responsibility for how one lives life. It is the will to live that keeps one alive; it is also the will to make your own decisions about life that gives life meaning. In making choices about how to live, one develops a system of values that will give structure and direction to life. Understanding what human life entails is not enough, however, because death is always there at the end with all its mystery. If we cannot be sure of some existence beyond this earthly life, we may have a hard time finding the answer to the question of why we are here on earth. However, just as understanding life is not enough, neither is "immanent morality" (O'Malley "Toward" 344) enough for most people to make meaning in their lives. In Rice's novels, Lestat must find a way to reconcile his vampirism with his desire to live as an honorable man; and as a non-religious man, Lestat reconciles himself to vampirism by carrying over his desire for goodness and love into his new life. However, since the innate morality of humans is relative and often not enough to give true meaning to life, his views of what constitutes goodness must change.

In *Danse Macabre* (1981), Stephen King argues that morality "lies ... in the hearts and minds of men and women of good will" (402). He defines morality as "a codification of those things which the heart understands to be true and those things which the heart understands to be the demands of a life lived among others ... [in] civilization" (403). For King, immorality lies in "lack of care" (403). However, there are also two dangers in subscribing to a natural morality as the true meaning of life: first, personal morality may replace the higher spiritual quest through which man evolves into a being deserving of immortality; and second, personal morality is relative and may change at any time at the will of the individual, so that what the person desires becomes more important than what salvation requires. Although Lestat has established a moral meaning for his life, and although he tries to live as a honorable man by helping those mortals whom he loves and by re-creating the family he has lost, when those acts fail to give his life value, he must change his views of what defines goodness. In order to discover what constitutes goodness in the life of a vampire, Lestat decides to search out other vampires for the history of what it is to be a vampire. What he hopes for is reassurance that his doctrine of goodness is not in vain; so, the answers to the questions of who he is and what he is rest on the results of this search.

On first becoming a vampire, Lestat had made a conscious choice to take the blood and the lives only of those he considered evil, in order to retain the goodness that was important to him in his mortal life, and that he felt might be lost to him as a vampire. However, later he begins to look at that decision as a petty attempt to seek the salvation of his soul despite being a vampire. Now, the system of dealing with his transformation by taking only the blood of evildoers no longer works for him. He feels that he needs to experience a stronger rapture, as he had when Magnus had shared his blood with him. Aware that his earlier victims had been "strong wine ... in chipped and broken vessels" (Rice *Vampire Lestat* 135), Lestat feels now that he needs that divine fire in his veins, a fire kindled by the innocence of the victim. When he sees his friend Nicholas again, he feels himself to be in the presence of that innocence; to him, Nicholas is "the priest with the golden chalice in his hands, and the wine inside it ... [is] the Blood of the Lamb" (135).

When Lestat finally gives in to his desire for innocent blood, though, it is by killing a beggar woman and her child. Through this act, he discovers again the love he felt when Magnus passed on the Dark Gift to him; "the very blood seemed warmer with their innocence, richer with their goodness" (Rice *Vampire Lestat* 142). Having now gone against his earlier doctrine of goodness by taking innocent blood, Lestat realizes that his world is a "Savage Garden" (143) where innocence falls victim to the

Four • Eros and the Thanatotic Hero

vampire's love. In this act of vampirism against innocent humans, Lestat senses that the "last barrier between [his] appetite and the world had been dissolved" (143) and rationalizes his need for blood as an aesthetically beautiful act of love and, therefore, of goodness. Lestat has been living by aesthetic principles only, because they can be verified through feelings, while spiritual meaning cannot be verified except by a faith in a remote God. Faith is something Lestat has always found in short supply; so, instead of the Garden of Eden, Lestat's world is a savage paradise where rightness is predicated on power, where survival of the fittest rules and innocence is strong wine to a vampire alienated and alone. For Lestat, blood represents more than life; it represents the meaning of life — love and goodness; but with the act of taking innocent blood, Lestat has now managed to adapt his morality to accommodate his desires of the moment.

He continues to rationalize his acts as goodness; and, when his dying mother, Gabrielle, arrives in Paris, he makes her a vampire not only to save her from a lingering death, but also from death itself. His first rationalization for making her a vampire is that he cannot bear the thought of her in a grave for eternity. However, in the back of his mind is also the possibility of having a family again. Once again, Lestat's desires are predicated on what he has lacked in the past, and these desires will control his definition of what is good. As a vampire, he desires the love of a family because a family who loved him is what he felt the absence of when he was a child. However, Gabrielle had never fulfilled all his desires or needs, even when he was a mortal child; and she will not now, either.

Vampirism is a personal experience. Having recognized the inevitability of her own death, and subsequently having been reborn as a vampire, Gabrielle has a different personal agenda than her son. Her death gives her the freedom to make her own choices, to fulfill her own desires; and as a vampire, she lives as though she is going to die soon, trying to experience everything she can. While Lestat wants the peacefulness of their tower sanctuary, where he can live his life as if he were still human, she only wants "experiment, adventure" (Rice *Vampire Lestat* 169). She also finds Lestat's desire to keep his mortal connections with friends and family hard to understand because, as a vampire, she feels detached from her past. Lestat's answer is indicative of his need for love and his insistence on making his own choices in life. His feeling is that even as a vampire one needs love, and he tries to make her understand that he did what he wanted in staying near those he loved. This is the narcissistic mortal still thinking only of himself. Doing what he wants, making his own choices, has always been important to Lestat, even as a mortal child; but he finds it hard to understand that Gabrielle might want the same right to make her own choices.

Lestat's will and his need to live his life as he chooses become even more clear when he and Gabrielle meet the Parisian vampires who have been stalking them. These vampires curse Lestat and his mother as "profaners ... [and] outlaws" (Rice *Vampire Lestat* 186) because according to their worldview as followers of Satan, Lestat and Gabrielle were made "in defiance of the coven" (214). They also are angry with Lestat for compounding the sin of his birth by continuing to live in the society of mortals as if he were still human. Their leader Armand articulates the philosophy of this coven: that vampires "walk the earth ... by the will of God, to make mortals suffer for his [His] Divine Glory" (219). However, Lestat did not seek out these vampires to learn of his nature from them, and he feels that they have nothing to teach him about the philosophy of vampirism. Armand then tempts Lestat with what he senses Lestat wants most — love. However, Lestat disagrees with Armand's philosophy and refuses his definition of love. He tries to explain to Armand that the human part of him wants meaning; but he does not realize that his meaning is simply different from Armand's. Again, as it did with Gabrielle, Lestat's egoism gets in the way of his full understanding of another's experience. Armand and his band of vampires have a history of religious belief from their human lives and, so, form the meaning of vampirism from that belief. Thus, they see themselves as vehicles through which God's wrathful side, his potential for what mortal's perceive as evil, is shown to the world. Since Lestat never believed in God, he does not believe in the Devil either. However, Lestat also wants the meaning of vampire life to fit his preconceived, mortal ideas of value. Instead of searching for the whole truth behind the vampire's existence, he is looking for validation of his own existence. He does not want to hear about meaning that may contradict his already established set of values.

While Lestat seeks a sense of his new existence that will enable him to retain his humanness, these Parisian vampires subscribe to the belief that their vampire nature is what gives them meaning. In these malevolent vampires, believing themselves the chosen of Satan, Armand posits a society with meaning, where only the strong survive. Armand then offers Lestat salvation of a sort, the saving grace of bonding together with your own kind and living by "the ancient ways" (Rice *Vampire Lestat* 230). Warned by one of the older members of the coven that his love for mortals can only end in madness or suicide, Lestat disagrees once again. His value system is based on love and on his desire to be human again, so he has continued to live among mortals. He has loved mortals from the beginning, he tells them, and feels that his love of humans is essential to his experience as a vampire.

Despite his lack of belief in God, Lestat's value system of love and goodness is stronger than Armand's philosophy of evil because Lestat's will to make his own choices drives his moral outlook, while Armand's will has been given over to Satan's control. Lestat will not accept any answer that does not fit with his own value system, because any realization that he had been wrong about the value of his life would mean that his life was meaningless and that, as he had told Nicholas when he was still mortal, would be chaos. His answer to Armand's philosophy, therefore, is that good and evil are both relative concepts. Lestat tells Armand that "forms of goodness change with the ages" (Rice *Vampire Lestat* 227) and so do the forms of evil. In a secular age, nothing is sacred; and new times call for a "new evil" (228). To find meaning for himself in the world, Lestat sees himself as that new evil—"the monster who looks exactly like everyone else" (228). However, this is simply his will controlling how he approaches his new nature. While the vampires of the Paris coven have a background of belief in God and, therefore, must find their own meaning within that construct of belief, Lestat is once again able to go his own direction and give meaning to his existence on a personal level. Still, what he would like to find is a group of vampires who reflect his own value system, because then he could be sure he was right in choosing goodness and love over evil.

The next step in Lestat's quest for a value system among vampires that reflects his need for goodness involves a search for the history of vampires. However, this search will not result in final answers for him, either. Armand's tale of Marius, his maker, and of Those Who Must Be Kept, the mother and father of all vampires over whom Marius watches, propels Lestat on a quest that finally takes him into Egypt. These older vampires are those who survived what John Clute calls "end times" (1), the passage over the threshold of time into a new millennium; and Lestat needs their history for reassurance of his own survival and of his concepts of goodness and love as his moral prime directives. If he is to live forever, he must live as an honorable person.

It is in Egypt that Gabrielle finally leaves him to make her own way. However, Marius finally finds him, and he and Marius begin to travel together as Marius tells him the story of his own vampire birth and life and of the making of the mother and father of all vampires, Akasha and Enkil, from the Egyptian rulers Isis and Osiris, respectively. The story of Osiris' death is symbolic of initiation and rebirth. Isis, the fertile goddess and mother of Horus, wife and sister of Osiris, recovers the pieces of Osiris' dead body after he has been dismembered by Set. Thoth restores Osiris' body to wholeness, and the regeneration of the agricultural cosmos is complete for another year. As a vegetation god, Osiris represents humanity more closely than any other god that Lestat has been exposed to in the past. Eliade has characterized Osiris as "taking on the destiny of man himself, like him experiencing passions, suffering, and death. Never had god been brought so close to man" (*Patterns* 98). However, Lestat will replace Osiris/Enkil as god/man. When Lestat finally is brought into the presence of Those Who Must Be Kept, Akasha stirs from her long sleep and eventually offers Lestat her blood to make him stronger. While this act does give him a connection to his history as a vampire, its results will later complicate his moral decisions.

The meaning Lestat might hope to gain from Marius' story is that in the beginning vampires were good, and, therefore, could be again in his *lifetime*; and this does seem to be the substance of Marius' history of vampires, who began as "benevolent rulers" (Rice *Vampire Lestat* 442), and whose legacy was perverted later by those who destroyed what Marius had built and who captured Armand and turned him toward Satan. In the end, however, Marius' experience is just as personal as Lestat's. Marius cannot tell Lestat the secrets of the universe or even why vampires exist; but he can tell him his own personal experience in hopes that the knowledge of what happened to him can help Lestat to survive. He warns Lestat that when his tale is finished, Lestat will be no closer to understanding why he exists. On this journey a man, or a vampire, must find his own way home. Psychologically, Lestat will end this part of his journey where he began it, as the master of his own fate, the ruler of his own will, seeking to formulate a value system that would provide the significance he craved and still craves.

Four • Eros and the Thanatotic Hero

Lestat's spiritual journey eventually takes him to Louisiana where he meets Louis de Pointe du Lac and makes him a vampire. Despite his new knowledge that vampires did indeed once embody goodness, and despite his disagreement with Armand over vampire philosophy, and his insistence that he is the new evil in the world, Lestat has now internalized some of Armand's philosophy and reorganized his own value system so that when he meets Louis he considers vampires to be part of God's "divine plan" (Rice *Interview* 83) in their ability to carry out cosmic retribution and salvation. However, just as Lestat had trouble accepting Armand's philosophy that vampires serve Satan with God's dispensation in order that mortals might suffer for the glory of God, Louis has trouble accepting Lestat's philosophy. Lestat is now in the position of a father with a recalcitrant child. Louis, however, like Armand, is trying to reconcile his human religious beliefs with his new vampire existence. Making another attempt to build a family structure, and hoping that the family will keep Louis submissive to his will, Lestat makes a child he calls Claudia into a vampire. However, this family structure only lasts a human lifetime of sixty-five years before Claudia rebels and convinces Louis to help her kill Lestat. Lestat's hunger has always been for more than blood, more than mere survival. The blood maintains the life, but life must have a deeper meaning. The cultural authorities of society, family, and religion have failed Lestat both as a mortal man and as a vampire; still, he hungers and "thirsts for *being*" (Eliade *Sacred and Profane* 64), for meaning and order to be born out of the chaos of his vampire existence.

The Hunger for a Higher Reality of the Soul

Lestat's spiritual journey will "reach beyond the limits of time and space" (O'Malley "Toward" 342) to a reality of higher consequence, a higher reality of the soul. Otto characterizes this reach beyond time and space as the yearning we have to transcend the sense of our own unworthiness in relation to the divine. This is the stage where the element of fascination that one feels upon experiencing the numinous operates, "where the living 'something more' ... is to be found" (Otto *Idea of the Holy* 35), the sense, as O'Malley defines it, that there is something more to life than simply surviving it. This something more is the need to create a connection, a bond, between the divine and the personal. As William James writes in *Varieties of Religious Experience* the world is an arena for the hero; and it is in heroism that he feels human beings discover the mystery of life. Having survived the attempts of Claudia and Louis to destroy him and the despair of a vampire who has lost the meaning of his existence and, therefore, his will to live, Lestat now sees his search for meaning as the quest of a hero.

The last time Lestat was above ground was 1929; and during this dormant existence underground, he has observed the world above him through the voices he heard "as a mortal does in sleep" (Rice *Vampire Lestat* 4). Through this somnolent education, he has begun to understand "the caliber of the changes that the world had undergone" (4). Realizing he is *alive* and "starved for living blood" (5), he rises once more to the surface to find "the dark dreary industrial world" (7) of 1929 is gone; and "the old bourgeois prudery and conformity [have] lost their hold on the American mind" (7). This new world of 1984 New Orleans reminds him of the days of his *youth* before the French Revolution. People are dressing more freely, showing their individuality; and in the arts, and even the language, he can see a combination of old and new. More importantly, Lestat discovers that in the 1980s "the Christian god [is] as dead as he had been in the 1700s. *And no new mythological religion [has] arisen to take the place of the old*" (9). Yet, in the activism of the people, who argue over capital punishment and abortion, and seek to wipe out such evils as hunger and pollution as zealously as earlier societies had fought against "witchcraft and heresy " (9), Lestat sees a "secular mortality as strong as any religious morality" (9). In this "sinless secular morality, this optimism" (10), Lestat finds a new and "brilliantly lighted world where the value of human life was [is] greater than it had ever been before" (10).

As far as Lestat can see, in this twentieth-century world, people make meaning for themselves in a secular way, just as Lestat the young mortal had before the French Revolution, and as Lestat the vampire has chosen to do since his transformation. While Lestat has loved mortals since his change, he now feels a kinship with them that is beyond that love because they show the same willfulness that he has always shown. He understands their motivations much more than he ever did Louis', or even his mother's, and certainly more than those of the vampire Armand and his band. His dilemma seems to be over — the meaning of his existence is clear. In the twentieth century, he can seek meaning in being the new evil for a new age, just as he told Armand he was doing over a hundred years before.

As he watches the movie *Apocalypse Now*, he is struck by the fact that "horror and moral terror ... have no real value" (Rice *Vampire Lestat* 10) or place in the twentieth-century world. Nor does "pure evil" (10). This means that Lestat, as a vampire, seemingly has no role in the world, other than in "the art that repudiates evil — the vampire comics, the horror novels, the old gothic tales— or in the roaring chants of the rock stars who dramatize the battles against evil that each mortal fights within himself" (10). In his irrelevance to the world, Lestat sees cause for despair, at least for "an old world monster" (10). However, he is a monster who changes with the ages, as he told Armand. His answer to the despair these new age attitudes might bring on is to create a secular meaning for his existence by becoming a rock star and a famous author. Like the secular answer to the old-world prophet or the new-age television evangelist, Lestat plans to bring other vampires "into the light" (10); but he will do it with his participation in the band Satan's Night Out and by publishing his story as Louis had done earlier in *Interview with the Vampire*.

Lestat is still something of a rebel for whom "old rules" (Rice *Vampire Lestat* 16) do not exist; he wants to bring together the vampires he has "known and loved" (16) and wants "mortals *to know*" (16) about them. In effect, he wants vampires to invest life with meaning, to be visible; and he wants to be the hero, the one to "lead them into the truth of it" (17). In exposing himself to the mortal world and the hidden world of other vampires to the light of publicity and fame, he might cause a revolution, "a great and glorious war" (17); but Lestat *wants* to live heroically. He loves the idea of rebellion, the heroics of it, whether in triumph or defeat, for "even at the moment of destruction" (17), he tells his readers, he would feel more alive than he had ever felt before. This may well be the feeling one gets from an experience of the numinous, that in facing death one finally feels more alive than ever before, because one is no longer indifferent to the world. The imminence of death heightens the senses and focuses the mind, so if one is not denying death anymore, but instead embracing the possibility, one becomes intimately aware of the joys and sorrows of life, and of the meaning of life. Like James' hero, Lestat is willing to risk death to find meaning. He joins the band, Satan's Night Out, offering them fame and fortune in order to be able to articulate his vampire nature instead of hide it; and to instigate some response from other vampires, he writes his story. As Coleridge's Ancient Mariner did, Lestat has attained the creative level of numinous contact and can, indeed must, tell his story. These acts are meant to give purpose to his existence, just as his formation of a family with Gabrielle and Nicholas, and later with Louis and Claudia, was meant to do. In this case, however, he is bringing the existence of vampires out into the open, outing them to the human world, as it were. This is a revolutionary move of which the larger vampire community does not seem to approve; and in response to their anger and violence, Lestat must become the hero he always has envisioned himself to be.

In *Queen of the Damned*, Lestat articulates even more clearly than before his need to be a hero. He describes himself as "the vampire who would have been a hero and a martyr finally for one moment of pure relevance..." (4–5). Calling himself the "James Bond of vampires" (8), he invites the reader once again to share in his heroic exploits. Lestat's choice of James Bond as a heroic model is telling, I think. As one of the more important culture heroes of twentieth-century literature and film, Bond is roguishly and erotically charming and rebelliously individual, much as Lestat so often describes himself in his narratives. Like Bond, who always identifies himself precisely to his enemies, Lestat refuses to be invisible. Admitting that he has brought disaster with his past attempts to reconcile his human values with his vampire existence, he still finds it unacceptable to walk in the shadows of life. "It's the risk that fascinates, the moment of infinite possibility ... [that] lures" (6) him on to continued immortality. That moment of possibility is the numinous, the threshold experience of dread and mystery and fascination where one is no longer indifferent to the divine; instead one is invested in the spiritual life of the cosmos. At that moment one must face not only the possibility of death, but also the possibility of the infinite and what life itself truly means. The moment when he was faced with the vampire Magnus and the possibility of immortal life, Lestat was no longer indifferent to the divine. Instead, as a result of his transformation, he feels he now knows the mystery of life; and this is the realm of the hero, as James has defined it.

To prolong that feeling of rapture, that moment when all is risked for the reward of higher understanding, Lestat now must do to others what was done to him. However, he needs more than the simple act of survival.

Four • Eros and the Thanatotic Hero

For vampires and humans alike the blood is the life, and regardless of the rapture Lestat feels when he feeds, blood is not enough to provide meaning in life. He finds this meaning in his interaction with others, both humans and vampires. Although, in *Queen of the Damned*, Lestat is "just a player" (Ramsland *Prism* 294), the several narratives by other older vampires come together in the end at the spectacle which he has engineered to bring the vampires out into the open. Through the various narratives, *Queen of the Damned* tells a story that encompasses the birth of the vampires and the history of various branches that have formed through the ages. The story culminates in a mythic, universal struggle between the forces of creation and destruction represented by the two strongest female vampires.

Akasha has destroyed her mate Enkil and come to Lestat in the United States. She is plotting to kill most of the male vampires and mortal men and to make slaves of those who are left. Katherine Ramsland argues that, as a figure of destruction, Akasha represents "the dark side of the feminine, an image of the ancient goddesses who demanded blood sacrifice" (*Prism* 296). Her intent, Ramsland writes, is to "create a new Eden" (300) and become its "divine meaning-maker" (300), ruling the world according to her own laws. Ramsland characterizes her as "a combination of object and goddess, both forms of existence which cancel the possibility of being human" (300–1). Having given her blood to Lestat a hundred years before, she now expects to enlist his help with her apocalyptic scheme. Akasha thinks that with the completion of her plan she will have "transcended history" (Rice *Queen* 399) and brought an end to the seemingly "endless cycle of human violence" (399). However, free will must be destroyed to do that. In this new Edenic existence, only she will "define goodness ... [and] peace" (401). Forgetting that the world she sees is the one she has selected to see and not the whole reality of existence, she refuses to acknowledge the changes that have been wrought over time as humans evolved and attempted to repair their previous mistakes.

Since Lestat sees in her global plan something of his own personal desire to do good, he accepts her offer to be her consort and helper at first. However, although Lestat initially helps her by killing the men on the island of Lykanos, he eventually realizes that while his plan had been to motivate people toward goodness, hers is simply to destroy those she perceives as evil. Lestat's personality, however, signals that there is more to his refusal of her plan than simply wanting to be good. He is, after all, still a rebel who makes his own choices and guides his life according to his own will. Losing his free will to someone like Akasha would mean giving up his own value system and losing his chance to be a hero. Never having struggled as Lestat has in order to maintain a sense of humanity, Akasha becomes the model for what Lestat does not want to be. To keep his will and value system intact, and to remain a hero, at least in his own mind, he leaves Akasha and joins the vampire forces ranged against her under the control of Maharet, a powerful witch from Akasha's past. In joining with the other vampires against Akasha, Lestat will learn another lesson about his search that will propel him on another path in his quest for meaning.

The group under Maharet's leadership pleads with Akasha to spare humans. Trying to convince her that they are not the enemy, Maharet tells her that it is the "irrational ... the spiritual when it is divorced from the material ... from the lesson in one beating heart or one bleeding vein" (Rice *Queen* 409) that is the enemy. Maharet's words echo Otto's insistence of a balance between the rational and irrational qualities of the divine, as well as Mircea Eliade's argument that a religious man lives in two existential situations: the profane world of empirical reality and the sacred world of the spirit. Once again, this is something Lestat never had as a child, since his family provided no religious upbringing and even went so far as to deny him a chance at spiritual meaning when he sought to join the monastery.

Lestat refuses to go with Akasha, reminding her "we're not angels ... we are not gods. To be human, that's what most of us long for. It is the human which has become myth to us" (Rice *Queen* 411). Where once he thought of himself as a dark god, striking down evil as God does, he no longer feels that way. He has, as Ramsland puts it, brought the human "closer to the surface" (*Prism* 296). In the battle that ensues, Akasha is killed and Mekare, Maharet's twin sister, becomes the head of the new coven of vampires that have chosen to protect the mortal world from destruction. However, Lestat is still plagued by the questions of goodness and meaning as he was when first made a vampire; and he realizes finally that what Marius had tried to tell him so long ago was that everyone, humans and vampires, must "wrestle forever with those questions" (Rice *Queen* 431) to which there are no simple solutions. He will never settle for

Four • Eros and the Thanatotic Hero

life in the shadows, however, because a hero never does; and he refuses Marius' request that he destroy the manuscript of his latest exploits. Humanity, he tells Marius, will only think this story is fiction as humans had when both *Interview* and *Vampire Lestat* were published, and "that's how it should be" (422). He feels now that there is no room for vampires or God or the Devil in the life of humans. Instead, they should be a "metaphor" (422), helping humans to find meaning in their own lives. Lestat is now moving in the direction of higher meaning — of becoming that meaning for others, just as the Ancient Mariner became his own message by becoming a metaphorical vampire.

At this point, Lestat seems to have given up on finding meaning either through power or through the secular rapture of rock music. He tells Louis he has no "designs on Western civilization" (Rice *Queen* 439) or even on his two million rock fans. His need is simple: to break the rules as he has always done, to find the fascination and the rapture in taking risks, in the pleasure of the individual experience. Nothing has changed. He still is the one who must have everything his own way; however, in speaking to Akasha of how all vampires want to be human again, Lestat has set himself up for his next heroic adventure and a further evolution as human/vampire/hero. Maharet has suggested that the spiritual and material should be wedded into one; and Lestat will attempt that wedding.

In *The Tale of the Body Thief*, Lestat, the self-proclaimed "man of action" (4), the "James Bond of vampires" (6) discovers what it is to be human again. Knowing he cannot be forgiven as a vampire, he still likes saving innocent lives by taking those of the evil humans who prey on them; at the beginning of the story he is tracking a serial killer. As he takes the killer's blood he sees the man's past, the cadavers of the old men and women who were his victims "floating in the current" (22), tumbling "against each other without meaning" (22). While he might make the connection at this point between himself and his own victim, Lestat does not see himself as that kind of cold-blooded, calculating killer. His own murders have meaning for him, since he feels he is protecting humans from evil. The blood is the life for human or vampire, and Lestat says "I wanted to be human, and feel human" (23). However, the evil victim's blood has never been enough to make this happen. Giving in to his need for more innocent blood, he kills the serial killer's victim, also; but even that now leaves him unfulfilled. The goodness and love he used to feel when drinking innocent blood no longer are enough to give him the rapture he craves. Lestat now must face the fact that he needs more than blood, however innocent that blood might be, to give himself a reason to survive. He needs that higher reality of the soul of which O'Malley writes to make his vampire life worth living.

With no rapture left in his life, he is in despair, as Armand had warned him might happen. Concluding that he cannot save his soul "through art or Good Works" (Rice *Tale* 39), he is more depressed than usual. "Sick and weary" (28), he travels to London to say farewell to his friend Talbot, superior general of the Talamasca, an organization formed to record incidents of the paranormal. Lestat tells him he has "figured a way to end it" (43). He feels he should have died the day he battled the wolves; and in the Gobi Desert he plans to fly as close to the sun as he can just before sunrise; then, when it is too late to retreat, the sun will rise and he will be burned to death. His plan for vampire suicide fails, though, because Akasha's stronger blood has saved him. Now he is tanned "almost like a man" (55); however, he is not the man he wants to be. Immortality truly has become a curse for Lestat, unless he can find a way to change and revitalize his life through new meaning. Therefore, when Raglan James approaches him and proposes that they exchange bodies, Lestat is tempted. He can become mortal again for a while; and this is what he wants most: "to be human again" (99), to be "innocent and alive" (100). His search for a confirmation that he has a soul takes him back into the body of a human being where he attempts to find the combination of spiritual and material of which Maharet spoke.

Once he exchanges bodies with Raglan James, however, his experience of being human does not live up to the memory. He is no longer so heroic or so rebellious as a human. Instead, Lestat concentrates on the physicalness of this experience — the cold, the sweat, the itching, the bleeding, the pain of a full bladder; and, right away, he decides he hates his human body "to the marrow of these human bones" (Rice *Tale* 177). He is disgusted by his mortal needs to eat, to defecate, to urinate; and even having sex does not fulfill him the way the blood drinking did. Now, without his vampire perspective, humans appear to him as "common ... utterly worthless" (190) things; and mortal life is "nothing but abysmal struggle and trivia and fear" (193). Mortality has no value to him, like it did when he was above it all and when humans had value because they had what he lacked. As he had felt that the Parisian vampires had wasted their immortality, so he feels that mortals have "wasted our [their] lives in foolish preoccupation" (193). However, when he wakes up in the morning to see his first sunrise in centuries, he perceives his human life differently. For Lestat, this sunrise, with all its connotations of rebirth and new chances, is the "biblical promise which had gone unfulfilled for two hundred years" (195) and "worth all the trials and the pain" (195) of mortality. Lestat has evolved, however, in the sense that he no longer finds aesthetics of goodness and love sufficient to give a life meaning. Nor are sunrises enough, since they represent only an aesthetic enjoyment of the moment. There is, as there always has been, the need for something more. The answer will only come when he can wed the spiritual and material as Maharet suggested. For now, he is stuck in a human body; and although the beauty of a sunrise may be sublime, although it may fill him with awe, love, and even a sense of goodness, it cannot relieve him of his physical pain or give him back the power he had as a vampire. In fact, his mortal pain increases, as he is struck with pneumonia. This illness, however, does lead him to someone who can teach him what being human means and, perhaps, how to combine the spiritual and material, the vampire and the human.

Taken to the hospital where he faces the possibility of dying, he begins to hallucinate that he sees Claudia and tells the nun Gretchen who is nursing him that he is a vampire. He also tells her that he "can't bear to be quiet and be nothing" (*Tale* 233) while mortals create and accomplish so much in their lives. He feels that to accomplish anything, to be the hero of his story, he once again must be immortal. While not believing he is a vampire, Gretchen tries to convince him that he came into the mortal body as Christ did for the same reason: for "redemption" (235). To her, redemption is in the small acts, and in her life these are the heroic acts. It does not matter if she affects the world in the larger scheme of things, only that she changes someone's life on a personal level. What one does to help others is what matters in the end. She tries to convince him that he did good when he made Claudia and Gabrielle vampires to save them from death, and that doing good is to "transcend doubt and something ... something perhaps hopeless and black inside" (247). This is what Lestat has always looked for in his hopelessness— reassurance that goodness can transcend despair and give life meaning.

Lestat finally he manages to re-inhabit his own body. He has had his chance at salvation in the human body and refused it; but he has learned something along the way, realizing that finding meaning as a human is no different than finding meaning as a vampire. From his experience as a human, he has learned that vampires and humans can all waste their lives in trivial pursuits. From Gretchen he has learned that salvation is in the small acts of kindness done for others. However, although many religious humans subscribe to a belief that good words and faith will get one into Heaven, this belief cannot give Lestat the answers to the question that he has avoided for so long. Goodness and evilness, being relative concepts, cannot give him anything but relative answers to his questions of whether he is a good person or not. Lestat finally must struggle with whether his goodness as a vampire ensures him a place in the afterworld or not. The search for answers to his question will take him to another level of numinous contact.

In *Memnoch the Devil* Lestat will finally seek the answers to his questions of good and evil and divine grace in the afterlife as he takes on the role of the cosmic hero who enters both Heaven and Hell in search of the ultimate higher meaning. In the Prologue, Lestat tells his audience that he has "set for [himself] the task of being a hero in this world" (Rice *Memnoch* 3). He adds, "I maintain myself as morally complex, spiritually tough, and aesthetically relevant" (3) because, as he says, he has "things to say" (3) both about being a vampire and about being human. Through his experiences, he has come to realize that humans and vampires have the same souls; and neither truly knows "what it means to die" (3). In fact, becoming a vampire is the ultimate denial of death in an acceptance of physical immortality. As a hero, Lestat is "searching desperately for the lesson, and for the song and for the raison d'être" (3); he wants to understand why he exists, and, like the Ancient Mariner, he wants his readers to understand, also.

Lestat's lesson will come from another experience of the numinous; but now that he, as a vampire, represents the numinous also, whatever divine figure opposes him must appear even more powerful than he is. The powerful entity that finally confronts him turns out to be the Devil himself. Lestat overhears a fragmented conversation between God and the Devil; and, without understanding all the words, he knows they are arguing about him. As he listens to them talk, he feels the "fabric of life ripping" (Rice *Memnoch* 15) and thinks the devil has come for him. Worried

Four • Eros and the Thanatotic Hero

about his fate at the hands of the Devil, he tells his friend David that his "views are changing" (106), that "the atheism and nihilism" (106) he subscribed to in his earlier life now seem "shallow, and even a bit cocky" (106). To add to his anxiety, the ghost of one of his victims has charged him with the responsibility of watching out for his daughter Dora, an evangelist in search of revelation; and so, Lestat's life has taken on some purpose after all. He also reminds himself that he has Mojo, the dog he inherited from his time inside the body Raglan James had inhabited. Although he laughs at the thought of resisting the Devil "on account of a flesh-and-blood dog" (109), he gives relevance to the possibility by deciding that stranger things have happened to humans. Still, these reasons to think his life has meaning are mundane; they do not provide for the higher meaning of the spirit that he requires. Lestat's spiritual journey must take him to a realm where he can confront his fears for his soul in order for him to find the true meaning of his existence and to make true moral meaning from his experiences. Despite his own supernatural power, once more Lestat has been affected by an experience of the numinous; but this time the initial fear is not dissipated in the rapture, as it was when Magnus turned him into a vampire. This time, a feeling of love cannot assuage his fear; and no aesthetic of goodness can help him deny the danger in which he perceives his immortal soul to be. Lestat is terrified because, if the Devil were to take his soul, Lestat would have an answer to the question of where he belongs in the spiritual scheme of things. This answer would not be one Lestat would find acceptable, because it would not validate his own sense of value and meaning. Like Jonathan Harker in *Dracula*, Lestat is aware that the span of his life may be over. For him, though, this realization is more problematic because, if the Devil claims his soul, the act would be a sign that he has been wrong all these centuries.

Lestat's cosmic journey begins when the Devil finally visits him. At first Lestat is surprised that the Devil appears, not as "some monstrous angelic being ... resembling more a Mesopotamian demon than an angel" (Rice *Memnoch* 31), but as an "Ordinary Man" (115). Despite the innocuous appearance of Memnoch the Devil, Lestat is reduced to tears at the thought that the Devil wants his soul. However, Memnoch wants more than that. He has been watching Lestat for centuries; and he wants Lestat to help him in his battle with God. The Devil offers Lestat a chance "to turn your [his] life from aimlessness and meaninglessness" (136) into meaning by helping win the "crucial battle for the fate of the world" (136). As the Devil often does, he tempts Lestat with precisely what Lestat has desired all these centuries—meaning in his life. If he helps the Devil, he will be a hero of cosmic proportions. However, his main reason for accepting the Devil's proposal is his hope that he will discover once and for all the meaning of his existence. Lestat has now taken up Louis' quest, in his need to know whether he serves God or the Devil. If he can have assurance from God that despite his disbelief there is a place for him in Heaven, then he will be reassured that his life has value regardless of his vampire nature.

In the spirit of an apocalyptic text, Rice has Memnoch propose that Lestat accompany him to Heaven to talk to God. Otto writes that in a state of spiritual bliss the shuddering horror, that sensation accompanying the *uncanny* and *aweful* daemonic dread, "appears in a form ennobled beyond measure where the soul, held speechless, trembles inwardly to the farthest fibre of its being" (*Idea of the Holy* 17). This ennobled terror is characterized by Rice as Memnoch and Lestat visit Heaven. When Lestat finally approaches God, he is overcome by the numinous and feels he is "on the verge of death" (Rice *Memnoch* 169). As God touches him, he feels "his body in all its solidity and fragility" (169). In that moment, he says, "I might have ceased to breathe ... or ceased to move with the commitment to life and might have died!" (169). The will that had made him immortal, and that had sustained him through countless years as a vampire, is in danger of being completely overwhelmed as he is embraced by God. When Memnoch pulls Lestat away into the whirlwind again, Lestat is left in "utter agony" (169), bereft of God's presence. Having now experienced belief in God as he encountered Him as an objective presence in Heaven, Lestat must now endure the loss of God when he is taken from His presence. Although he does not feel the same level of alienation from God that Louis or Armand did as religious men turned vampires, Lestat still suffers the sadness of loss. However, the fact that God knows his name, and that as God's children even Lestat the vampire and Memnoch the Devil seemingly can enter Heaven at will, fills Lestat with excitement and hope, despite his realization that salvation cannot be that easy.

Memnoch continues his campaign to enlist Lestat by showing him the angels fall from grace, the earth through all its history, and all the terrible things that have happened since creation, blaming all of them on

Four • Eros and the Thanatotic Hero

God's indifference to humanity. When Lestat is shown the crucifixion of Christ, he is offered the Blood of Christ and drinks from Christ's wounds; he is also given Veronica's Veil, a veil with Christ's blood on it, which he keeps with him as he travels into Hell with the Devil. In Hell, Lestat is confronted by his dead victims and urged to "learn" (Rice *Memnoch* 315) about what evil he has done. He cries out for God's help but realizes that his cries cannot be heard anymore than can the incessant cries of the dead, whose only excuse seems to be that they "did not know" (315) the consequences of their actions would result in their being consigned to Hell. Lestat has never realized his own indifference to consequences, just as he did not see his own parallel with the serial killer in his last adventure. Now he does not want to face his own guilt over what he has become and what he has done in making other vampires like Nicholas and his mother, Louis and Claudia. With the examples of the death of Christ and the souls of his own victims in Hell before him, Lestat understands that salvation is a difficult state to attain. One does not simply live a life of personal goodness and love, but, like Christ, must act heroically in the world and be willing to give up their life in service of another's salvation.

However, Lestat's vampire divinity offered no salvation to the innocents he took; they have ended up in Hell with no hope of getting God's attention, let alone of getting into Heaven. If his victims ended up in Hell, Lestat must realize that his place is there with them eventually. Like those souls in Hell, Lestat also must realize that he has ignored the consequences of his actions as a vampire. In maintaining his moral doctrine of goodness and love that served him as a mortal, and in not searching for a deeper meaning to life, he has settled for earthly morality over a spiritual meaning. Accused by his victims, his own words coming back to haunt him, Lestat refuses the Devil's earlier offer. However, his refusal is not due to his desire to become one of God's chosen. Feeling that God is "blind" (Rice *Memnoch* 317), and that both Memnoch and God are "mad" (317), Lestat escapes from Hell; and although he loses an eye in the encounter, he does manage to keep hold of the Veil. On his return to earth, Lestat brings back his story and the Veil to Dora and his friends; but he tries to tell them all that the Veil is no proof of his experiences or of the existence of God or Christ. He is ambivalent about what he has seen because the Devil was his guide and the Devil could have been lying about it all.

Armand and Lestat end their relationship where they started in Paris,

The Vampire as Numinous Experience

arguing about whether vampires serve God or the Devil; and Lestat reasserts his belief that "we have conceived better rules" (Rice *Memnoch* 331) of personal morality than either the Devil or God could offer. His belief that personal doctrines of goodness and love are better than the rules offered by either side of the cosmic equation indicates that he has given up on salvation for himself, or rather, rejected it. In the end, the consensus of the group to whom he has told his story is that even the ultimate experience of meeting God and the Devil cannot give one spiritual surety. However, when he gives the Veil to Dora, she is overcome by the revelation of God's face appearing on it. Despite her despair at the possibility of never knowing for sure that God exists, she still believes in Him. For Lestat, however, the Veil is no proof his experience; it is only a piece of cloth with what appears to be blood in the image of Christ on it. Lestat himself cannot be entirely sure the whole experience was real; and the one proof he has—Christ's blood in his own veins—he will not offer to them. Although Armand asks him for a taste and assures him that he would know the blood of Christ when he tasted it, Lestat refuses. He does not want to put the reality of his experience to the test because living with the possibility allows him to continue to live with his relative morality as a foundation. Living with the possibility of its truth is faith of a sort, for Lestat, because, after all, faith is by definition belief in that which we cannot prove empirically to be true.

Although Lestat warns them all that his story is no proof of truth, nor is the Veil, when Armand sees God's face in the Veil, he falls to his knees in awe. As humans rush to see the revelation of the Veil, vampires also come into its presence and are convinced by the sight of it that redemption lies in immolating themselves. Armand is one of the first to walk into the fire to his death; and, though Lestat is anguished by this act, he still is caught between a desire to believe and his will not to believe. For Lestat to admit his proof, his blood, into evidence for the other vampires would be to give up his free will and his hero status, to relinquish his autonomy and purchase the surety of spiritual knowledge with a loss of power. This would place him second in authority to God or the Devil; and neither position is acceptable to him. Rejecting both God and the Devil as arbiters of meaning, Lestat falls back on the personal ideals and philosophy that have always characterized his journey. He is no longer an atheist, if he ever truly was one, but instead more of an agnostic, harboring some small hope that there is a place in Heaven meant for him.

Four • Eros and the Thanatotic Hero

The Desire to Expend One's Life in Service to Mankind

Through his visits to Hell and to Sheol and the visions of human history the Devil has provided for him, Lestat has come to value humans for their faith in the divine and their struggle to survive in an indifferent world watched over by an indifferent God. While, in his adventure within the human body of Raglan James, he came to despise humans for wasting of their own lives, he now sees the struggle they have gone through because of the perceived indifference of God. Though Lestat refused to take either side in the cosmic battle, he did bring back the Veil, and the miracle of the Veil itself gives "a new infusion of blood into the very religion that Memnoch loathed" (Rice *Memnoch* 341). Lestat, however, feels that by bringing back the Veil he has served a God he still hates and is angered by his unintended collusion. However, then he receives a note from Memnoch and is led to believe that all along he was "Memnoch's servant; Memnoch's prince" (351). Once again in an ambiguous position, he is no happier about this turn of events than he was about unintentionally helping God with the miracle of the Veil. However, Lestat is a changed vampire now, despite his hatred of both God and the Devil, and resolves never to "take a human *life*" (348) again as long as he lives. He has made his decision finally about how to live an honorable life; and his service to mankind will be a vow to resist consigning another victim to Hell. He finishes his tale with a message to his readers that is much like Marius' earlier warning to him: this is his experience and the breadth of his knowledge and that is all there is.

Eliade writes that "to relate a sacred history is equivalent to revealing a mystery" (*Sacred and Profane* 95); and the characters in those histories are "gods or culture heroes" (95). Still "the hero of [his] own dreams" (Rice *Memnoch* 354), Lestat wants to "pass now from fiction into legend" (354). Like Marius, his meaning is found in this transcendence. In *End Times*, Clute writes that "we need to believe we make sense; we need stories to live by" (44). As the Ancient Mariner became his own message, Lestat has become the story. His apocalyptic tale is in a sense a myth, and, as such, it is sacred history; but what has been his message to the world of humans? His message seems to be that the answers to our questions— about the nature of good and evil, the existence of the divine, and how we make meaning in our lives— do not lie within the artificial constructs that deny the true reality of human existence or with the knowledge of others whom we expect to give us easy answers. The true spiritual journey takes place within us; and the potential for meaning in life lies also within a constantly seeking soul, searching for something more than rational reality can give. Meaning lies in the will to search for that meaning and in the will to make one's own choices about how to live and what life means and what death means. To develop a system of morality based on love and goodness helps an individual to survive in the short term; but to give the system of personal morality a more cosmic meaning, one must make the spiritual choice to live in a reality of higher consequences by serving mankind and assuring their salvation, instead of our own. However, one can never truly be sure of the reality of the spiritual quest or the answers it provides except as they are represented by the individual experience. Lestat does not ask the others to believe in his experience because he knows that the way to spiritual knowledge is the individual journey of discovery. The spiritual quest is a personal journey; and the answers gained at the end are just as personal and will only hold up to the scrutiny of our own hearts. In the end, all we can offer someone else who is searching for spiritual meaning is what Lestat offers his friends and his readers: "this is what I know! This is *all* I know" (Rice *Memnoch* 353). Believe it or not, as you choose.

• CONCLUSION •

Vampires for a New Age

At the ends of centuries and millenniums, many people suffer what John Clute describes in *The Book of End Times: Grappling with the Millennium* as "cultural despair, storylessness, dread, anxiety" (41), perceiving these thresholds of time as the possible end of time itself and, therefore, the end of human history. This threshold is a numinous place, where the magnitude of time passed and the possibility of its sudden absence come together. At this intersection, fascination and fear create a natural hesitation and anxiety. We are in awe of, we dread, the power and energy that could put an end to time; yet, we are curious to see if we will survive the apocalypse. While there is always the possibility that one will join God's angels at end time, there is also the possibility of finding oneself on the edge of the abyss, and that nothing is all one can expect to find on the other side of that fateful midnight. It is here that our fears and hopes collide, here that faith becomes of the utmost importance to our survival.

Yet, Clute writes, what survives the dread and anxiety, the possible "storylessness" (41) of the end of time " is not exactly the silence of the tomb" (33). There is a story here, the framework of which is as old as time itself: the story of renewal. We have survived as a species before and we can again. Hopefully. Humanity can rise again in the new century or millennium, like the vampire has in the past in its guise as Ancient Mariner, Dracula, or Lestat. In light of the tragic and seemingly apocalyptic circumstances that have ushered in this fledgling twenty-first century, however, the question seems to be whether our renewal will be positive or negative.

The ambivalence of expectations as to what the new century might hold allows writers to employ the numinous in order to address the spiritual fears of their respective societies. The difference between centuries lies in how these fears are resolved by each society. The literature I have chosen to use as representative of the vampire as numinous figure in each period is also representative of how many of the people of that period answered the questions that their fears about the end of time produced. In order to explore the idea that the figure of the vampire conveys a human sense of alienation from the divine and a desire to overcome that alienation, this study has argued that a textual experience of the numinous in the form of the vampire causes at least one of the characters in the text to embark on a spiritual journey.

In "The Rime of the Ancient Mariner," Romantic poet Samuel Taylor Coleridge portrays an individual's journey away from traditional religious systems to the higher understanding signified by the cosmic relationship of human and divine. Separated from his God, as well as from humanity, the Mariner, as cosmic hero, suffers through the experience of a numinous contact and evolves into the numen/artist who must carry the lesson of his experience to others. In his representation as the Romantic artist, the Mariner allows the primitive numinous to come to the surface as he creates his tale for the audience who is in need of the lesson embedded in it. Although considered a negatively numinous figure because of his hypnotic influence over people and his haggard and frightening appearance, the Mariner is nevertheless a vehicle for revelation and transformation for the Romantic period.

A century later, many Britons still were searching for a relationship with the divine. This search often led them to occult practices, but at the same time, they feared the influence that the primitive occult might have on their larger society and on their families. While in "The Ancient Mariner" grace comes through the individual act of telling a penitential tale, the salvation of the group in *Dracula* is gained through a more primitive and community-based act, the resacralizing of the British world through the ritual staking of the vampire. The community of heroes in Stoker's novel choose to approach the numinous of the vampire not as something that might be integrated into their lives, but as something that must be destroyed to maintain order. To conquer their anxieties and fears, they strengthen the previously constructed Victorian reality represented by their society and deny the numinous its rightful place in their lives by taking away its power.

During the twentieth century, the cultural systems that had given meaning and structure to the lives of humans seemed to be shifting more than ever due to the rapid increases in technological and scientific advancements. Families and societies also seemed more fragmented; and for many people traditional forms of religion no longer served as a vehicle for divine faith. In Anne Rice's *Vampire Chronicles*, Lestat represents the human condition; and through his adventures, Rice shows the reader the anxiety of the twentieth-century individual over his inability to construct a system that will satisfy his desire for significance in both the mundane and the spiritual worlds. Like the humans he represents, the vampire Lestat is on a spiritual journey, searching for meaning to deny his fear of death and to alleviate the anxiety that his questions about existence produce in him. As in "The Ancient Mariner," these questions must be asked for healing or making meaning to take place. Lestat's search for answers evolves over several adventures to an understanding that meaning is complicated and found only within the individual. From Lestat's experience, we humans might conclude that we are in charge of whether we believe in God or not, of whether we believe in an afterlife or not, and of whether we wish to be good or evil. However, the most important thing to understand is that, regardless of how one answers these questions of existence, life on earth ultimately has moral meaning only in how one accepts the responsibility of being human.

If in "The Rime of the Ancient Mariner" and *Dracula* the sin lies in forgetting our sacred connection with the world, then in Anne Rice's vampire novels the sin lies in being forgotten. For Rice's Lestat, because he sees himself as a hero, the sin lies in having no meaning in life and, therefore, nothing for which to be remembered. While, in most senses of the word, the Mariner does serve as the hero of his tale, having a voice and taking action, albeit involuntarily, to create meaning in the world, Dracula is in no way the hero of his tale. He has no real voice in the novel and the change that his presence can bring to the British world is not the kind the Victorian society of the novel desires. In Rice's novels, however, Lestat is definitely the hero; in representing the human condition, he underscores for the rest of us that meaning in life comes from our confrontation with the terror of death through the numinous and from the resulting questions about our existence.

Although Lestat is much like the Mariner in his moral dilemma, his journey is more like Dracula's in some ways. While Dracula never questions his role as vampire, he clearly understands the lack of heroic avenues available to him. Where once he was a hero of his people, those days are gone. Motivated as Lestat is by free will, just as Dracula appears to be, the world is what he wants it to be or he will make it so. Yet, by the time Lestat has lived more than two hundred years, he is changing. Since, nothing that he has done to make meaning in his life has worked, his hero's quest becomes a search for the possibility of personal transcendence and salvation. Despite the fact that the Mariner's tale and the tales of the group of human characters in *Dracula* both reflect their individual experiences of the numinous, at the end of their respective tales the Mariner and the human characters of *Dracula* articulate the importance of the community in spiritual or sacred issues. In the *Vampire Chronicles*, however, Lestat is very much the rebel and the loner, despite his seeming need to create a vampire family; and, as such, he underscores the modern American position of individual choice and free will as the only acceptable moral and spiritual stand by refusing to give proof of his journey.

The Future of the Vampire in Gothic Literature

In his discussion of the origins of the Gothic, Fred Botting, lecturer on Romanticism at Lancaster University, argues that "'Gothic romance'" is a more definitive term for the genre than "'Gothic novel'" (24) because the description of Gothic as a romance connects its origins to its progenitors: "medieval romances, the romantic narratives of love, chivalry and adventure" (24). In Botting's estimation, these early romances "blurred boundaries between supernatural and illusory dimensions and natural and real worlds [and] loosened the moral and rational structures that ordered everyday life" (28). Many of the Gothic tales written over the last three centuries posited "an order based on divine or metaphysical principles that had been displaced by enlightenment rationality, a way of conserving justice, privilege and familiar and social hierarchies" (47). However, in order to represent the established systems of culture, the Gothic genre had to "exceed the boundaries of reason and propriety" (47). In this way, Botting argues, the Gothic is meant to "interrogate, rather than restore, any imagined continuity between the past and present, nature and culture, reason and passion, individuality and family and society" (Botting 47).

In its interrogative aspect, Gothic literature is a literature of thresholds,

Conclusion • Vampires for a New Age

where both character and reader face the anxieties and fears of human life and of the times in which they live. However, the messages of the Gothic are ambivalent at best, for the answers to the questions brought up by the anxiety and fear felt by the characters, and through them by the reader, are found only within the individual. This individual experience of the character positions the character outside society and results in a quest for a way to be reintegrated. For Botting, "the romance quest provides the structure of a male fantasy of sacred, immortal power ... restored in the present by violent, sacrificial energy" (Botting 154).[1]

In the twentieth century, Botting argues, the "Gothic is everywhere and nowhere" (Botting 155). In that amorphous space "ideas of human individuality and community ... are sacralised" (Botting 157) through the "loss of human identity and the alienation of self from both itself and the social bearings" (157) which are the foundation of the individual's sense of reality. In this ambivalent space the position that the truth of any experience "can be discovered by the individual through his senses" (Watt 12) becomes problematic as one realizes that, if experience is judged through the individual's senses, each individual must have his or her own version of that experience. Gothic literature is characterized by its multiplicity of interpretations, which I feel is aptly represented by the many faces and forms the vampire has taken over the centuries and, hopefully, will continue to take in this twenty-first one.

In the postmodern Gothic, it is the "play of fear and laughter" (Botting 168) that characterizes the "escalating anxiety" (169) over how the individual fits into social constructs as they are reflected in literary constructs. The question for this conclusion is: what will the role of the vampire be in the first decades of this new millennium? The psychological theories of Freud, Jung, and Kristeva discussed in the introduction may provide some answers. All three theories define the sense of otherness caused by the horror of the uncanny, visionary, and abject feeling of helplessness as in some way sacred because of its mysterious power. For Freud, the uncanny's mystery is part of its qualities of secretness, of hiddenness from public knowledge. Human fear of otherness is a narcissistic fear that what we see reflected in the other may be what we really are. Freud's theory of the uncanny is based on repressions of fears of castration or on surmounted primitive beliefs resurfacing in the human psyche. That these repressed ideas are secretly familiar frightens us because these impulses or ideas are considered unacceptable within the wider cultural codes of society. Echoing Freud, Jung's theory of psychology maintains that visionary literature, such as the Gothic, provides the reader with uncanny, primordial visions of the unacceptable spiritual and psychical aspects of human experience. Kristeva's theory, articulated in *Powers of Horror*, relates the sense of sacredness in the horror of the other, even more strongly than either Freud or Jung, as a sense of helplessness, abjection, and oppression. Arguing that cultural structures, such as society, family, and religion, are the codes by which we deny or repress our sense of abjection, she maintains that no one would want to admit that they are powerless. Like Otto, she believes that to admit that one is helpless diminishes one in his or her own eyes. Recognition of the repressed sense of abjection is apocalyptic for the individual and that is where the horror, the terror, lies.

In *Danse Macabre* Stephen King defines terror as the emotion that arises when one suffers "a pervasive sense of disestablishment" (9). He argues that social contact is an illusion, albeit a necessary one. "Feelings of love and kindness, the ability to care and empathize" (12) are all we can know of the spiritual world while we are still alive. "Horror, terror, fear, panic: these are the emotions which drive wedges between us" (13), which isolate us and make us feel alone in the world. To handle real horrors of the world we make up fictional ones through which we can have a cathartic release of our feelings. In late twentieth-century Gothic, particularly in the novels of Anne Rice, one sees an exploration of the individual experience through the perspective of the isolated individual.

In the past the self seems to have reflected the ideas behind the social systems that helped to create it; however, in the Gothic, as Botting argues, these social forces are always problematic. In the horror of the Gothic of the last decades of the twentieth century, one sees the beginnings of an examination of problematic areas, most often dealing with issues and voices that have been considered marginalized and unacceptable in earlier periods and societies. These marginalized areas include issues of lesbian and gay culture, women's issues, and issues of race. Identification with the characters is the key to understanding any idea represented in literature; and when an author invites identification and understanding through a character considered *other*, the stifled and repressed voices that each of us hide within are given prominence over the idealized, socially controlled ones.

Conclusion • Vampires for a New Age

In an introduction to the paperback edition of Jeffrey N. McMahan's *Somewhere in the Night: Eight Gay Tales of the Supernatural* (1989), Jewelle Gomez, author of *The Gilda Stories* (1991), makes the same point Rice has so often, and so deftly, made in her fiction. Asking the reader to envision the abyss, that mysterious and fearful place where darkness reigns, Gomez argues that "horror stories have always lived in the dark, in those fearsome places we've been taught to hate. Yet writers are continually drawn to them" (1). We are drawn to the darkness because the darkness illuminates what is hidden and because, as Otto writes, we are fascinated by the mystery of it. What is hidden in the darkness is often a reflection of us. Where, for Rice, homosexuality seems to be a constant undercurrent of the work, Jeffrey N. McMahan's writing turns a spotlight on the complexities of the gay world in its context as underground to the outwardly heterosexual world. In the title short story of his collection "Somewhere in the Night; Cruising with Andrew" and in *Vampires Anonymous* (1991), his full-length novel, McMahan's protagonist — a gay, boutique night clerk and vampire named Andrew — faces the dilemma of his condition with a humor as sharp as the switchblade he uses to dispatch his victims.

In her own novel *The Gilda Stories* (1991), Jewelle Gomez examines the dynamics of race and class, gender and sexuality. Her vampire fantasy extends from the time of slavery in the Southern United States to a period two hundred years later when much of the natural environment has been destroyed. In it, the organization of the female vampires is based on their views about what is important in life rather than on the power acquired by banding together or on the abilities of each member of society to contribute to the larger cause or code system. In this vampire novel, blood drinking becomes a shared, almost sacramental, event, instead of a vicious act of survival.

In the last decade of the twentieth century, other writers dealt with lesbian issues through the vampire figure. *Daughters of Darkness: Lesbian Vampire Stories* (1993), edited by Pam Keesey, brings together ten stories of female vampires including "Carmilla" by J. Sheridan LeFanu and the original short story behind Jewelle Gomez's *The Gilda Stories*. Keesey maintains that early writers most often associated the vampires with the dreadful aspect of the goddess. According to Keesey the vampire as goddess, or the goddess as vampire, is connected historically to the Judeo-Christian philosophy of evil because the figure of the goddess "embodied all that was evil" (8) in that philosophy, being "female, sexual, pagan" (8) entities who "embraced death as part of the cycle of life" (8).

Keesey traces the appearance of lesbian vampires in nineteenth-century British literature to Samuel Taylor Coleridge's "Christabel" (1817), a text she argues that "clearly condemns homosexual love between women" (8). She calls "Carmilla" (1871) "the most famous and influential lesbian vampire story" (9) but again maintains that it censures the lesbian relationship. In *Dracula*, also, she finds a homosexual theme. Of course, this undercurrent of meaning is effectively castigated, perhaps one might even say castrated, with the staking of the vampire by Victorian social forces. The vampire tales in Keesey's anthology all involve "female vampires that have sought out one-to-one relationships with other women" (16); most were written by lesbian writers for a lesbian audience. However, they all investigate the point where sexuality and violence come together; and, at this point of convergence, most women can find some measure of identification.

In the introduction to *Night Bites: Vampire Stories by Women* (1996), edited by Victoria A. Brownworth, Brownworth and Judith M. Redding argue that "anyone can become a vampire simply by being in the wrong place at the wrong time" (ix). As an anthology of vampire stories written entirely by women, *Night Bites* offers "a feminine and feminist perspective on the genre" (xiv); and the problems of women in modern culture— motherhood, adolescent rebellion, domestic violence, and homelessness— are all treated in this anthology. They interpret Rice's novels as a blend of "vampire myth with the politics and paradoxes of postmodernist nihilism" (xiii).

Now we are in the twenty-first century; having survived with us the crossing into a new time, the vampire is still a significant figure in Gothic literature. Anne Rice continues to produce novels that examine the human condition through the lives of vampires; Lestat is still telling his story of spiritual survival. In *Merrick* (2000), Rice uses another vampire, former Talamascan David Talbot, to tell the story of Merrick Mayfair, witch turned vampire; however in reference to Lestat's continuing journey, it is David's characterization of Lestat as "stunned spiritually" (77) by his experiences with Memnoch that is important. Like the Wedding Guest in "The Ancient Mariner," Lestat is "of sense forlorn" (Gardner *The Annotated*

Ancient Mariner lines 655–56), lying in a stupor on the floor of St. Elizabeth's Chapel. Eventually, he does come to his senses to help David and takes his place again as hero—"a Savior ... come in answer to directionless prayers" (Rice *Merrick* 282). In the twenty-first century, Lestat is still searching for the spiritual. After Lestat, David and Merrick save Louis from death, Lestat questions him about what he saw; and Louis must reply "nothing—empty, colorless, timeless. Nothing." (296). Lestat's part in this narrative is short and mostly uneventful, for him; however, the characterization of his spiritual condition does take the reader further along the road of his journey.

In *Blackwood Farm* (2002), Rice once again characterizes Lestat through another character, Stirling Oliver, a current member of the Talamasca. Telling Lestat that the Talamasca has watched him while he was at his most vulnerable, sleeping on the floor of the chapel, Stirling describes Lestat as "a dark King Arthur waiting for England to need him again" (26). Like Holmwood, in Stoker's *Dracula*, Lestat is being connected symbolically to this heroic figure, whose legend implies resurrection in time of trouble. Lestat has been resurrected numerous times throughout the telling of his life stories, having gone underground and risen again repeatedly over the centuries of his vampire existence. Moreover, in his many reincarnations, he has gone from fact to fiction to legend and back to fact again, as Stirling confesses that the reason he has confronted him is to see for himself face to face if Lestat really exists.

However, it is in Rice's most recent novel *Blood Canticle* (2003) that we see Lestat as a main character again, describing his spiritual journey. He now sees himself as "a supernatural hero" (206) and tells the reader he wants to be "a saint " (3), saving souls and fighting evil. Returning to his fans in this new *Chronicle*, he characterizes himself as answering the desire of his readers for more stories "like Superman dodging into the all–American phone booth" (7). He also allies himself more closely than ever before with organized religion, calling himself "a Roman Catholic storyteller par excellence" (7). He wants to be the religious hero now, the one humans pray to for help and reassurance. Like the Ancient Mariner, he would fulfill a role of transformation and revelation. Where once he searched desperately for meaning in his own life, now he wants to *be* the meaning, the message, for others. About his fantasy of being a saint, he writes,

> I answer everyone. Peace, the certainty of the sublime, the irresistible joy of faith, the cessation of all pain, the profound abolition of the meaninglessness.
> I am relevant. I am vastly and wondrously known. I am unavoidable! I have pierced the current of history!....
> And meantime, I'm in Heaven with God. I am with the Lord in the Light, the Creator, the Divine Source of All Things. The solution to all mysteries is available to me [9].

This, after all, is the "proper work of a great saint" (9), to manifest himself to people and work miracles for their benefit.

Lestat is a vampire for the new millennium; and as such, he has much to say about apocalyptic anxieties. Speaking of the passage of time, Lestat writes that we make a mistake "perceiving every new development as a culmination or a climax" (11); he calls that attitude "a constitutional fatalism" (11), a condition in which we humans view "the 'now' as the End Time" (11). We have, he warns, "an Apocalyptic obsession" (11). Instead, he says, we should think in terms of being at the threshold of "a sublime age" (11). This attitude is one of renewal and rebirth, of looking forward with hope instead of with fear and despair; and that is the heroic stance James wrote of in *Varieties of Religion*. Lestat maintains that we live now in a world where technological and scientific advancements, like "a compilation of wonders that borders on the miraculous," (Rice *Blood Canticle* 11) give us almost constant labor pains. In order to maintain our significance in this world, we must, in effect, be reborn ourselves. We must be willing to reevaluate the secular in terms of the spiritual because secular Western culture has been so influenced by Judeo-Christianity that "its profound tenets have been internalized by the most remote and intellectual agnostics" (11), including Lestat himself, of course.

History has become what Eliade refers to as sanctified history, made sacred by the presence of Christ in the world (*Sacred and Profane* 111). Even a vampire like Lestat, once an avowed atheist, now reads the *National Catholic Reporter* and can recite scripture and Latin benedictions. Lestat's fantasy of being a saint goes so far that in his dreams he visits the Pope and lectures him on how Christ will "triumph in the Third Millennium as the supreme emblem of Divine Sacrifice and Unfathomable Love" (Rice *Blood Canticle* 12). He reiterates several times his desire not to do evil, but it is only a fantasy. He realizes that he "can't save the world" (14) because he is "ritually impure" (14).

Yet, later he characterizes himself as "the ultimate Christian" (Rice *Blood Canticle* 19). Like the Ancient Mariner before him, he sees "God's gifts in everyone" (19) and believes in Divine redemption and in a "God who can sanctify ... suffering" (26) and can purify through that sanctification and forgiveness. After his experiences recorded in *Memnoch the Devil*, he feels that "God tolerates us" (49). Bitter about Memnoch, he still contemplates God and his doubts about the truth of his experience in Heaven and wonders if his desire to disbelieve came from a sense of fear and emptiness or a feeling that the cosmos as he saw it during those experiences was "simply ... unendurable" (49). Not sure of the status of his experience as vision or illusion, he offers Mona Mayfair, a fledgling vampire, a vision for the future. His vision is one he has been perfecting for centuries: vampires can be powerful and yet benevolent. They do not have to hurt those who are "good and kind" (50). Like the Ancient Mariner's victims, Lestat's are seemingly "soulless mortals" (57), taking no notice of the world around them. He describes his victims as "cosmic trash" (60) and the "misbegotten of Hell" (60).

Although he is not a saint, Lestat still has a "passion to be officially canonized" (Rice *Blood Canticle* 65), to be recognized in the world as a spiritual being. Where once his tales were vehicles of rebellion, meant to show the world the existence of vampires like himself, now he sees the consequences of that kind of recognition. As he tells two rogue vampires, his tales are not a "model in all things" (68) for them. Accusing them of not having learned from his experiences, he says "You think I confessed what I did for you to follow my example? My faults were no template for your abominations" (68). Like the Mariner's tale, his novels are now meant to stand as narratives of the spiritual quest and as a warning for others not to ignore the spiritual for the material side of existence.

The questions that Lestat so often asked in the earlier *Chronicles* now are being investigated by young Mona, but all Lestat can do is encourage her. He cannot give her answers he is not yet sure of himself. For Lestat, the experience of vampirism is "weightless, timeless, apocalyptic" (Rice *Blood Canticle* 115). However, he now considers himself one of "the faithful" (117) and has replaced his aesthetic vision of the world as Savage Garden with a "belief in the Maker ... who put it all together with love and purpose" (141). For him, now, "God has to be an all-merciful God. Nobody is beyond redemption" (151). The weight of his faith is that everyone, including vampires, is capable of change, growth, and learning. He tells Mona that, as vampires, "we do not leave behind the Natural Law when we receive the Blood. We are principled creatures" (213). As such, they are all redeemable in the end.

Like Coleridge's tale of the Mariner and the manuscript put together by Mina Harker in *Dracula*, Lestat's confessions are part of the redemptive process. He sees writing as "an age-old form of public confession ... sacrosanct.... A book goes forth quietly into the world, labeled fiction, to be perused, pondered, passed from one to another, ... to endure if valued" (Rice *Blood Canticle* 273), much like a human being born into the world must also. After all, every life "is a story" (Clute 96). The message of Lestat's tale is that everyone should "beware the ordinary life.... Reach for something finer, greater" (Rice *Blood Canticle* 293). It is this striving for the higher reality of his soul, as it was in the earlier stories of his life, that keeps Lestat invested in the world. As Maharet tells him in her letter at the end of the novel, she has every confidence that he will "behave according to the highest standards" (295) that he has established for his own conduct. His "moral evolution" (295), as she terms it, "simply doesn't allow for anything else" (295). Lestat lives now in "the past, the present, the future" (298). Though he suffers at the thought of being "damned" (306), he tells the reader "my heart cries out, my heart will not be still, my heart will not give up, my heart will not give in —" (306). Still the hero, taking a heroic stance in the world, he must always reconcile his need for physical survival with his need for spiritual survival. In the end, it is spiritual truth that sustains us. Solomon-like, a wiser Lestat can now articulate his own Song of Songs, "— the blood that teaches life will not teach lies, and love becomes again my reprimand, my goad, my song" (306).

Having survived the passage into the new millennium, we humans also have been transformed, renewed, and resurrected; in answer to our resurrection we must find a new spirituality to serve as a guide for the new century. This new spirituality should show us that we have faced the death of time and survived, and that the numinous is, therefore, within each of us. In the first century of the new millennium, the question remains: how do we human beings make meaning to give ourselves cosmic significance? The use of the vampire figure in our literature may continue to provide a clue in our search for significance. Fear is a universal emotion: fear of alienation, of abandonment, of death; yet, as the technological advances of the late twentieth and the newly entered twenty-first century isolate us further from personal contact and increase our fears and anxieties for the future, spirituality remains the key to meaning. The vampire figure can still make meaning because vampires and humans will both survive until the end of time and neither knows when that will be.

In his book *Dreams of Millennium: Report from a Culture on the Brink*, Mark Kingwell maintains that, as a literary figure, "the vampire is the millennial standard-bearer" (284) because he or she combines "gory mortal threat with profound, even insistent, erotic appeal" (284). As a representative of both Thanatos and Eros, the vampire can seduce, as well as frighten; and, just like humans, the vampire has the ability to become whatever it chooses, whatever form will obtain for it what it wants most in life. As the shape-changer that it is, in literature, the vampire figure contains the possibility of being whatever we want it to be, also: warning, enemy, mirror of ourselves.

The first years of this new millennium are designated as an Age of Aquarius bringing enlightenment and transcendence (Prophet 15), so perhaps the new vampire, whoever he or she might be, and whoever's hand might pen his or her story, will take a page from Lestat's many adventures and show us the way to meld the spiritual and material of a twenty-first century vision into a cosmically significant whole that has the power to reunite us with the divine in its true essence and to give the marginalized voice a resonance that can be heard. If the writers of the twenty-first century take their cue from Anne Rice, and the other writers previously discussed in these chapters, they will use the vampire to illuminate not only the spiritual conditions of humanity, but also those systems of culture that break down when the spiritual side of life is not providing the support it should. Hopefully, in this new century, the vampire can serve as an interrogator of the outsider's point of view, not only for questions about the human relationship with the divine, but also for questions about the more earthly aspects of our lives such as society, gender, race, and family, which are all influenced by our relationship with the divine.

Who will be the new vampires of the twenty-first century? Will they be villains or heroes? Will they represent our political, economic, philosophic, or religious enemies, or relate to us in evangelical tones the doctrines of our salvation? Will they be marginal creatures who represent us in our human struggle toward goodness despite ourselves? In light of circumstances since the turn of the century/millennium, we can no longer deny our individual or cultural mortality. We live now in an apocalyptic culture, ripe for revelation about ourselves.

Chapter Notes

Chapter One

1. See also Freud's *Totem and Taboo* (1913) and the essay "The Group and the Primal Horde" (1920–22) in his collected works.

Chapter Two

1. Shelley's *Frankenstein* shows several clear influences from Coleridge's "The Ancient Mariner." Not only does the frame of the story allow Victor to tell his story of sin and retribution to the sailor Walton, but also Shelley makes it clear in chapter one of volume three that Victor views the creature and the fear and guilt he engenders as a weight equal to the Mariner's albatross. Then, in chapter five of the same volume, Victor paraphrases the Mariner again in speaking of what he has suffered and what he has yet to suffer because of his sin; and in chapter seven, he echoes the Mariner's speech on the gentleness of sleep. However, the most obvious of references which Shelley makes is early in the novel, in chapter four of volume one, just after Victor has given life to and then repudiated his creation. As he roams the streets of Ingolstadt afraid he will meet the creature around each corner he turns, he is overcome by alternating fits of weakness and frenzy; and he quotes the passage from "The Ancient Mariner" in which the Mariner is fearful because he has seen the fiend that follows him and now has knowledge of the danger he faces.

2. Harry Stack Sullivan originally coined the terms prototaxic, parataxic, and syntaxic to identify these modes of numinous contact in *The Interpersonal Theory of Psychiatry*, edited by Helen Swick Perry and Mary Ladd Gawel (New York: W. W. Norton, 1953).

3. The text used in this chapter's discussion is the original 1798 version as published in Martin Gardner's *The Annotated Ancient Mariner* (New York: Bramhall House, 1965). However, citations will be made by line number rather than page number.

4. Coburn connects entry 1383 — "Inopem me copia fecit" — in Coleridge's *Notebooks* to this passage of "The Ancient Mariner" and links it to the story of Narcissus and Echo in Ovid's *Metamorphoses*, Book III. In this tale, Narcissus discovers that what he desires most, himself, is what he cannot have. If one looks at the other tales of Book III, one can see that Coleridge may have gotten inspiration for his becalming of the Mariner's ship from the tale following that of Narcissus. In the tale of Bacchus and the pirates, the pirates unknowingly commit a crime against the gods by taking Bacchus hostage, and Bacchus becalms the ship and turns the sailors all into creatures of the sea as punishment. The one sailor who attempts to stop the crime is allowed to live and sail the ship to port. Coleridge's library contained the 1801 edition of the Garth/Dryden translation of *Metamorphoses*. See Ralph J. Coffman's *Coleridge's Library: A Bibliography of Books Owned or Read by Samuel Taylor Coleridge* (Boston: G. K. Hall, 1987. 156).

5. In his early journals Coleridge writes of a slave who dreams of "imaginary freedom" and who, realizing he is sleeping and may wake from this dream soon, "contrives to slip into a deep pool where he can neither touch the bottom nor swim to the surface" (Coburn *Notebooks*, 44). Coburn notes that this transcription of Coleridge's is "of interest as an indication of his awareness thus early of the wish-fulfilment element in dreams" (44) formulated by Freud a century later. For a further discussion of wish-fulfillment in dreams, see Sigmund Freud's *The Interpretation of Dreams* (New York: Avon, 1965), originally published as *Die Traumdeutung* (Leipzig and Vienna, 1900), and first translated into English by A. A. Brill (London: George Allen; New York: Macmillan, 1913).

6. (See *Mesmerism: The Discovery of Animal Magnetism*. Translated by Joseph Bouleur. Edmonds, Washington: Holmes, 1998.)

Chapter Three

1. Known members of The Hermetic Order of the Golden Dawn include William Butler Yeats, Algernon Blackwood, and Aleister Crowley, among others.

2. This and all future references to *Dracula* are from the World's Classics paperback edition published by Oxford University Press in 1983.

3. In *Vampires: Lord Byron to Count Dracula*, Christopher Frayling reproduces sections of Stoker's research notes from Emily Gerard's book. Stoker's working and research notes for *Dracula* are housed at the Rosenbach Museum in Philadelphia.

4. Leonard Wolf, in *The Essential Dracula* (an annotated version of *Dracula*, New York: Plume/Penguin, 1975) and Raymond McNally and Radu Florescu, in their *The Essential Dracula* (annotated version of *Dracula*, New York: Mayflower Books, 1979) all note that the "white lady" of Whitby Abbey is thought to be the ghost of St. Hilda, the first abbess of Whitby monastery in the seventh century. *Brewer's Book of Myth and Legend* (J. C. Cooper, ed.) defines the "white lady" as a "kind of spectre, the appearance of which generally forebodes death in the house" (301).

5. In the early eighteenth century, Daniel Defoe alleged "that men often disposed of unwanted wives" (McCandless 339) in private asylums. Elaine Showalter's *The Female Malady: Women, Madness, and English Culture, 1830–1980* (New York: Random House, 1985) contains an interesting study of the treatment of women diagnosed as insane during the nineteenth century.

6. Highwaymen also found this spot particularly attractive for their activities, and the Spaniard's Inn, on the edge of Hampstead Heath, where Professor Van Helsing and the others dine, was the setting for Alfred Noyes poem "The Highwayman."

7. For more information on the *New Woman* and the role of sexual freedom in *Dracula*, see: C. F. Bentley's "The Monster in the Bedroom: Sexual Symbolism in Bram Stoker's *Dracula*" (*Literature and Psychology* 22 [1972]: 27–34); Phyllis A. Roth's "Suddenly Sexual Women in Bram Stoker's *Dracula*" (*Literature and Psychology* 27 [1977]: 113–21); and John Allen Stevenson's "A Vampire in the Mirror: the Sexuality of *Dracula*" (PMLA 103 [March 1988]: 139-49).

8. Hungarian physician and disciple of Caesar Lombroso, Max Nordau's (1849–1923) most famous work, *Degeneration*, published in 1892, argued that culture had deteriorated and retrogressed, and that criminals, prostitutes, the insane, and artists were degenerate types. Lombroso (1836–1909), known by many as "the father of modern criminology" (Wolf 403), argued a theory that the congenital criminal is an aberrant mental type showing regression to primitive behavior.

9. Discussions of the fear of reverse colonization in *Dracula* can be found in chapter five of Carol A. Senf's *Dracula: Between Tradition and Modernism* (New York: Twayne/Prentice Hall, 1998) and in Stephen D. Arata's article "The Occidental Tourist: *Dracula* and the Anxiety of Reverse Colonization" (*Victorian Studies* 3, no. 4 Summer 1990: 621–45).

Chapter Four

1. See "Let Us Prey: Religious Codes and Rituals in *The Vampire Lestat*" by Aileen Chris Shafer in *The Gothic World of Anne Rice*. (Ed. Gary Hoppenstand and Ray B. Browne. Bowling Green: Bowling Green State University Popular Press, 1996. 149–161) for an in-depth discussion of how Lestat challenges religious rules.

2. Another discussion of Stoker's *Dracula* and Rice's *Vampire Chronicles* is included in Kathryn McGinley's chapter "Development of the Byronic Vampire: Byron, Stoker, Rice" published in *The Gothic World of Anne Rice* (eds. Gary Hoppenstand and Ray B. Browne. Ohio: Bowling Green State University Press, 1996).

3. The books of the *Vampire Chronicles* that will be dealt with in this chapter include only those written during the twentieth century: *Interview with the Vampire* (Ballentine, 1976 paperback), *The Vampire Lestat* (Ballentine, 1985 paperback), *Queen of the Damned* (Alfred A. Knopf, 1988 hardback), *The Tale of the Body Thief* (Alfred A. Knopf, 1992 hardback), and *Memnoch the Devil* (Alfred A. Knopf, 1995 hardback). Those published after the turn of the millennium will be dealt with in the concluding chapter of this book.

4. See "Living with(out) Boundaries: The Novels of Anne Rice" by Lynda and Robert Haas (*A Dark Night's Dreaming: Contemporary American Horror Fiction*, edited by Tony Magistrale and Michael A. Morrison. Columbia, SC: University of South Carolina Press, 1996) for a discussion of Lestat as social outsider. The article discusses how Rice revises the elements of history and identity to represent the postmodern individual as one without spiritual hope, as one who must continually search for identity in order to survive.

5. Rice seems to have had a similar epiphany in college at Berkeley. She had been smoking pot and suddenly had this insight that "we might not even know when we died what this [existence] was all about" (Ramsland *Prisms* 100). Like Lestat, she was devastated by this revelation, because she had hoped that at death would come some higher knowledge and understanding of what life had been about.

Conclusion

1. For a further discussion of how the romance genre became internalized, see editor Harold Bloom's "The Internalization of Quest-Romance" in *Romanticism and Consciousness: Essays in Criticism* (New York: W. W. Norton, 1970).

Works Cited

Abrams, Meyer Howard. *The Milk of Paradise: The Effect of Opium Visions on the Works of DeQuincey, Crabbe, Francis Thompson, and Coleridge.* Folcroft, Pa.: The Folcroft Press, 1934; 1969.
Adderley, Charles. "Speech on the Australian Colonies Bill." *The Annual Register, or a View of the History and Politics of the Year 1850.* London: F. and J. Rivington; Longman, 1851.
Andriano, Joseph. *Our Ladies of Darkness: Feminine Daemonology in Male Gothic Fiction.* University Park: Pennsylvania State University Press, 1993.
Armour, Richard W., and Raymond F. Howes. *Coleridge the Talker: A Series of Contemporary Descriptions and Comments.* Ithaca: Cornell University Press, 1940.
Baring-Gould, Reverend Sabine. *Curious Myths of the Middle Ages.* Edited by Edward Hardy. New York: Crescent Books, 1987.
Barnes, Thomas. "On the voluntary Power which the Mind is able to exercise over Bodily Sensation." In *Memoirs of the Literary and Philosophical Society of Manchester*, 451–66. Vol. 3. Warrington, Eng.: T. Cadell, 1790.
Becker, Ernest. *The Denial of Death.* New York: Free Press, 1973.
Belford, Barbara. *Bram Stoker: A Biography of the Author of Dracula.* New York: Alfred A. Knopf, 1996.
Bhalla, Alok. *The Cartographers of Hell: Essays on the Gothic Novel and the Social History of England.* New Delhi: Sterling, 1991.
_____. "Sacred and Desecrated Space: The Cathedral and the Ruin in the Gothic Novel." In *The Cartographers of Hell: Essays on the Gothic Novel and the Social History of England.* New Delhi: Sterling, 1991. 71–106.
Bodkin, Maud. *Archetypal Patterns in Poetry: Psychological Studies of Imagination.* London: Oxford University Press, 1934.
Bogatyrëv, Pëtr. *Vampires in the Carpathians: Magical Acts, Rites, and Beliefs in Subcarpathian Rus'.* Translated by Stephen Reynolds and Patricia A. Krafcik. Classics of Carpatho-Rusyn Scholarship. New York: Carpatho-Rusyn Research Center, 1998.
Bostetter, Edward E. "The Nightmare World of *The Ancient Mariner.*" In *Coleridge: A Collection of Critical Essays*, ed. Kathleen Coburn, 65–77. Englewood Cliffs, N.J.: Prentice-Hall, 1967.
Botting, Fred. *Gothic.* New York: Routledge, 1996.
Boulger, James D, ed. *Twentieth Century Interpretations of The Rime of the Ancient Mariner.* Englewood Cliffs, N.J.: Prentice-Hall, 1969.

Works Cited

Brownworth, Victoria A, ed. Introduction. *Night Bites: Vampire Stories by Women*. Seattle, Wash.: Seal Press, 1996. ix–xvi.

Buchan, A. M. "The Sad Wisdom of the Mariner." In *Twentieth Century Interpretations of The Rime of the Ancient Mariner*, ed. James D. Boulger, 92–110. Englewood Cliffs, N.J.: Prentice-Hall, 1969.

Burke, Edmund. *A Philosophical Enquiry into the Origin of our Ideas of the Sublime and Beautiful*. Edited by James T. Boulton. Notre Dame: University of Notre Dame Press, 1968.

Carlyle, Thomas. *The Works of Thomas Carlyle*. Edited by H. D. Traill. Vol. 13, *Life of John Sterling*. New York: Peter Fenelon Collier, 1897.

Carter, Margaret L. *Dracula: The Vampire and the Critics*. Ann Arbor: UMI Research Press, 1988.

Clute, John. *The Book of End Times: Grappling with the Millennium*. New York: HarperCollins/HarperPrism, 1999.

Coburn, Kathleen, ed. *Coleridge: A Collection of Critical Essays*. Englewood Cliffs, N.J.: Prentice-Hall, 1967.

_____. *The Notebooks of Samuel Taylor Coleridge*. 2 vols. London: Routledge and Kegan Paul, 1957.

Coleridge, Henry Nelson, ed. *The Literary Remains of Samuel Taylor Coleridge*. Vol. 1. London: William Pickering, 1836. Reprint, New York: AMS Press, 1967.

Coleridge, Samuel Taylor. *Biographia Literaria*. Edited by John Calvin Metcalf. New York: Macmillan, 1926.

_____. *The Complete Works of Samuel Taylor Coleridge*. Edited by Ernest Hartley Coleridge. 2 vols. Oxford: Clarendon Press, 1912.

Cooper, J. C., ed. *Brewer's Book of Myth and Legend*. New York: Cassell, 1992.

Cooper, Lane. "The Power of the Eye in Coleridge." In *Language and Literature in Celebration of the Seventieth Birthday of James Morgan Hart*, ed. Clark Sutherland Northup, et al., 78–121. New York: Henry Holt, 1910.

Darwin, Charles. *Voyage of the Beagle*. New York: Penguin, 1989.

De Quincey, Thomas. *Collected Writings of Thomas De Quincey*. Edited by David Masson. Vol. 2. London: A. and C. Black, 1896.

_____. *The Confessions of an English Opium-Eater*, with an introduction by John E. Jordan. London: Dent, 1967; 1960.

De Selincourt, Ernest, ed. *The Early Letters of William and Dorothy Wordsworth (1787–1805)*. Oxford: Clarendon, 1935.

Eliade, Mircea. *Images and Symbols: Studies in Religious Symbolism*. Translated by Philip Mairet. Princeton: Princeton University Press, 1991.

_____. *The Myth of the Eternal Return, or, Cosmos and History*. Translated by Willard R. Trask. Princeton: Princeton University Press, 1971.

_____. *Occultism, Witchcraft, and Cultural Fashions: Essays in Comparative Religions*. Chicago: University of Chicago, 1976.

_____. *Patterns in Comparative Religion*. Translated by Rosemary Sheed. Lincoln: University of Nebraska Press, 1996.

_____. *The Sacred and the Profane: The Nature of Religion*. Translated by Willard R. Trask. San Diego: Harcourt Brace, 1987.

Ferriar, John, M. D. "Of Popular Illusions, and particularly of Medical Demon-

Works Cited

ology." In *Memoirs of the Literary and Philosophical Society of Manchester*. Vol. 3. 31–116. Warrington, Eng.: T. Cadell, 1790.

Florescu, Radu R., and Raymond T. McNally. *Dracula, Prince of Many Faces: His Life and Times*. Boston: Little Brown, 1989.

Frayling, Christopher. *Vampires: Lord Byron to Count Dracula*. London: Faber and Faber, 1991.

Freud, Sigmund. *The Future of an Illusion*. Translated by James Strachey. New York: W. W. Norton, 1961.

——. "The 'Uncanny'." *The Standard Edition of the Complete Psychological Works of Sigmund Freud*. Vol. 17 (1917–1919). Translated by James Strachey. London: Hogarth Press, 1955. 218–252.

Gardner, Martin, ed. *The Annotated Ancient Mariner*. New York: Bramhall House, 1965.

Gerard, Emily. *The Land Beyond the Forest: Facts, Figures, and Fancies from Transylvania*. New York: Harper and Brothers, 1888.

Giussani, Luigi. *The Religious Sense*. Montreal: McGill-Queen's University Press, 1997.

Gomez, Jewelle. *The Gilda Stories*. Ithaca: Firebrand Books, 1991.

——. Introduction. *Somewhere in the Night: Eight Gay Tales of the Supernatural*. 2nd ed. By Jeffrey N. McMahan. New York: alyson books, 1997. 1–4.

Gowan, John Curtis. *Trance, Art, and Creativity*. Buffalo, N.Y.: Creative Education Foundation, 1975.

Gregory, Lady Augusta. *Gods and Fighting Men: The Story of the Tuatha De Danaan and of the Fianna of Ireland, Arranged and Put into English by Lady Gregory*. London: John Murray, 1904.

Haney, John Louis. "The Color of Coleridge's Eyes." *Anglia* 23 (1901): 424–426.

Harding, D. W. "The Theme of the Ancient Mariner." In *Coleridge: A Collection of Essays*, ed. Kathleen Coburn, 51–64. Englewood Cliffs, N.J.: Prentice-Hall, 1967.

Hennelley, Mark M., Jr. "*Dracula*: The Gnostic Quest and Victorian Wasteland." In *Dracula: The Vampire and the Critics*, ed. by Margaret L. Carter. 79–92. Ann Arbor: UMI Research Press, 1988.

Hoppenstand, Gary, and Ray B. Browne, eds. *The Gothic World of Anne Rice*. Bowling Green: Bowling Green State University Popular Press, 1996.

House, Humphrey. "The Ancient Mariner." In *Twentieth Century Interpretations of The Rime of the Ancient Mariner*, ed. James D Boulger, 48–72. Englewood Cliffs, N.J.: Prentice-Hall, 1969.

James, William. *The Varieties of Religious Experience: A Study in Human Nature*. Longmans, Green, 1902. New York: Penguin Books, Penguin Classics, 1985.

Jung, Carl G. "On the Relation of Analytical Psychology to Poetry." In *The Spirit in Man, Art, and Literature*. Translated by R. F. C. Hull. Bollingen Series XX. Princeton: Princeton University Press, 1966. 65–83.

——. "Psychology and Literature." In *The Spirit in Man, Art, and Literature*. Translated by R. F. C. Hull. Bollingen Series XX. Princeton: Princeton University Press, 1966. 84–105.

——. *The Spirit in Man, Art, and Literature*. Translated by R. F. C. Hull. Bollingen Series XX. Princeton: Princeton University Press, 1966.

Works Cited

Kant, Immanuel. *Observations on the Feeling of the Beautiful and Sublime.* Translated by John T. Goldthwait. Berkeley: University of California Press, 1960.
Keesey, Pam, ed. Introduction. *Daughters of Darkness: Lesbian Vampire Stories.* San Francisco: Cleis Press, 1993. 7–17.
King, Stephen. *Danse Macabre.* New York: Berkley Publishing, 1981.
Kingwell, Mark. *Dreams of Millennium: Report from a Culture on the Brink.* Boston: Faber and Faber, 1996.
Kristeva, Julia. *Powers of Horror: An Essay on Abjection.* Translated by Leon S. Roudiez. New York: Columbia University Press, 1982.
Lasch, Christopher. *The Culture of Narcissism: American Life in an Age of Diminishing Expectations.* New York: W. W. Norton, 1979.
Lowes, John Livingston. *The Road to Xanadu: A Study in the Ways of the Imagination.* Princeton: Princeton University Press, 1927.
MacKillop, James. *Fionn mac Cumhaill: Celtic Myth in English Literature.* Syracuse: Syracuse University Press, 1986.
Magistrale, Tony, and Michael A. Morrison, eds. *A Dark Night's Dreaming: Contemporary American Horror Fiction.* Columbia: University of South Carolina Press, 1996.
Magnuson, Paul. *Coleridge's Nightmare Poetry.* Charlottesville: University Press of Virginia, 1974.
Marrs, Edwin W., Jr, ed. *The Letters of Charles and Mary Lamb.* Vol. 1, *The Letters of Charles Lamb (1796–1801).* Ithaca: Cornell University Press, 1975.
Mayhew, Henry. *London Labour and the London Poor.* Vol. 3, *Those that will not work.* London: Griffin, Bohn, 1862.
McCandless, Peter. "Liberty and Lunacy: The Victorians and Wrongful Confinement." In *Madhouses, Mad-Doctors, and Madmen: The Social History of Psychiatry in the Victorian Era*, ed. by Andrew T. Scull. 339–362. Philadelphia: University of Pennsylvania Press, 1981.
McCarthy, James B. *Death Anxiety: The Loss of the Self.* New York: Gardner Press, 1980.
McKeon, Michael. *The Origins of the English Novel 1600–1740.* Baltimore: The Johns Hopkins University Press, 1987.
McMahan, Jeffrey N. *Somewhere in the Night: Eight Gay Tales of the Supernatural.* 2nd ed. New York: alyson books, 1997.
_____. *Vampires Anonymous.* Boston: alyson books, 1991.
Mellett, D. J. (David J.) *The Prerogative of Asylumdom: Social, Cultural, and Administrative Aspects of the Institutional Treatment of the Insane in Nineteenth-Century Britain.* New York: Garland Publishing, 1982.
Melton, J. Gordon. *The Vampire Book: The Encyclopedia of the Undead.* Detroit: Visible Ink Press, 1999.
Memoirs of the Literary and Philosophical Society of Manchester. Vols. 2 and 3. Warrington, Eng.: T. Cadell, 1790.
Mishra, Vijay. *The Gothic Sublime.* Albany: State University of New York Press, 1994.
Murgoci, Agnes. "The Vampire in Roumania." In *The Vampire: A Casebook*, ed. by Alan Dundes, 12–34. Madison: University of Wisconsin Press, 1998.
Nagy, Joseph Falaky. *The Wisdom of the Outlaw: The Boyhood Deeds of Finn in Gaelic Narrative Tradition.* Berkeley: University of California Press, 1985.

Works Cited

Nordau, Max. *Degeneration.* New York: D. Appleton, 1895; Lincoln: University of Nebraska Press, 1993.
Ó hÓgáin, Dr. Dáithí. *Myth, Legend and Romance: An Encyclopedia of the Irish Folk Tradition.* New York: Prentice Hall, 1991.
O'Malley, William J. *God: The Oldest Question.* Chicago: Loyola Press, 2000.
_____. "Toward an Adult Spirituality." *America* (November 18, 1989): 341–344.
Otto, Rudolf. *The Idea of the Holy: An Inquiry into the non-rational factor in the idea of the divine and its relation to the rational.* Translated by John W. Harvey. New York: Oxford University Press, 1958.
_____. *Naturalism and Religion.* Translated by J. Arthur Thomson and Margaret R. Thomson. London: Williams and Norgate; New York: G. P. Putnam's, 1907.
Prophet, Elizabeth Clare, Patricia R. Spadaro, and Murray L. Steinman. *Saint Germain's Prophecy for the New Millennium.* Corwin Springs, Montana: Summit University Press, 1999.
Ramsland, Katherine, ed. *Anne Rice Reader: Writers Explore the Universe of Anne Rice.* New York: Ballantine Books, 1997.
_____. "Let the Flesh Instruct the Mind: A *Quadrant* Interview with Anne Rice," in *Anne Rice Reader: Writers Explore the Universe of Anne Rice*, ed. Katherine Ramsland (New York: Ballantine Books, 1997), 55–73.
_____. *Prism of the Night: A Biography of Anne Rice.* New York: Dutton, 1991.
Rank, Otto. *Will Therapy and Truth and Reality.* Translated by Jesse Taft. New York: Alfred A. Knopf, 1972.
Rice, Anne. *Blackwood Farm.* New York: Alfred A. Knopf, 2002.
_____. *Blood Canticle.* New York: Alfred A. Knopf, 2003.
_____. Interview with Bryant Gumbel. *Today.* NBC. New York. 25 July 1995.
_____. Interview with Charlie Rose. *The Charlie Rose Show.* 25 July 1995.
_____. Interview with Larry King. *Larry King Live.* CNN. Atlanta. 27 July 1995.
_____. *Interview with the Vampire.* New York: Alfred A. Knopf, 1976.
_____. *Memnoch the Devil.* New York: Alfred A. Knopf, 1995.
_____. *Merrick.* New York: Alfred A. Knopf, 2000.
_____. "A Message from Anne Rice." *Interview with the Vampire.* Produced by Stephen Woolley and David Geffen. Directed by Neil Jordan. 123 minutes. Geffen Pictures, 1994; Warner Home Video, 1995. Videocassette.
_____. *Queen of the Damned.* New York: Alfred A. Knopf, 1988.
_____. *The Tale of the Body Thief.* New York: Alfred A. Knopf, 1992.
_____. *The Vampire Lestat.* New York: Alfred A. Knopf, 1985.
Roth, Phyllis A. *Bram Stoker.* Boston: Twayne, 1982.
Schellinger, Sharon Jones. "The Three Faces of Imagination." Ph.D. diss., University of Dallas, 1998.
Scherman, David E., and Richard Wilcox. *Literary England: Photographs of Places Made Memorable in English Literature.* New York: Random House, 1943–44.
Schneider, Kirk J. *Horror and the Holy: Wisdom-Teachings of the Monster Tale.* Chicago: Open Court Press, 1993.
Scull, Andrew T., ed. *Madhouses, Mad-Doctors, and Madmen: The Social History of Psychiatry in the Victorian Era.* Philadelphia: University of Pennsylvania Press, 1981.
Senf, Carol A. *Dracula: Between Tradition and Modernism.* New York: Twayne, 1998.

Works Cited

Shapiro, Karl, and Robert Beum. *A Prosody Handbook*. New York: Harper and Row, 1965.
Shelley, Mary (Wollstonecraft). *Frankenstein, or the Modern Prometheus*. Edited by M. K. Joseph. Oxford: Oxford University Press, 1980.
Sidgwick, Eleanor Mildred. *Phantasms of the Living: Cases of Telepathy Printed in the Journal of the Society for Psychical Research during Thirty-five Years*. 2 Vols. New Hyde Park, N.Y.: University Books, 1962.
Sjoestedt, Marie-Louise. *Gods and Heroes of the Celts*. Translated by Myles Dillon. Berkeley: Turtle Island Foundation, 1982.
Smith, Jennifer. *Anne Rice: A Critical Companion*. Westport, Connecticut: Greenwood Press, 1996.
Snyder, Edward D. *Hypnotic Poetry: A Study of Trance-Inducing Technique in Certain Poems and its Literary Significance*. Philadelphia: University of Pennsylvania Press, 1930.
Stoker, Bram. *Dracula*. Oxford: Oxford University Press, 1983.
Strozier, Charles B., and Michael Flynn, eds. *The Year 2000: Essays on the End*. New York: New York University Press, 1997.
Summers, Montague. *The Vampire in Europe*. London: Routledge and Kegan Paul, 1929. Reprint, New Hyde Park, N.Y., 1961; New York: Gramercy Books, 1997.
Tave, Katherine Bruner. *The Demon and the Poet: An Interpretation of "The Rime of the Ancient Mariner" according to Coleridge's Demonological Sources*. Salzburg, Austria: Institut für Anglistik und Amerikanistik Universität Salzburg, 1983.
Tennyson, Alfred, Lord. "In Memoriam." In *The Poetic and Dramatic Works of Alfred, Lord Tennyson*. Student's Cambridge Edition, ed. by W. J. Rolfe. Boston: Houghton Mifflin, 1898.
Todorov, Tzvetan. *The Fantastic: A Structural Approach to a Literary Genre*. Translated by Richard Howard. Ithaca: Cornell University Press, 1973.
_____. *Genres in Discourse*. Translated by Catherine Porter. Cambridge: Cambridge University Press, 1990.
_____. *Introduction to Poetics*. Translated by Richard Howard. Minneapolis: University of Minnesota Press, 1981.
_____. "Reading as Construction." Translated by Marilyn A. August. In *The Reader in the Text: Essays on Audience and Interpretation*, ed. by Susan R. Suleiman and Inge Crosman. 67–82. New Jersey: Princeton University Press, 1980.
Turner, the Reverend William. "An Essay on Crimes and Punishments." In *Memoirs of the Literary and Philosophical Society of Manchester*. Vol. 3. 293–325. Warrington, Eng.: T. Cadell, 1790.
Twitchell, James B. *The Living Dead: A Study of the Vampire in Romantic Literature*. Durham: Duke University Press, 1981.
_____. *Romantic Horizons: Aspects of the Sublime in English Poetry and Painting, 1770–1850*. Columbia: University of Missouri Press, 1983.
Updike, John. "The Future of Faith." *The New Yorker* (November 29, 1999): 84–91.
Varma, Devendra P. *The Gothic Flame, Being a History of the Gothic Novel in England: Its Origins, Efflorescence, Disintegration, and Residuary Influences*. London: Arthur Barker, 1957.
Varnado, S. L. "The Daemonic in *Dracula*." In *Haunted Presence: The Numinous in Gothic Fiction*. Tuscaloosa: University of Alabama Press, 1987. 95–114.

Works Cited

———. *Haunted Presence: The Numinous in Gothic Fiction*. Tuscaloosa: University of Alabama Press, 1987.
Walker, Barbara G. *The Woman's Encyclopedia of Myths and Secrets*. San Francisco: Harper and Row, 1983.
Ward, R. H. *A Drug-taker's Notes*. London: Victor Gollancz, 1957.
Watt, Ian. *The Rise of the Novel: Studies in Defoe, Richardson and Fielding*. Berkeley: University of California Press, 1957.
Whalley, George. "The Mariner and the Albatross." In *Coleridge: A Collection of Critical Essays*, ed. Kathleen Coburn, 32–50. Englewood Cliffs, N.J.: Prentice-Hall, 1967.
Williams, Anne. *The Art of Darkness: A Poetics of Gothic*. Chicago: University of Chicago, 1995.
Williams, Niall. *As It Is in Heaven*. New York: Warner Books, 1999.
Wolf, Leonard, ed. *The Essential Dracula: The Definitive Annotated Edition of Bram Stoker's Classic Novel*. New York: Penguin/Plume, 1993.

Index

A priori ideas 20, 33
Abrams, Meyer Howard 42–43
Adderley, Charles 91–92
All Hallows' Eve 114
All Saints' Day 114
"The Ancient Mariner" (House) 64
Andriano, Joseph 92, 109
animal magnetism 71
Anne Rice: A Critical Companion 136
The Annotated Ancient Mariner 51, 53, 56, 76, 96, 176, 183n.3
apocalyptic 32, 134, 137, 157, 164, 167, 169, 174, 178–179, 182
Arata, Stephen D. 107, 184n.9
Archetypal Patterns in Poetry 59, 61
archetypes 5, 12–13, 19, 33–35, 41–43, 55, 57, 59, 61, 65, 70, 73–75, 83–85, 92, 118, 125
Armour, Richard W. 44–45
Art of Darkness 64
As It Is in Heaven 129
atheism 8, 145–146, 163
autochthony 97

Bacchus 183n.4
Baring-Gould, the Reverend Sabine 123–124
Barnes, Thomas 70
Becker, Ernest 131–132, 138, 181; Eros 131, 133, 181; Thanatos 131, 133, 181
Belford, Barbara 87
Beltane 114
Beum, Robert 77, 79
Bhalla, Alok 97
Biographia Literaria 45, 76
Blackwood Farm 10, 177

Blood Canticle 10, 177–180
Bodkin, Maud 59, 61
Bogatyrëv, Pëtr 122
Böhme, Jakob 23
Bond, James 156, 159
The Book of End Times 151, 167, 169, 180
Bostetter, Edward E. 50
Botting, Fred 172–174
Bram Stoker 87, 184n.7
Bram Stoker: A Biography of the Author of Dracula 87
Brewer's Book of Myth and Legend 113, 184n.4
Browne, Ray B. 134
Brownworth, Victoria A. 176
Buchan, A. M. 53, 82
Budge, E. A. Wallis 101
Burke, Edmund 13, 19, 52, 64–65, 75, 77, 139
Burke, Kenneth 60

cannibalism 111–112
"Carceri d' Invenzione" 42
Carfax Abbey 97–100, 115, 117
Carlyle, Thomas 44–45
The Cartographers of Hell 97
catharsis 33, 37
"Christabel" 1, 4, 176
Clute, John 151, 167, 169, 180
Coburn, Kathleen 45, 52, 183n.4, 184n.5
Coleridge, Henry Nelson 39
Coleridge, Samuel Taylor 1, 3, 4–9, 28, 39–85, 88–89, 96, 133, 135–136, 145, 156, 159, 162, 167, 169–172, 176–177,

Index

179–180; Gothic art as numinous 39; numinous contact 42–46; the sublime and the divine 39; the sublime and the Gothic 39
Coleridge the Talker 44–45
Coleridge's Nightmare Poetry 52–53
"Coleridge's Revision of 'The Ancient Mariner'" 46
Collected Writings of Thomas 55
collective unconscious 33, 41
"The Color of Coleridge's Eyes" 44
The Confessions of an English Opium-Eater 42
Cooper, J. C. 113, 184n.4
Cooper, Lane 44
Critique of Judgement 20
Critique of Pure Reason 20
Cruikshank, John 55
The Culture of Narcissism 129–130, 136
Curious Myths of the Middle Ages 123–124

Danse Macabre 147–148, 174
A Dark Night's Dreaming 129
Darwin, Charles 86, 111
Daughters of Darkness 175–176
Death Anxiety 129
De Fascinatione 71
Defoe, Daniel 11, 184n.5
Degeneration 109
The Demon and the Poet 49, 54, 56–57, 59, 61–62, 67–68
The Denial of Death 131–132, 138
De Quincey, Thomas 42, 55
De Selincourt, Ernest: Coleridge's eyes 44
De Spectris 56
Devil 9, 14, 95, 122–123, 134, 137, 162–167
Dracula (Stoker) 1, 3, 7, 6–8, 28–29, 86–128, 89, 91, 95, 102, 133, 135–136, 139, 142–143, 145, 163, 169–172, 176–177, 180
Dracula: Between Tradition and Modernism 86, 107, 119, 184n.9
"*Dracula*: The Gnostic Quest and Victorian Wasteland" 101
Dracula, Prince of Many Faces 106, 184n.4

dragons 90, 105, 122–125, 143
dreams 18, 29, 41, 43, 45, 52, 54–55, 59, 61, 75, 85, 116, 143, 146, 184n.5
Dreams of Millennium 181
A Drug-taker's Notes 68, 82

The Early Letters of William and Dorothy Wordsworth 44
ego (self) 4–5, 31, 40–41, 48, 50, 53–54, 57, 62, 67, 73, 83–84
Eliade, Mircea 7, 12, 89–91, 92, 94, 95–99, 100, 101, 106, 107, 110–114, 117–119, 120–122, 125, 126, 127, 140–141, 142–143, 145–146, 148, 152, 153, 167, 178
Eros 131, 133, 181
"An Essay on Crimes and Punishments" 64
The Essential Dracula 93, 98–99, 101, 110, 112, 124, 184n.4, 184n.8

faith 6–8, 10, 20, 36–37, 49–50, 54, 86, 88, 105, 126–131, 134–135, 141–142, 145, 162, 166–167, 179
the fantastic 11, 14–19, 25–26, 29–31
The Fantastic: A Structural Approach 14–21, 25–26, 29–31, 143
Fascinans (fascination) 24, 26, 31–32, 36, 142–143, 149, 153, 169
Faust 113, 133
Ferriar, John, M. D. 46, 56, 71
Fichte, Johann Gottlieb 22
Fionn mac Cumhaill 103
Florescu, Radu R. 106, 184n.4
Flynn, Michael 137
Frankenstein 1, 37, 39, 183n.1
Frayling, Christopher 101, 184n.3
Frazer, Sir James 103, 112–13
Freud, Sigmund 27–31, 34–35, 42, 130, 142, 173, 183n.1, 184n.5; death instinct 59; ego 4–5, 31, 40–41, 48, 50, 53–54, 57, 73, 83–84; id 4–5, 40, 53
Frye, Northrop 12
The Future of an Illusion 27–28
"The Future of Faith" 130

Gardner, Martin 51, 53, 56, 76, 96, 176, 183n.3
Genesis 22, 60
Genres in Discourse 15–17

196

Index

Gerard, Emily 92, 106, 108, 123, 184n.3
The Gilda Stories 175
Giussani, Luigi 82
God: The Oldest Question 141, 144–145
Gods and Fighting Men 103–104
Gods and Heroes of the Celts 114
The Golden Bough 103, 112–13
Gomez, Jewelle 175
Gothic 1–2, 5–6, 19–20, 35–36, 39, 88–89, 97–98, 155, 172–174
Gothic 172–174
The Gothic Flame 19
The Gothic Sublime 19–20
The Gothic World of Anne Rice 134
Gowan, John Curtis 4, 40–41, 47, 51–55, 61, 63–64, 71–72, 81; collective preconscious 41
Gregory, Lady Augusta 103–104

Hallowtide 114
Hampstead Heath 97, 100
Haney, John Louis 44
Harding, D. W. 53
Haunted Presence 7, 21, 23, 76, 89
Hazlitt, William 45
Hennelley, Mark M., Jr. 101
Hermetic Order of the Golden Dawn 86–87, 184n.1
Hoppenstand, Gary 134
Horror and the Holy 92
House, Humphrey 64
Howes, Raymond F. 44–45
hypnosis 4, 41, 67, 70–72, 74–80, 82, 87–88, 136, 170
Hypnotic Poetry 74–80

id 4–5, 40, 53
The Idea of the Holy 2, 7, 19–26, 31, 36, 39, 43, 53, 60, 69, 75, 87, 89, 93, 95, 97, 109, 122, 132–133, 139, 141–145, 153, 158, 164, 174–175
Images and Symbols 90, 92, 94, 112, 115, 122, 126
imitatio dei 118, 143
"In Memoriam" 86
instincts 33–34, 131–132
Interview with the Vampire 153, 155, 159
Introduction to Poetics 16–18

Irving, Henry 87, 113
Isis 152

James, William 132, 154–55, 178
Jung, Carl G. 33–35, 41; instincts and archetypes 33–34, 59, 61, 73–75, 83, 118, 125; night sea journey 59; visionary experiences in literature 34–35, 174

Kant, Immanuel 20, 22
Keesey, Pam 175–176
King, Stephen 147–148, 174
King Arthur 103–104
Kingwell, Mark 181
Kristeva, Julia 31–33, 35, 142, 173–174

Lamb, Charles 45
The Land Beyond the Forest 92, 106, 108, 123, 184n.3
Lasch, Christopher 129–130, 136
Lavater 56
"Let the Flesh Instruct the Mind" 133, 135
The Letters of Charles and Mary Lamb 45
Lévi-Strauss, Claude 12
Leviticus 112
"Liberty and Lunacy" 100, 184n.5
Literary England 100
Literary Remains 39
The Living Dead 3, 5, 46–47, 56, 62, 68, 84
Lombroso, Cesare 107, 184n.8
London Labour and the London Poor 100
Lowes, John Livingston 46, 49, 52, 55
Lyrical Ballads 45–46, 66

MacCumhal, Finn 103–104
MacKillop, James 103
Magistrale, Tony 129
Magnuson, Paul 52–53
"The Mariner and the Albatross" 64
Marrs, Edwin W., Jr. 45
Mayhew, Henry 100
McCandless, Peter 100, 184n.5
McCarthy, James B. 129
McElderry, Jr., B. R. 46
McKeon, Michael 12–14

Index

McMahan, Jeffrey N. 175
McNally, Raymond T. 106, 184n.4
Mellett, D. J. (David J.) 100
Melton, J. Gordon 106
Memnoch the Devil 9, 137, 162–168, 179
Memoirs of the Literary and Philosophical Society of Manchester 46, 64, 70
Mephistopheles 113, 133
Merrick 10, 176–177
Mesmer, Franz Anton 71; Mesmerism 47, 71–72, 85, 184n.6
"A Message from Anne Rice" 133
A Midsummer Night's Dream 44
The Milk of Paradise 42–43
Mishra, Vijay 19–20
Morrison, Michael 129
The Mummy: Chapters in Egyptian Funereal Archeology 101
Murgoci, Agnes 124
Museums of Madness 99
Mysterium (mystery) 21, 27–28, 35–36, 48, 75, 132, 143
Myth, Legend and Romance 114
The Myth of the Eternal Return 125

Nagy, Joseph Falaky 103
narcissism 32, 130, 145, 150, 173
Narcissus 183n.4
Naturalism and Religion 20
New Woman 101, 184n.7
Night Bites 176
"The Nightmare World of *The Ancient Mariner*" 50
Nordau, Max 107, 109, 184n.8
The Notebooks of Samuel Taylor Coleridge 45, 52, 183n.4, 184n.5
numinous 2–11, 15, 19–26, 29, 31, 33–38, 120, 127, 141–142, 169–171, 180; artistic mode 41, 48, 55, 59–66, 70, 73, 83–85; creative mode 41, 48–49, 63–64, 66–67, 70, 73–74, 83–85; definition of 20–25, 141; as inexpressible 11, 20–21, 26, 29, 33, 35, 39, 51, 84; levels of numinous contact 4–5, 40–41, 183n.2; *mysterium horrendum* 23, 56, 67, 109; *mysterium tremendum* 21–23, 41, 43, 50, 95, 143; *mysterium tremendum et fascinans* 21, 89; negative numinous 6, 23, 35–38, 48, 56– 57, 67, 89, 95, 105, 109, 118, 122, 128, 135, 141–142, 170; and opium use 42–43, 45; primitive mode 41, 43, 48–58, 62, 65, 67–70, 83–85; and the vampire 2–4, 35–38, 48–49, 82–83, 170

Observations on the Feeling of the Beautiful and Sublime 22
occult 86–87, 170
Occultism, Witchcraft, and Cultural Fashions 127
"Ode to the Departing Year" 43
Ó hÓgáin, Dr. Dáithí 114
O'Malley, William J. 137, 141, 144–145, 147, 153, 160
"On Popular Illusions and Particularly of Medical Demonology" 46, 56, 71
"On the Relation of Analytical Psychology to Poetry" 33–34
"On the Voluntary Power Which the Mind Is Able to Exercise Over Bodily Sensation" 70
The Origins of the English Novel 1600–1740 12–14
Osiris 152
Otto, Rudolf 2, 7, 19–26, 31, 36, 39, 43, 53, 60, 69, 75, 87, 89, 93, 95, 97, 109, 122, 132–133, 139, 141–145, 153, 158, 164, 174–175; numinous, definition of 20–25, 141
Our Ladies of Darkness 92, 109
Ovid's *Metamorphoses* 183n.4

"Pains of Sleep" 43
Patterns in Comparative Religion 152
Phantasms of the Living 87
A Philosophical Enquiry into the Origins of Our Ideas of the Sublime and Beautiful 19, 52, 64–65, 75, 77, 139
The Philosophy of Literary Form 60
Piranesi, Giovanni Batista 42
"A Poem of Pure Imagination: An Experiment in Reading" 49
"The Power of the Eye in Coleridge" 44
Powers of Horror 31–33, 35, 142, 173–174
The Prerogative of Asylumdom 100
Prism of the Night 134, 157–158, 185n.5

Index

Prophet, Elizabeth Clare (with Patricia R. Spadaro, and Murray L. Steinman) 181
A Prosody Handbook 77, 79
"Psychology and Literature" 34–35

Queen of the Damned 156–159
quest 19, 88, 101, 131, 137, 144, 148, 151, 154, 158, 164, 168, 172–173, 179, 185n.1

Ramsland, Katherine 133, 134, 135, 157–158, 185n.5
Rank, Otto 110–111
"Reading as Construction" 16–17
realism 11–14, 88; and the fantastic 14–15, 17, 20, 25–26
The Religious Sense 82
Rice, Anne 3, 8–10, 29, 129–168, 133, 137, 138–168, 171–172, 175, 176–180, 181; interview with Bryant Gumbel 134; interview with Charlie Rose 134; interview with Larry King 133–135
"The Rime of the Ancient Mariner" (Coleridge) 1, 3, 4–9, 28, 39–85, 88–89, 96, 133, 135–136, 145, 156, 159, 162, 167, 169–172, 176–177, 179–180; as a vampire text 5, 46–48
The Rise of the Novel 11–14, 173
Road to Xanadu 46, 49, 52, 55
Romantic Horizons 58
Roth, Phyllis A. 87, 184n.7

"Sacred and Desecrated Space" 97
The Sacred and the Profane 90–91, 95–99, 101, 107, 110–114, 117–119, 121–122, 126, 140–141, 145–146, 153, 167, 178
"The Sad Wisdom of the Mariner" 53, 82
St. George 105, 123–124
St. George's Eve 106, 123
Saint Germain's Prophecy 181
Samhain 114
Schellinger, Sharon Jones 84–85
Scherman, David E. 100
Schneider, Kirk J. 92
Scholomance 123
Scull, Andrew T. 99

Senf, Carol A. 86, 107, 119, 184n.9
Sennertus 71
sensory deprivation 51, 54–56, 72, 74
Seward's insane asylum 97, 99–100
Shapiro, Karl 77, 79
Shelley, Mary (Wollstonecraft) 1, 37, 39, 183n.1
Shelley, Percy Bysshe 47
Sidgwick, Eleanor Mildred 87
Simoom 108
Sjoestedt, Marie-Louise 114
Smith, Jennifer 136
Snyder, Edward D. 74–80
Society for Psychical Research 87
Somewhere in the Night: Eight Gay Tales of the Supernatural 175
space 13–14, 17–18, 20, 40, 42, 50–51, 54–55, 58, 62–63, 81, 83, 91–112, 114, 118, 121–122, 128, 137, 153
"Speech on the Australian Colonies Bill" 91–92
Stoker, Bram 1, 3, 6–8, 28–29, 86–128, 87–88, 133, 135–136, 139, 142–143, 145, 163, 169–172, 176–177, 180
Stoker, Charlotte 87
Strozier, Charles B. 137
sublime 5, 19–20, 22, 32, 39, 44–45, 49, 51, 53–54, 57–58, 75, 161, 178
Sullivan, Harry Stack: levels of numinous contact 183n.2
Summers, Montague 98, 106, 123–124
superego 31, 53, 64

The Tale of the Body Thief 159–162
Tave, Katherine Bruner 49, 54, 56–57, 59, 61–62, 67–68
Tennyson, Alfred, Lord 86
Tepes, Vlad 105–106
Thanatos 131, 133, 181
"The Theme of 'The Ancient Mariner'" 53
"The Three Faces of Imagination" 84–85
time 2, 13–14, 16–17, 20, 40, 42, 50–51, 54–55, 62–63, 69, 83, 90, 112–126, 128, 137, 143, 153, 169–70, 178–180
Todorov, Tzvetan 4, 14–21, 25–26, 29–31, 40–41, 47, 51–55, 61, 63–64, 71–72, 74, 81, 143

Index

"Toward an Adult Spirituality" 137, 141, 147, 153
Trance, Art, and Creativity 4, 40–41, 47, 51–55, 61, 63–64, 71–72, 81
tremendum (dread) 21–24, 36–37, 41, 48, 71, 108–109, 127, 132, 142–145, 169
Turner, the Reverend William 64
Twitchell, James B. 3, 5, 46–47, 56, 58, 62, 68, 84

uncanny 15, 25, 29–30, 32–35, 41, 107, 164, 173–174
"The 'Uncanny'" 29–31, 142
Updike, John 130

The Vampire Book 106
Vampire Chronicles 3, 8–9, 29, 171–172, 176–177, 179
vampire, definition as numinous 35–38
Vampire in Europe 123
"The Vampire in Roumania" 124
The Vampire Lestat 138–156
Vampires Anonymous 175
Vampires in the Carpathians 122
Vampires: Lord Byron to Count Dracula 101, 184n.3
Varieties of Religious Experience 132, 154–55, 178
Varma, Devendra P. 19
Varnado, S. L. 7, 21, 23, 76, 89, 91, 95, 102; on *Dracula* 7, 89, 91, 95, 102; numinous 7, 21, 76
Voyage of the Beagle 111

Walker, Barbara G. 103, 114
Walpurgis Night 113–114
Ward, R. H. 68, 82
Warren, Robert Penn 49
Watt, Ian 11–14, 173
Whalley, George 64
whirlpool 67, 92, 118
whirlwind 108, 164
Whitby Abbey 96–98, 117, 184n.4
Wilcox, Richard 100
Will Therapy and Truth and Reality 110–111
Williams, Anne 64
Williams, Niall 129
The Wisdom of the Outlaw 103
Wolf, Leonard 93, 98–99, 101, 110, 112, 124, 184n.4, 184n.8
The Woman's Encyclopedia of Myths and Secrets 103, 114
Wordsworth, Dorothy 44
Wordsworth, Willia 5, 44–46, 45–46, 66
The Works of Thomas Carlyle 44–45

The Year 2000 137